CENTRAL AMERICA

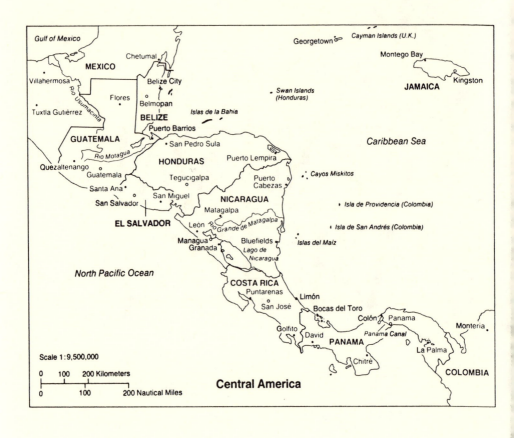

Central America

Scale 1:9,500,000

Gulf of Mexico

Georgetown   Cayman Islands (U.K.)

Montego Bay

MEXICO

Chetumal

Villahermosa

Belize City

Swan Islands
(Honduras)

JAMAICA

Kingston

Flores

Belmopan

Caribbean Sea

Tuxtla Gutiérrez

BELIZE

Islas de la Bahía

Puerto Barrios

GUATEMALA

San Pedro Sula

Rio Motagua

HONDURAS

Puerto Lempira

Quezaltenango

Guatemala

Tegucigalpa

Puerto
Cabezas

Cayos Miskitos

Santa Ana

San Miguel

NICARAGUA

San Salvador

Isla de Providencia (Colombia)

EL SALVADOR

Matagalpa

León

Rio Grande de Matagalpa

Isla de San Andrés (Colombia)

Managua

Bluefields

Granada

Lago de
Nicaragua

Islas del Maíz

North Pacific Ocean

COSTA RICA

Puntarenas

Limón

San José

Bocas del Toro

Colón   Panama

Golfito

David

Monteria

PANAMA

Panama Canal

La Palma

Chitré

COLOMBIA

Rio Usumacinta

Scale 1:9,500,000

0   100   200 Kilometers

0   100   200 Nautical Miles

CENTRAL AMERICA

Democracy, Development, and Change

Edited by

John M. Kirk and George W. Schuyler

With the Assistance of Sylvia Mattinson, Sandor Halebsky, James Sacouman, and Henry Veltmeyer

PRAEGER

New York
Westport, Connecticut
London

Library of Congress Cataloging-in-Publication Data

Central America: democracy, development, and change / edited by John
   M. Kirk and George W. Schuyler with the assistance of Sylvia
   Mattinson ... [et al.].
      p. cm.
   Bibliography: p.
   Includes index.
   ISBN 0-275-93049-1 (alk. paper)
   1. Central America—Politics and government—1979–
2. Representative government and representation—Central America.
3. Central America—Economic policy.   4. Central America—Social
conditions—1979–   I. Kirk, John M.   II. Schuyler, George W.
JL 1402.C46 1988
972.8′053—dc19   88-6922

Praeger Publishers, One Madison Avenue, New York, NY 10010
A division of Greenwood Press, Inc.

Printed in the United States of America

The paper used in this book complies with the
Permanent Paper Standard issued by the National
Information Standards Organization (Z39.48-1984).

10 9 8 7 6 5 4 3 2 1

Contents

Part III   Change

Abbreviations

AGA	Association of Guatemalan Agriculturists
AID	Agency for International Development
ANACH	National Association of Honduran Campesinos
APROH	Association for the Progress of Honduras
BEP	Student Production Brigade
BID	Inter-American Development Bank
CACIF	Coordinating Committee of Agricultural, Commercial, Industrial, and Financial Institutions
CAUSA	The anticommunist, quasi-fascist political section of the Unification Church
CCTD	Costa Rican Confederation of Democratic Workers
CONADI	National Investment Corporation
COSEP	Higher Council of Private Enterprise
COSUFA	Armed Forces Superior Council
CPDH	Permanent Human Rights Commission
CUS	Confederation of Union Unity
DIT	Technical Investigation Department
DNI	National Intelligence Department
ERET	Rural Work-Study Schools
FDR	Revolutionary Democratic Front
FENACH	National Federation of Honduran Campesinos
FENAGH	National Federation of Farmers and Cattle-Raisers
FMLN	Farabundo Martí National Liberation Front

FSLN	Sandinista National Liberation Front
FUSEP	Public Security Forces
GAM	Mutual Aid Group
ICE	Costa Rican Institute of Electricity
IMF	International Monetary Fund
INA	The Agrarian Institute
INSSBI	Nicaraguan Institute for Social Services and Welfare
INTA	Institute for National Agrarian Transformation
MIDINRA	Ministry of Agricultural Development and Agrarian Reform
NGO	Non-Governmental Organization (Canadian)
ORIT	Inter-American Regional Labor Organization
PDC	Christian Democratic Party
PID	Institutional Democratic Party
PLN	National Liberation Party
PSD	Social Democratic Party
PUN	National Union Party
UNC	National Peasants Union
UN-ECLAC	United Nations Economic Commission for Latin America and the Caribbean
UNTS	National Unity of Salvadorean Workers
UPD	Popular Democratic Unity
UPR	United to Reconstruct

Preface

Scholars and activists do not always mix easily, but in March 1987 they came together for a superb conference on Central America. This book reflects the dual nature of that conference—an effort to inform and to identify paths of action. The organization and content of the conference gradually emerged from the sometimes conflicting perceptions of scholars and community activists about appropriate themes and priorities. We debated vigorously—and sometimes bitterly—but finally understood that we must work together for change in Central America.

First and foremost therefore, we are deeply grateful for the enormous contribution made by members of the Halifax-Dartmouth community. The Latin American Information Group, Save the Children Canada, Tools for Peace, and the Atlantic Chapter of the Canadian Association of Latin American and Caribbean Studies stand out among the several groups that offered ideas, time, and expertise. Dozens of individuals helped in various ways but Eleanor O'Donnell, Beth Abbott, Pat Schuyler, and Sylvia Mattinson proved indispensable. Dalhousie University, Saint Mary's University and its International Education Centre, the Public Participation Program of the Canadian International Development Agency, and the Social Sciences and Humanities Research Council of Canada contributed generously to the costs of the conference. Special acknowledgment should be given to Dr. Joseph Jabbra, Academic Vice President, Saint Mary's University, and to Dr. Robert Fournier, Vice President Research, Dalhousie University, for their support and advice.

In preparing this volume, we are indebted to the sixteen contributors who responded promptly (and we hope, cheerfully) to our demands for material. Sylvia Mattinson worked long hours and with meticulous care

to put the manuscript on computer disks. Sandor Halebsky, James Sacouman, and Henry Veltmeyer read and edited portions of the manuscript. Alison Bricken, Omar Dahbour, and an anonymous copy editor,
all of Praeger Publishers, helped to improve and prepare it for publi-
cation.

On behalf of all our contributors, we hope this volume helps to illuminate some of the more popularly-held myths about our Central American neighbors—and about ourselves.

John M. Kirk
George W. Schuyler

Introduction

John M. Kirk and George W. Schuyler

To many people in Canada and the United States, what has happened in Central America[1] in recent years—and what continues to happen— simply defies logic and explanation. In El Salvador the murder of Archbishop Romero, the rape and murder of four U.S. women religious workers, and the seemingly random massacre of tens of thousands of peasants, is confusing enough. In Guatemala and Honduras, military forces exercise veto power over so-called democratic governments and, together with paramilitary death squads, are responsible for thousands of deaths and disappearances. In Nicaragua, before the recent devaluation, inflation raged at 1,400 percent (1987) devouring its currency, the *córdoba*. The U.S.-backed Contras are called the "democratic resistance." They specifically murder teachers, health workers, and rural workers— and indiscriminately kill men, women, and children—in order to terrorize the population. When one adds to this the distortions and lies revealed in the Iran-Contragate hearings, the personal obsession of President Ronald Reagan with Central America, the antics of General Noriega in neighboring Panama, and generally poor media coverage of the region, the resulting obfuscation is hard to clear up.

The images flickering on a television screen are particularly hard to decode in a meaningful way. In 90-second clips, we see an apparently endless stream of reports on guerrillas, civil wars, human rights atrocities, elections, religious polarization, military engagements, and the like. The alphabet soup of acronyms held by various groups and factions helps only to muddy the waters. To make matters worse, network correspondents become "instant experts," spouting "journalese," as they stand, bedecked in their flak jackets, in front of the latest round of carnage. Meanwhile, the *New York Times* states in a page one headline that the "Central American Plight is People in Abundance."[2]

What can we make of all this? Middle America clearly wants no direct military involvement in Central America although, in ever-diminishing percentages, it still supports President Reagan. For many people, the memory of the Indo-China engagement is still fresh. The spectre of televised reports in U.S. living rooms once again of "American boys" fighting abroad—and the steady flow of body bags returning stateside—is clearly unpalatable. On the other hand, there is still much confusion. According to a *New York Times*/CBS poll taken in the summer of 1987, nearly two-thirds of Americans are *still* unsure of where Nicaragua is.[3]

How, for example, can one decipher the "newspeak" concerning elections in the region? North Americans actually saw Salvadoreans lining up for blocks to exercise their democratic rights in what was presented as a burst of patriotic fervor. The images of people muscling their way in to the polling booths haunt others, better informed, who point out that the elections were a sham: that voting was obligatory; that rumors circulated that the death squads would murder all those who could not prove that they had voted (a threat taken seriously in a country where the "security forces" have murdered more than 60,000 since 1979); that government employees would not be paid unless they produced proof of voting; that all ballots were *numbered*, with the number of each ballot being entered into government ledgers (so that it was possible to see how people had voted); that the ballots were placed in a clear plastic ballot box, for all to see; that there were only candidates from the center-right (since the major centrist and left-of-center parties, correctly fearing for their lives, refused to run candidates); and that the government of El Salvador, helped by slick U.S. public relations outfits, deliberately limited the number of polling stations to provide "photo opportunities" for the army of foreign journalists who were there to "report" the event.

A similar predicament faces those who speak positively about Nicaragua. In the view of the Reagan administration and its publicists, "Nicaragua is bad—they're communists; El Salvador is good—they want freedom." The tens of thousands of North Americans who have actually travelled to the region are regarded with tremendous suspicion and occasional hostility when they suggest that Central American reality is not what the U.S. president and his cohorts present. If they explain, for instance, that despite horrendous economic problems the Sandinistas are still popular, they are labelled "naïve." To talk about legislation protecting the autonomy of the indigenous peoples, the massive reduction of illiteracy, the elimination of polio and other diseases, a sweeping land reform, and the redistribution of medical services throughout Nicaragua, is to invite scorn and derision—and to be labelled "a useful fool."

The following anthology continues the debate and seeks to demystify some of the key issues in Central America. Three central themes, democracy, development, and change, are discussed throughout the text. These problems need to be addressed if we are to understand our neighbors to the south.

Democracy is an issue frequently raised by the United States—it must be considered in an anthology of this nature. But what sort of democracy is found in Central America? Racial and class antagonisms divide Central Americans, conditioning attitudes so that demands for change fall on the deaf ears of light-skinned and powerful elites. Effective political participation is limited by massive illiteracy and poverty, the destruction of popular organizations, and the fear of death. Military and paramilitary forces often operate outside constitutional and judicial boundaries but, strengthened by U.S. military aid, no political institution can bring them to heel. For Central Americans, unlike North Americans, press censorship is less important than control of radio stations. Many people cannot read—but everyone listens to the radio. Thus Central American governments carefully control radio stations, as do the governments in almost every Latin American country, including elected democracies.

Given this context, what are the effects of U.S. aid to the "re-democratized" government of El Salvador—the showcase of Reagan's policy in the region? Is the western, liberal concept of democracy *the* model to be emulated in Central America (as the White House would have us believe)? Why can't a revolutionary model embody the principle of "rule by the people"? How has Guatemala fared in the transition to the civilian presidency of Vinicio Cerezo—after thirty years of direct military rule, 38,000 disappearances and 100,000 deaths? Is the democratic welfare state surviving in Costa Rica, the only country without a standing army? What about democracy in Honduras, the site of a large U.S. military base and the recipient of an apparently unending stream of military aid?

To shed light on these complex questions, we have assembled the interpretations of specialists from very different backgrounds. The analysis of democracy begins with El Salvador, the subject of extensive media coverage in recent years. Guillermo Ungo, leader of the opposition *Frente Democrático Revolucionario*, the former vice-presidential running mate of El Salvador's President José Napoleón Duarte, and a member of the 1979 "revolutionary junta," writes insightfully about the much vaunted "democratization" of his country. In January 1988, Ungo returned to El Salvador to mobilize opposition political forces. He wears a bulletproof vest at public meetings because his physical survival is an open question. Liisa North follows with a broader historical overview that places the current Salvadorean political scenario in its historical context.

The remainder of Part I examines other countries of the region, and how they approach democratic government. In Guatemala, as in El Salvador, a Christian Democrat recently won the presidency after many years of military rule. Jim Handy shows that the situation is far less promising than at first it would appear, partly because the military's historical control of the countryside obstructs the democratic transition. Nicaragua's ambassador to Canada, Sergio Lacayo, offers a detailed summary of a radically different model and explains the democratic nature of many of the initiatives undertaken in revolutionary Nicaragua. Judith Weiss rounds off this section with an essay on Honduras, the "banana republic par excellence." She examines both the role of the military and that of the unions and popular organizations that have emerged in recent years.

If the democracy theme is subject to much political and journalistic manipulation, the same can be said about the portrayal of various development issues. Too often the mainstream media assures us that there really *is* a meaningful agrarian reform in El Salvador, and that if the Duarte government could only be left alone by fanatics of the right and left, then meaningful socioeconomic progress would result. Similarly, they tell us that in Guatemala, President Cerezo has made giant strides in helping the less fortunate, particularly the indigenous population, for whom "model villages" (read concentration camps) have been especially constructed. On the other hand, negative views of Nicaragua's social and economic development often accompany the much-maligned image of its "democracy." The general image is of a war-mongering, totalitarian octopus, struggling to smash private enterprise and wrest control of all facets of private ownership from those best qualified to plan the economy rationally. About tiny Costa Rica, that anomaly in all of Latin America, we hear almost nothing; it is generally treated with paternalistic and benign neglect.

Part II of the anthology explores aspects of the development process in Central America. The goal is to consider development as an extraordinarily complex, multifaceted dynamic linked to international and national variables. James Petras and Morris Morley analyze in detail three basic development models in the region: "dependent-welfare" in Costa Rica, "authoritarian" in El Salvador, Guatemala and Honduras, and "revolutionary" in Nicaragua. Four contributions follow on specific dimensions of these models: the political origins of the modern Costa Rican welfare state (Anthony Winson); the impact of development on the Guatemalan Indian (George Lovell); the importance of democratic educational reforms in Nicaragua (Gordon West); and the failure of the military presence in El Salvador (Charles Clements).

Panamanian economist Xabier Gorostiaga notes that ". . . change is a prerequisite for peace, development and democracy in Central America. Change is also an essential condition for the security of the United States in its own backyard."[4] If change is essential, from where will it emerge? Part III thoughtfully probes this often-neglected question. Underpinning this section (and other chapters throughout the collection) is the conviction that fundamental change *is* taking place in Central America—despite massive infusions of military aid, an attempt to convert a "North-South" conflict into an "East-West" one, and an appalling disregard for the most elementary human rights.

The degree of change differs in Central America, depending on a host of historical and socioeconomic variables. Yet it appears in union organizations demonstrating in San Salvador, in Christian base communities in Managua or Guatemala City, in Honduran refugee camps in Honduras, and in the beginnings of an independent policy of President Oscar Arias in Costa Rica. And in North America, where the battle for Central America must also be won, there are signs of change: for every Ben Linder murdered by the Contras,[5] several more volunteers go to work in Nicaragua. Throughout "middle America," church members assist refugees at great personal risk, while academics and journalists belatedly realize that the "Teflon" coating of the Reagan administration is badly flawed. Despite agonizing setbacks, Central Americans and North Americans, linked by solidarity, replace their losses and continue the fight for change.

The essays in Part III capture the vibrancy of this movement. James Petras opens with a provocative analysis of the burgeoning new social movements in Central and South America. Two brief chapters follow on the role of the clergy and Christians seeking change: Blase Bonpane, formerly a Maryknoll priest in Guatemala, criticizes "traditional" theology, and argues for a revitalized, pertinent religious praxis. Mary Ann Lundy, a "middle American" who in many ways symbolizes the rising wave of awareness in North America, and who suffered U.S. government harassment because of her "practical" religion, describes the spectacular growth of the Sanctuary Movement.

The last four contributors focus on change in the United States. They collectively see the Reagan administration as the greatest supporter of the status quo in Central America, and hence the greatest obstacle to meaningful change. They include academics Walter LaFeber, Susanne Jonas, and Sandor Halebsky; a 24-year State Department veteran turned academic, Wayne Smith; and the well-known actor and activist on Central America, Ed Asner. Despite varied backgrounds and experiences, they all point an accusing finger at short-sighted, impractical, and immoral U.S. policies toward Central America—policies that have resulted in the death of more than 100,000 Central Americans during the last eight years alone. As in Vietnam, the Middle East, the Caribbean, and elsewhere in the Third World, the United States government fails to comprehend the complex dynamics of these societies, preferring to see them only through the distorted lenses of its own image and interests. Meanwhile, the mounting corpses bear eloquent testimony to this selfish folly.

Unless the body politic of North America comes to realize the extent of its involvement, the tragedy of Central America will continue for years to come, undoubtedly accompanied by the "insight" of countless politicians and media pundits who try to "tell it like it is." If, however, we are to begin to understand the reality of life in that region, we must step outside the one-dimensional, stereotypical images given to us in the mainstream media. We can start by questioning government policy, demanding explanations for unacceptable behavior by our officials, and pushing for our own form of honesty, integrity, and *glasnost*. A healthy cynicism will help to puncture the many myths currently foisted off as "the truth." The contributions in this collection present insights that bear on such myths. The challenge is to remain vigilant and to speak out so that they do not resurface—if for no other reason, we owe it to the 100,000 who have paid for them with their blood since 1980.

NOTES

1. Central America includes seven countries: Belize, Panama, Costa Rica, Nicaragua, Honduras, El Salvador, and Guatemala. Since the crisis of Central America principally revolves around the last five countries, this anthology focuses on them.

2. *New York Times*, 6 September 1987.

3. Cited in *Access, Cooperative Newsletter of the American Forum* (New York), no. 75 (January 1988): 6. "Slightly less than one-third of Americans can correctly place Nicaragua in Central or Latin America. Another third said they did not know. Twenty-one percent said it is in South America. The remaining 15 percent placed it in the Middle East, Africa, or Asia."

4. NACLA, *Report on the Americas* (July/August 1987): 10. Gorostiaga is a Jesuit who currently heads the Regional Office for Economic and Social Research in Managua.

5. Ben Linder, an unarmed American volunteer working on agricultural projects in Nicaragua, was shot at point blank range by Contra troops in early 1987.

PART I
DEMOCRACY

1
El Salvador: "Democratization" to Halt the Insurgency

Guillermo Manuel Ungo

The false process of "democratization" urged by the Reagan administration is just one of the political components of the U.S. counterinsurgency efforts in El Salvador. It is a case of "democracy of the right and for the right," complete with state of siege, political persecution, imprisonment, assassination, and the deprivation of political liberty for all those considered to be the "insurgents," "subversives," or "terrorists." It is, of course, interesting to remember that these same epithets now tossed around by Mr. Duarte to discredit progressive political, social and union organizations, are the very same ones received by the Christian Democrats themselves in the 1970s when we were allies in opposing the proimperialist military regime of the oligarchy.

Ingenuous or biased opinions, particularly those close to international Christian Democrat positions, or perhaps with exaggerated devotion to the appearance of democracy, believe that a modest process of democratization has taken place in El Salvador. According to this line of thought, such a process has begun with the reactivation of the political right wing of the country, and now only needs a similar development from the democratic left. The elections held in El Salvador illustrate clearly this belief.

What is certain is that before this counterinsurgency project began, complete with the participation of the Salvadorean Christian Democrats, the right wing had very little political expression. Rather, they exercised influence through their powerful associations, the control of the government and state apparatus, the media (which they monopolize completely), and—through the army—totally directed by the oligarchy. Thanks to the government of Magaña and Duarte the right wing grew politically, with several political parties, as they exploited the space now closed to the progressive and popular forces. State terrorism on a massive scale, in which "security forces" assassinated more than 60,000 persons, then took charge of this singular and exclusive "democracy." Let us not forget that Somoza, too, held elections, and that Stroessner is a product of Paraguayan electoral "democracy." This is why we consider it important to distinguish clearly between democratization, a democratic opening, a political opening, or simply the existence of some space for social and political activity.

It is difficult to talk of democratization when there is a war of counterinsurgency, one in which the internal enemy is the very people itself—the most oppressed and exploited sectors who are now organized in their opposition. It is precisely because they have been violently excluded—through repression and death—from any participation in meaningful political, economic and social development, that they have had to opt for armed resistance, for legitimate defense, and their right to survive. They have joined the insurgency after decades of suffering fraud, persecution, torture, imprisonment, exile, and death—first by the hundreds, and subsequently in the thousands.

It is also difficult to talk of democratization when there exists a power structure in which the machinery designed precisely to assassinate people is untouchable, and functions in perfect accord with the needs and interests of the dominant minority. It is clear in El Salvador that after assassinating tens of thousands of compatriots—as Pinochet did at the outset in Chile—this state terrorism has become more selective and better organized. No one is ever found responsible for these political crimes: it is as if there were an exterminating angel who descends from heaven every day. No Salvadorean can be ignorant of these functional, organic activities of the so-called "death squads," which depend on the repressive military apparatus of the regime. It is not by chance that, as a result of the state of siege, these political crimes are committed when the army and the security forces control the cities and the streets, especially at night.

Nor can we talk of a democratic opening, since the political process has opened solely for the fascists and rightists in general. Mr. Duarte invited us to participate in elections, in a move which was false, hypocritical, and dishonest. Everybody understood that it was merely an invitation for us to engage in collective suicide. To show up in order to be assassinated: a deadly jest. At the very least, this invitation could be considered a hoax of hypocritical Christians who tie your hands behind your back and then invite you to play basketball. Let us not forget that the power structure, including the Military High Command, treats us as "subversives," to be dealt with through persecution, imprisonment and death. The cemeteries bear eloquent witness to their policies, for democracy continues to be seen as "subversive."

Consequently, one cannot claim that Mr. Duarte's regime has brought about a simple political opening, one that is limited and controlled—as is the case in Guatemala. There, several moderate leftist political groups that "behave themselves" *can* participate in political life, although groups which might threaten the status quo are still excluded. In other words, the motto appears to be: "Welcome—as long as you do not endanger our interests."

Unfortunately, the Duarte regime can't provide even this small luxury. Its power is too weak and precarious, and as a result even a minimal participation by the FDR would destroy this unstable balance, leaving Duarte in a greater, more accelerated, crisis. We do not forget that the Christian Democratic party in El Salvador has taken advantage of the repression to occupy—temporarily—some of our traditional political space, with the illusion that people must choose them as the lesser evil. The problem facing Mr. Duarte and the Christian Democrats, though, is their growing isolation and weakness; it is increasingly difficult to regard them as the "lesser evil" in the midst of an acute economic, social, and political crisis. In the end it is preferable to struggle for improvement rather than to choose an evil which strikes all so profoundly. If there were any doubts concerning the political opening of this regime, one has only to read the declarations and speeches of their principal leaders, observations which are increasingly menacing, accusing almost everyone of being a "subversive."

The image of Mr. Duarte as the democrat, a Christian fervently interested in dialogue, is rapidly disappearing. His responsibility in the repressive, antidemocratic and counterinsurgency process is clear. His inability to develop a serious dialogue, to fulfill the agreements we arrived at with him and his representatives at La Palma and Ayagualo, and the interruption in this dialogue for more than two years, have removed his credibility as a man of peace. Moreover, with regard to his conduct as a Christian, it is worth recalling an article of Gabriel García Márquez, who pointed out that Duarte's Christianity was based upon his having sent thousands of Salvadoreans to heaven, as a result of state terrorism.

When Mr. Duarte has travelled abroad to visit political leaders who are friends of ours, he has had to refer to leaders of the FDR in positive terms as a means of ingratiating himself with them. He has invited us to return to El Salvador, to join his "democratic process," and has assured us that there is no danger of political persecution. (One can cite, for example, his declarations to the Madrid daily, *El País*, in November 1985). Just a few weeks later the dishonesty of this position was made abundantly clear, in December of that year, when he threatened to imprison an FDR delegation which had made public its objective of entering the country to participate in a peace forum, organized by the University of El Salvador.

Nobody gives away what they do not possess. A regime which has no democratic nature or character, which responds as it has to the insurgency, and which refuses to seek a peaceful solution by means of dialogue, can neither democratize the country, guarantee a democratic avenue, or even propose a political opening. The recent amendments to the electoral law, for the exclusive benefit of the Christian Democrats, represent yet another step against meaningful pluralism.

All of this leads us to examine the problem of political space. That is something quite different. Some kinds of political space are indeed found in Chile and Paraguay, and also in El Salvador. In our country the existing spaces are found principally in the area of civil society, even though they may have a political dimension. The unions, professional associations, civic groups, and those dealing with human rights have greater and better possibilities of action—although they are the victims of covert, or even overt repression when the regime is unable, or refuses, to absorb social protest. It goes without saying that activities from the right wing, even when they favor the idea of a military coup, are not the objects of any repression.

But if there is, then, what can be termed limited social space in El Salvador, this space is sharply reduced when it is a matter of specific political activity. It is then that the repressive framework enters into play. Despite this, the popular struggle has continued to open up greater space for political action. Moreover, this space will continue to widen, with the growth of popular mobilization, as the crisis deepens in the country.

The regime's counterinsurgency effort requires an acceptable human face. The Christian Democrats provide it and the regime therefore allows a limited space, giving the appearance of a degree of democratization. The dilemma confronting the present regime lies in the fact that the increase in the popular movement could become a major political earthquake unless it is stopped through repressive means. If the regime then resorts to violence and repression, we will see a confrontation between popular mobilization and state repression. That, however, would be the final stage of the counterinsurgency project, since as General Blandón, Head of the General Staff of the Armed Forces, has himself said, this war cannot be won unless the minds and the hearts of the people are also won. Fortunately, our people are not masochists.

2

Democratization in El Salvador: Illusion or Reality?

Liisa L. North

Christian Democratic Party leader José Napoleón Duarte was inaugurated president of El Salvador in June 1984 following national elections which he won with a plurality. In the subsequent Legislative Assembly elections of March 1985, his party obtained a majority of the seats. If elections actually determined who governs in El Salvador, as of mid-1987, the Christian Democratic Party (PDC) had exercised both executive and legislative power for more than two years. In reality, the capacity of elected officials to initiate and implement policy was painfully constrained by the historic power of the country's economic elite and military institutions, and by its overwhelming dependence on the United States.

Moreover, both the presidential and Legislative Assembly elections were held only among parties on one side of a civil war. The conditions were not present for participation by the leftist opposition—the Revolutionary Democratic Front (FDR) and its allied guerrilla movement, and the Farabundo Martí National Liberation Front (FMLN). In addition to the fact that the elections were nonrepresentative, they were also marred by corruption, intimidation, and fraud. Nevertheless, international observers, including official Canadian and U.S. delegations, certified the honesty of Duarte's election and contributed an aura of legitimacy to the new government. The mass media followed suit. They interpreted the electoral process as having created the conditions for advancing democratization and moderate reform.

The major proposals in Duarte's campaign platform promised a movement toward democratization. Most importantly, they included: first, dialogue with the revolutionary opposition in order to create the conditions for peace and for their future participation in the political process;

secondly, respect for human rights, including prosecution of gross offenders; and thirdly, agrarian reform and other redistributive measures designed to improve the living standards of the majority of the population who subsisted in abject poverty.

Movement toward peace through dialogue, respect for human rights and redistributive reforms were not only necessary but also interrelated components of democratization in El Salvador. Each was required and one could not exist without the other. Without peace, the country's profound economic crisis could not be resolved nor could reforms be effectively carried out. But advances toward peace and reform required dialogue with the FDR/FMLN, for they represented a broad spectrum of the population, especially those sectors historically excluded from the political process and denied the benefits of the economic growth which El Salvador had experienced in the past. Democratic competition, opposition organization, and critical thought per se could not develop without respect for political human rights, including the FDR/FMLN's. Political rights, in turn, were of limited value to individuals if their basic social and economic needs were not satisfied. Is it possible to consider a society democratic if more than half the population barely subsists due to the maldistribution of income and other resources?

The revolutionary opposition in El Salvador emerged in the 1970s precisely because peaceful efforts to obtain redistributive reforms were repressed by the military-oligarchic coalition which had ruled the country since the late nineteenth century. Violence against the majority of the population was woven into the social and political fabric of this regime which has been described as a "reactionary despotism."[1]

Inaugurated president in June 1984, with majority legislative support since March 1985, Duarte and the PDC have had the opportunity to demonstrate that elections in the context of civil war could make a difference in policy-making in El Salvador. This chapter seeks to evaluate his administration's record with reference to the different aspects of movement toward democracy as formulated above. It then places his presidency within the historical context of United States foreign policy, and concludes with remarks on Canadian foreign policy toward El Salvador.

DEMOCRATIZATION

In the fall of 1984, shortly after Duarte's inauguration, his government and the revolutionary opposition held two sets of widely publicized conversations. The talks largely responded to the buildup of popular pressure, both within the PDC and the general public, and sought to evaluate the conditions under which the FDR/FMLN might participate in the political process. During the next two years, no further conversations took place despite the FDR/FMLN's repeated offers to deepen the dialogue. Finally, following preliminary private meetings under Mexican auspices, the government agreed to a third round of peace talks to be held in September 1986 in the town of Sesori. A few days before the scheduled date, the Salvadorean armed forces violated the security arrangements on which Duarte had agreed. The Arce Battalion, commanded by Colonel Roberto Mauricio Staben—an officer implicated in corruption and human rights abuses—surrounded the town. Under the circumstances, the FDR/FMLN refused to send its representatives to Sesori on the grounds that their physical security was not guaranteed. In response, rather than confront the military, Duarte accused the FDR/FMLN of lacking serious interest in negotiations.

The regional peace accord signed by the Central American heads of state on August 7, 1987 in Guatemala introduced new incentives as well as complications for the renewal of talks. Among other things, it committed the signatory governments to seek dialogue with "all unarmed internal opposition groups and with those who have availed themselves of the amnesty."[2] This formulation was designed to pave the way for the disbandment of the Contras who lacked popular support inside Nicaragua and depended on United States aid to sustain their war from bases in Honduras. Contrary to the Reagan administration's demands, the Guatemala accord did not require the Sandinista government to negotiate with the Contras. But neither did it require Duarte to negotiate with the FDR/FMLN, which conversely enjoys widespread popular support inside El Salvador and has sustained its war without major external assistance. Nevertheless, the accord raised expectations of renewed dialogue once again.

Steps in that direction were likely to be slow and difficult. In three years, Duarte had devoted little energy to preparing the ground for peace talks or creating the political conditions in which the physical security of FDR/FMLN leaders would be guaranteed. Indeed, it may be argued that, following the initial round of conversations in the fall of 1984, the government—in accordance with the military's counterinsurgency campaign—adopted an increasingly hard line toward the revolutionary opposition.

In the fall of 1985, for example, a local peace group announced that representatives from all parties, including FDR leaders in exile, would be invited to attend a forum on "ending the war." Instead of welcoming this initiative to generate momentum for negotiations, Duarte responded that FDR leader Guillermo Ungo

"and other rebel political officials are subject to arrest because they are aligned with the main guerrilla alliance, the . . . FMLN."
Duarte said the rebel leaders must "answer to all of the crimes committed by

the FMLN. They have to answer before a judge and they can only be freed by a (legislative) amnesty."

Asked directly what would happen to rebel officials if they tried to return from exile, Duarte said, "the most probable thing is that the security forces would take responsibility in that regard."[3]

Subsequently, the armed forces issued a communiqué confirming that FDR representatives, should they return, would be arrested as "common criminals."[4] Duarte had also referred to FMLN leaders as "delinquents."[5]

Statements such as these, in effect, denied the legitimacy of the country's principal opposition forces. They also belied the government's assertion that the FDR/FMLN could have laid down their arms and participated without fear of reprisals in the 1984 and 1985 elections.

To be sure, the limited "political opening" introduced with Duarte's election was not without positive conseqences. It permitted the development of a nonpartisan popular movement in the major cities, with urban labor most visible within it. However, even the organizations participating in that movement faced repression. Their activists and leaders were regularly harassed; arbitrary arrests, disappearances, and torture continued; assassinations were carried out although not with the frequency of the early 1980s. To recall recent history, more than 5,000 members of the labor movement and an entire generation of its leaders were killed by death squads and the military between 1978 and 1982.[6] Altogether, some 50,000 individuals had lost their lives in El Salvador's civil war prior to Duarte's election. By mid-1987, the death toll had climbed to over 60,000. As before, the great majority of the victims were noncombatant civilians.

In sum, only the political rights of groups vociferously on one side of the civil war were fully respected. That was the bottom line beyond which the "political opening" did not advance. Even the nonpartisan organizations which called for the implementation of Duarte's election promises—including human rights, humanitarian and church groups —functioned under threat. Government propaganda linked them to "communist-inspired destabilization" and "even terrorism".[7] Meanwhile, political parties to the right of the PDC campaigned freely and the government called on them to work "for national unity in the face of the 'common enemy'. "[8] A new movement, Patria Libre, was launched by the resurgent right in September 1985.

Continuing human rights violations reflected the limitations of the "political opening." In its review of the situation in 1985, the Americas Watch Committee concluded that "the abuse of human rights had settled into a routine" in El Salvador. According to the tabulations of Tutela Legal, the human rights office of the Archdiocese of El Salvador, there were at least 1,913 victims of abuses in 1985: "1,740 at the hands of the

armed forces and death squads linked to them; 173 at the h
guerrillas."[9] These figures included 1,045 civilian noncomb
resulting from military operations, 136 targeted death squad vicu.
104 targeted assassinations by government military and security force
The most frequently singled out for assassination were precisely those
individuals actively involved in or leading the popular movement.

The Canadian nongovernmental organization (NGO) and church-
sponsored "Mission for Peace," which visited El Salvador in late 1986,
reported 1,576 victims during that year.[10] These included forty-five targeted assassinations by death squads and seventy-eight by government
military and security forces.[11]

The 1985 and 1986 figures certainly represented a decline with reference
to previous years: approximately 9,000 victims in 1980, 12,501 in 1981,
5,399 in 1982, 5,142 in 1983 and 2,881 in 1984.[12] Nevertheless, the frequency of human rights violations during Duarte's presidency remained
at a monstrous level. Repression simply became more sophisticated and
selective as the massive and indiscriminate violence of the previous years
was finally deemed politically counterproductive by the United States
and by sectors of the Salvadorean civilian and military elites. If the country's human rights abuses during 1985–86 had been recorded in Nicaragua, they would have generated front page headlines; it is indicative
of media bias that they were simply endorsed as signs of progress.

While President Duarte pointed to the "crimes" of the revolutionary
opposition, Salvadorean officers remained immune from prosecution for
human rights violations. Only soldiers implicated in the killings of United
States citizens were tried and sentenced. Their commanders and other
officers who directed the continuing terror were even rewarded with
promotions. The structures of repression remained intact.[13]

The growth of the refugee and displaced populations also reflected
the continuing high level of human rights abuses. Approximately one-
quarter of the Salvadorean population was displaced or fled into exile
during the course of the civil war. Roughly half a million entered the
United States; more than 248,000 escaped to other Central American
countries and Mexico; some 468,000 remained displaced within El Salvador.[14] The ebb and flow of refugees correlated with army sweeps in
the countryside. Following Duarte's election, the United States Congress
increased both economic and military aid to reward and fortify the transition to civilian rule. As a consequence, the armed forces intensified
their counterinsurgency campaign and the "political opening" did not
extend to the rural areas.

Since civilians living in guerrilla-controlled or contested areas were
considered FMLN supporters, "the army generally treat[ed] them as legitimate targets. In fact, Salvadorean army officers have admitted that
their main tool for convincing rural inhabitants to stop helping the guer-

rillas is terror."[15] In other words, most civilian casualties and refugees were victims of politically motivated violence rather than accidental casualties of war. The military's counterinsurgency strategy relied heavily on forced mass displacements which also involved the destruction of homes and crops. During 1985–86, indiscriminate attacks against civilians actually increased[16] rather than decreased as could have been expected if the government were attempting to create the political environment for negotiations.

In short, dialogue did not advance in El Salvador and the human rights situation remained dreadful. Popular expectations concerning redistributive reforms and improvements in living standards remained unrealized.

The agrarian reform law decreed in March 1980 was partly implemented before Duarte assumed the presidency. As of 1986, approximately 22 percent of the agricultural population, which makes up approximately half of the total labor force, had technically benefitted to varying degrees. Observers generally agreed that, in most cases, the benefits were marginal or undercut by the effects of war. Some thought that no positive change had taken place. A professor of sociology at the University of Central America argued that "[t]he agrarian reform hasn't solved the agricultural crisis in El Salvador because it hasn't changed the way capital is accumulated. The oligarchy is more powerful now. If anything, the reforms aggravated the wide differences in wealth."[17] Moreover, there were no plans for extending or deepening the reform program. This meant that most rural inhabitants who could not meet their basic needs in 1980 continued to live in conditions of abject poverty.[18] Neither did employment opportunities improve—at least 40 percent of agricultural laborers worked less than six months per year. Meanwhile, unemployment in the cities increased with the influx of refugees from the countryside and the continuing economic decline.

A spectacular increase in U.S. aid (see Table 2.1) could not reverse the economic decline and the deterioration of mass living standards caused by continued war and depressed international markets for El Salvador's exports. By 1986, per capita income had fallen 32 percent with respect to 1979, and the prospects for improvement were dim.[19] According to official government statistics, unemployment stood at 31.1 percent of the labor force.[20] The multiple costs of war—destruction of infrastructure, crop losses, capital flight, the price of diverting resources and personnel from civilian to military functions, the drain of skills through emigration, the loss of productive capacity produced by population displacement—argued for a negotiated settlement which, according to polls, 80–90 percent of Salvadoreans favored.[21] Instead, the government continued to pursue war and, in January 1986, introduced an austerity budget to deal with the deepening economic crisis and the

Table 2.1

U.S. AID TO EL SALVADOR (thousands of $ U.S.)

Year	Economic	Military	Total
FY 1980	58,549	6,200	65,749
FY 1981	116,349	30,500	146,849
FY 1982	185,676	80,500	266,166
FY 1983	261,867	81,300	343,167
FY 1984	224,302	206,550	430,852
FY 1985	432,231	136,250	568,481
FY 1986	—	—	545,000
FY 1987	—	—	770,000

Sources: Americas Watch Committee (May 1986), p. 150 for 1980-1985; *Newsweek* (March 1987) for 1986-1987.

increasing military expenditures. The austerity measures hit precisely those sectors of the population who could least afford them; the business elites successfully derailed proposed taxes which would have made them pay a greater share of the costs of war.

As a consequence of the government's failures to advance the peace process and implement promised reforms, popular opposition increased dramatically in 1986–87.[22] Even Christian Democratic control of its affiliated worker and peasant movement—the Popular Democratic Unity (UPD)—slipped. A new broadly based center-left coalition of unions, peasant associations and other popular organizations—the National Unity of Salvadorean Workers (UNTS)—was founded to oppose the austerity program and declining real wages. It attracted unions and activists who had been traditionally allied to the PDC. The government's incapacity to respond to the extensive damage caused by the October 1986 earthquake and the spread of corruption in Duarte's administration further deepened disillusionment.[23] The increasing popular protest provoked increasing repression—the historic vicious circle of Salvadorean politics.

THE HISTORICAL CONTEXT

How can the lack of progress on all the dimensions of democratization be explained? Insufficient political will on Duarte's part does not provide a sufficient explanation, although the statements cited above reflected it. Essentially, the president was blocked by a triple alliance whose members included the military and security forces, the economic elite, and the Reagan administration. U.S. policy rested on strengthening the military and business elites. All three were convinced that the revolutionary opposition could be militarily defeated, and that was their goal. Correctly, they perceived negotiations, the prosecution of human rights violators and redistributive reforms as policies inimical to their interests since those policies necessarily implied a diminution of their power.[24]

The United States played a critical role in the power equation: its massive aid program fortified the institutions and social classes that had historically repressed popular organizations and opposed even the mildest of reforms. El Salvador's oligarchy, backed by military force, organized the inequitable and oppressive system that eventually spawned the civil war that entered its eighth year in 1987.[25]

The roots of this system extend back to the Spanish conquest. However, it was in the 1880s that "liberal reforms" accelerated the dispossession of the Salvadorean peasantry by eliminating the legal recognition of communal landownership. The reforms were inspired by large landowners allied to merchant and banking interests attracted by the possibilities of expanding coffee exports. This modern and market-oriented oligarchy embarked on the wholesale and violent expropriation of the lands of the communal indigenous peasantry. They created police and specialized security forces and modernized the army to carry out these "reforms" whose goal was to convert communal property owners cultivating food crops into a landless and cheap labor force for export production.

Although the Salvadorean economy diversified and grew rapidly following World War II, the benefits of growth did not "trickle down" as expected. To the contrary, the diversification of export production (cotton and sugar) led to increased concentration of land in large estates and the growth of unemployment and underemployment in the rural areas. While the percentage of the agricultural population with no land or less than one hectare moved up from 52.6 percent in 1961 to 75 percent in 1972, estate owners mechanized production and hired labor only at peak seasons.

Industrial promotion policies, beginning in the mid-1950s, led to the growth of urban production but the use of capital-intensive technology meant relatively few employment opportunities. In short, a system which denied income-earning property or employment at reasonable wage rates to the majority of the population was put in place in the late nineteenth century and it further consolidated during subsequent decades.

When civil war broke out in 1980, 68.1 percent of the total population (57.6 percent in the urban areas and 76.4 percent in the rural areas) could not meet their basic needs according to studies conducted by the United Nations Economic Commission for Latin America and the Caribbean (UN-ECLAC).[26] The poorest 20 percent of the population (with an average income of $46.50 per year) received an estimated 2 percent of national income while the top 20 percent concentrated 66 percent. El Salvador's people had the lowest caloric intake in Latin America. Its socioeconomic and political structures systematically produced and reproduced injustice.

The revolutionary opposition organized to redress these conditions which were the causes of the civil war. Since its outbreak, mass living standards have deteriorated and Duarte's administration has not been able to halt that deterioration. His economic strategy relied on reactivating the private sector and did not deviate fundamentally from the failed policies that produced the civil war. Despite his intentions, the ability of Duarte and his party to promote positive changes—to move toward democratization and address the causes of war—was severely restricted because winning elections in 1984 and 1985 did not mean winning effective power in El Salvador. As one observer noted, land reform

would alienate the business class whose support he needs to rebuild the economy and attract foreign investment. To prosecute military officers for human rights abuses would alienate the high command whose cooperation has never been more than grudging. To talk to guerrillas about "humanizing the war," as the Catholic church proposes, would disturb both. And to overcome such opposition by mobilizing the Christian Democrats' traditional constituency—workers, peasants, middle class professionals—Duarte would run the risk of setting off again the kind of death-squad violence that had punished these same groups between 1980 and 1983.[27]

UNITED STATES POLICY

The United States has kept the civil war going through military aid, and the private sector afloat through economic aid. In the 1980s, El Salvador, a small country of 5,000,000 people, became the third largest recipient of U.S. economic aid in the world. In per-capita terms, it ranked at the top. The total aid package increased from $65.7 million in fiscal year 1980 to approximately $770 million in 1987 (see Table 2.1), and these figures did not include all forms of aid. [Although U.S. government reports classified 80 percent of the total as economic, the arms control and foreign policy caucus of the U.S. Senate concluded that 60 percent went to military purposes, and only 15 percent to urgently needed reform and development projects.[28]] Military expenditures soaked up some 40 percent of El Salvador's public spending.[29]

U.S. aid fueled the growth of El Salvador's military and security forces from 16,850 men in 1981 to 57,640 in 1986.[30] Sophisticated weapons and communications systems were added to their arsenal. Training programs enhanced their capacity not only to wage war but also to manage the so-called civic action projects which were incorporated into their counterinsurgency and pacification strategies. The various components of those strategies were brought together in the military's own development program—"United to Reconstruct"—announced in mid-1986, independent of the civilian political authorities. Towards the end of that year, Western diplomats in San Salvador observed that the "military [was] larger, better armed and more politically savvy than ever."[31]

The aid priorities of the United States represented a vote of confidence in the very institutions which defended oligarchic privilege, repressed popular organizations, and were responsible for monstrous human rights abuses. It clearly signalled the U.S. commitment to a military solution that would deny a political role to the revolutionary opposition which championed popular demands for effective redistributive reforms.

The military's violation of the terms on which Duarte had agreed to hold conversations with the FDR/FMLN in 1986 reflected their increasing power, their capacity to block negotiations and their confidence in U.S. support for such actions. A shocking indicator of all this was that the commander of the operation that surrounded Sesori, Colonel Roberto Mauricio Staben, had successfully defied Duarte's efforts to arrest him earlier that year. Colonel Staben, "a powerful officer friendly with U.S. military advisers and a man feared for his death-squad activities," had been identified as the leader of a gang of right-wing officers that "specialized in posing as guerrillas and kidnapping rich businessmen."[32]

The strengthening of El Salvador's military institutions contradicts the possibilities of progress toward democratization. The militarization of society is likely to deepen for two basic reasons. First, the armed forces are extending their functions through psychological operations and the management of the "reconstruction and development" projects previously considered civilian responsibilities. Second, and amazingly enough, the FMLN succeeded in resisting the almost quadrupled manpower and weaponry of the armed forces. During the twelve months ending May 31, 1986, the Salvadorean armed forces "suffered 477 dead, 2,482 wounded and 50 missing."[33] Having reorganized into smaller, more mobile units and adopted new tactics, in March 1987, the FMLN partly destroyed the country's second-largest military base—El Paraíso—which was considered impregnable. In addition to engaging the army in several provinces, in May, the FMLN executed another major attack on an important garrison. All this demonstrated that the war was far from over.

CANADIAN POLICY

Canada's November 1986 statement on the Salvadorean human rights situation at the United Nations included praise for improvements in respect for human rights, support for dialogue with the FDR/FMLN and an endorsement of the 1984 election results. With reference to the latter, the statement read: "since the 1984 elections in El Salvador were seen by Canada as being valid and representative of the popular will, we do not view the two sides as being equal in legitimacy." It was on the basis of this type of evaluation that Canada, in late 1984, announced that it would renew bilateral aid. That decision was implemented in 1986 despite objections raised by Canadian nongovernmental organizations and church groups.[34] Aid had been suspended in 1980 due to the prevalence of gross and systematic human rights abuses.

If the analysis presented here is valid, renewed bilateral assistance will not promote democratization in El Salvador. Rather, it legitimizes a regime in which the military exercises considerably more than veto power, and in which luxury exists for the few and abject poverty for the many. The Duarte government is clearly incapable of dismantling the organizations and transforming the structures which systematically violated political, social and economic human rights; continued a war against representative popular organizations; and subordinated development and reform programs to military objectives.

Moreover, the Canadian statement of support for dialogue cannot be taken at face value since it did not accord equal legitimacy to the parties in conflict, and identified the 1984 election results as "representative of the popular will." Bilateral aid should have followed, rather than preceded, negotiations and the attainment of peace. Humanitarian aid could have continued and even been increased through NGO and church channels while the Canadian government encouraged negotiation. Although Canada and the United States differ significantly on Central America and the peace process, they follow similar policies toward El Salvador. With the renewal of bilateral aid, Canada converted itself into a minor partner in a war sustained by the United States and designed to shore up an archaic regime that obstructs long overdue political and socioeconomic changes. The path toward democratization in El Salvador has yet to be pursued with any seriousness: it remains essentially an illusion.

NOTES

1. Enrique Baloyra, "Reactionary Despotism in El Salvador," in *Trouble in Our Backyard: Central America and the United States in the Eighties,* ed. Martin Diskin (New York: Pantheon Books, 1983).

2. *New York Times,* 12 August 1987.

3. Cited from the *Miami Herald,* in Americas Watch Committee, *Settling into Routine: Human Rights Abuses in Duarte's Second Year* (New York: Americas Watch Committee, May 1986), 117.

4. Ibid.

5. Ibid.

6. Ibid., 104, quoted from the *Wall Street Journal.*

7. Latin American Working Group, "Taking Sides: Canadian Aid to El Salvador," *LAWG Letter* (Toronto) 10, no. 1 (1987): 16; Inter-Church Committee on Human Rights in Latin America (ICCHRLA), *Newsletter, Annual Reports 1987* (Toronto), nos. 1 & 2 (1987): 25.

8. Latin American Working Group, "Taking Sides," 16.

9. Americas Watch Committee, *Settling into Routine*, 2–3.

10. Mission for Peace, *Interim Report* (Toronto, December 1986): 2. See also ICCHRLA, "1986 Annual Report on the Human Rights Situation in El Salvador," *Newsletter, Annual Reports 1987* (Toronto, January 1987).

11. ICCHRLA, *Newsletter, Annual Reports 1987*, no. 4 (1987): 2.

12. Liisa L. North, "El Salvador," in *International Handbook of Human Rights*, eds. Jack Donnelly and Rhoda Howard (Westport, Conn.: Greenwood Press, 1987).

13. Americas Watch Committee, *Settling into Routine*, 45.

14. William Dean Stanley, "Economic Migrants or Refugees from Violence: A Time-Series Analysis of Salvadoran Migration to the United States," *Latin American Research Review* 10, no. 1 (1987): 134, 136–37.

15. Ibid., 136.

16. Ibid.

17. *New York Times*, 28 September 1987; See also Laurence R. Simon and James C. Stephens, *El Salvador Land Reform, 1980–81: Impact Audit* (Boston: Oxfam America, 1981), for a discussion of the limitations of the law itself.

18. UN-ECLAC Mexico City Office, "The Crisis in Central America: Its Origins, Scope and Consequences," *CEPAL Review*, no. 22 (April 1984): 62.

19. *Latin America Monitor-Central America Region* (London: Latin America Monitor, 1987).

20. *Central America Report* 14, no. 30 (August 7, 1987): 236.

21. Tom Barry and Deb Preusch, "The War in El Salvador: A Reassessment," *Monthly Review* 38, no. 11 (April 1987): 43.

22. See, for example, Joseph Contreras, "Duarte's Unkept Promises: Attack from All Sides," *Newsweek* (March 2, 1987): 35; Philip Bennett, "Discontent Growing in El Salvador," *Boston Globe*, 10 August 1987.

23. Chris Norton, "Christian Democrats Gripped by Corruption," *In These Times* 11, no. 32, (August 19–September 1, 1987): 9.

24. See, for example, Jefferson Morley, "Prisoner of Success," *New York Review of Books* 33, no. 19 (December 4, 1986): 15–20; NACLA, "Duarte: Prisoner of War," *Report on the Americas* 20, no. 1 (January /March 1986).

25. For a review of the historical process, see Liisa North, *Bitter Grounds: Roots of Revolt in El Salvador*, 2nd ed. (Toronto: Between the Lines, 1985). For a detailed discussion of the period extending from the commencement of the civil war to 1983, see Raymond Bonner, *Weakness and Deceit: U.S. Policy and El Salvador* (New York: Times Books, 1984).

26. UN-ECLAC, "Crisis in Central America," 20.

27. Morley, "Prisoner of Success," 20.

28. *Latin America Monitor-Central America Region*.

29. ICCHRLA, *Newsletter, Annual Reports 1987*, 22.

30. *New York Times*, 19 April 1987.

31. *New York Times*, 21 September 1986.

32. Morley, "Prisoner of Success," 20.

33. ICCHRLA, Newsletter, *Annual Reports 1987*, 21.

34. See Latin American Working Group, "Taking Sides," for a critical analysis of Canada's bilateral program.

3

Democracy, Military Rule, and Agrarian Reform in Guatemala

Jim Handy

> The Constitution of the Republic tells us this: (And hear me well, I am not going to supercede the law if the law stops me. I am going to supercede the law if the law is not functioning and does not work for the people).
>
> Article 34 of the Constitution that the deputies passed two years ago and is now in effect says: "Social interest prevails over private interest. . . ."
>
> Social interest is the interests of thousands of you. . . .
> —Padre Girón at a sermon discussing
> land reform in Nueva Concepción,
> Escuintla, Guatemala, Feb. 22, 1986

Between 1982 and 1987 Guatemala experienced some rather startling changes. Probably none of them was so startling as the military's acceptance of relatively free elections and then allowing the Christian Democrat candidate, Vinicio Cerezo Arévalo, to take the president's office in January 1986. The inauguration of Cerezo after many years of military dominance in Guatemala was widely applauded from diverse sides of the political spectrum in Central America and elsewhere.[1]

Some observers did not share in the general euphoria accompanying the election, however, and remained cynical about the prospects of enduring democracy in Guatemala. They suggested that the military either stepped aside briefly to allow a civilian government to take the blame for predicted economic troubles, or that military acquiescence was a temporary policy used to win much needed foreign economic and military assistance for Guatemala.[2]

The key to understanding the repeated interventions of the Guatemalan military in the political process lies in Guatemala's rural heartland, the highlands and the Pacific Coast, where the military has long been the undisputed power. Any significant social and economic change must also begin here. A substantial agrarian reform remains the key to both economic development and any level of functioning democracy in Guatemala. But agrarian reform entails, by necessity, the mobilization of the peasantry and the rural poor. The military has repeatedly demonstrated that it will not countenance such mobilization. This chapter provides a context for understanding the severe limits to the current democratic interregnum in Guatemala and the prospects for enduring democracy there. It first outlines the reasons for military involvement in the political process and then discusses the current pressures for agrarian reform in Guatemala.

MILITARY INTERVENTION IN GUATEMALA

The military has always played an important role in Guatemala's political process. As early as the 1920s, observers divided the dominant Liberal party into a civilian and military wing. The two streams could usually unite in opposition to the Unionist and Conservative parties, but otherwise bitterly fought each other for predominance within the party and government. Even within the military faction there was serious conflict, best represented by the feud between Generals Lázaro Chacón and Jorge Ubico. During Ubico's long dictatorship he so dominated the military and politics that there was little serious opposition. As part of his penchant for centralization, the military permeated every nook and cranny of rural Guatemala and completely controlled rural society, primarily through the militia, military commissioners, and the civil guard.[3]

Ironically, a "revolution" from 1944 to 1954, inspired partly by an antimilitary sentiment among the civilian middle class, resulted in further involvement of the military in the administration of Guatemala—and the most serious challenge to its predominance in rural areas, with the spread of a peasant league, rural workers' union, and popular political parties. The revolution also clearly demonstrated the extent of factionalism within the army as officers disagreed over government economic and social policy.[4]

The overthrow of democratically elected president Jacobo Arbenz in 1954 only occurred after most of these factions reached an agreement on the need for intervention. This is an important point. In 1954, 1963, and 1982 the Guatemalan military has directly intervened to replace constitutional, if at times fraudulently elected, administrations. On each of these occasions the military acted only when its control over rural society was threatened, and the threat temporarily united the various factions within the institution.

Of these three interventions, the 1954 coup is the most important. The decade of reform from 1944 to 1954 was initiated by a combination of civil protest from elements of the middle class and a military coup. The first administration of the revolution, that of Juan José Arévalo, was marked by moderate and cautious reforms and extremely violent pressure from opposition civilian and military groups. Arévalo survived most of this opposition because the mainstream of the military refused to support a coup. The most serious challenge came in 1949 when, following the killing of the chief of staff, Colonel Francisco Arana, a widespread military revolt occurred. While civilians played an important role in putting down this uprising, it was unsuccessful primarily because major elements in the army and air force did not support it.

By the time the second president of the revolution came to power in 1951, the military had been purged of its most conservative officers. More than a quarter of the active officers were discharged following the 1949 revolt alone. Other smaller uprisings led to similar purges. In addition, Jacobo Arbenz, a colonel and former commander of the military academy's cadet battalion, had significant support and influence within the military.

Arbenz met less opposition from the military during his term in office and was freer to implement economic and social reforms. Indeed, there was a conscious effort to involve the military in the government's economic policies and numerous officers close to Arbenz were given important administrative posts in the government.[5] Nevertheless, following the passage of an agrarian reform law in 1952 and its often violent application from 1952 to 1954, the military command refused to defend Arbenz against the attack of a tiny "Liberation" army that invaded from Honduras and forced him from office. Most often the explanation for this event has centered around the pressure the United States placed on the military and the actions of the American ambassador, John Peurifoy. These accounts point to the agrarian reform as important in the overthrow of Arbenz because the expropriation of land from the United Fruit Company supposedly prompted the U.S. action.[6]

But the Guatemalan military, while affected by the U.S. pressure and concerned about the hostility of neighboring countries, acted for its own reasons against Arbenz. It was most concerned about the activities of agrarian organizers in the countryside and a concurrent reduction of military power in rural Guatemala. These organizers, intent on implementing the agrarian reform law, attempted to manipulate local appointments to the two remaining institutions essential for the military's control of rural Guatemala: military commissioners and the civil guard. (The rural militia had been disbanded in 1944). With the support of Arbenz, the leaders of the two most important popular rural organizations, the peasant league and rural workers' union, influenced the replacement of military commissioners and civil guard commanders by individuals sympathetic to their goals.

At the same time, the implementation of the agrarian reform law heightened violence and unrest in the countryside. A brutal conflict erupted between peasants and workers who demanded land, and the large landowners and their agents. Peasant organizers were beaten up, shot, hung, burned and run over throughout rural Guatemala in 1953 and 1954. Peasants fought back with machetes, stones, and the sheer force of numbers. In addition, bitter battles developed between communities and between peasants and workers as they fought over redistribution of the most important local resource: land.

This mounting unrest, the growing influence of organizers many in the military believed to be communist, and the military's diminished power in the countryside caused increasing agitation among officers. Citing the "total lack of control and absolute military disorganization" in the countryside, a commission of the Superior Defense Council called for immediate remedial action in 1954.[7] On June 5, top army commanders presented President Arbenz with a list of questions concerning the agrarian reform and communist organizers. They compelled Arbenz to attend a meeting on June 14 where the same questions and an ultimatum were presented to him by a larger group of officers. A few days later, when Central Intelligence Agency-supported "liberation forces" invaded Guatemala, senior commanders, with the support of virtually the entire officers' corps, surrounded the presidential palace and demanded Arbenz's surrender.

At the time of the overthrow of Arbenz, various issues divided the Guatemalan army. Many officers supported most of the economic policies of the administration, while some even approved of the agrarian reform, and others opposed both vehemently. The military did not act against the Arbenz regime because they supported the traditional landowning elite, nor did they act primarily because of United States pressure. Sufficient consensus for change emerged only when the military institution felt itself challenged by the actions of Arbenz and the agrarian organizers, and alarmed by the spreading rural unrest.

Following the overthrow of Arbenz, serious divisions continued within the military. Friction developed between Liberation officers being integrated into the army and regular army officers. The clearest demonstration of that conflict occurred with the attack of cadets from the military academy against Liberation soldiers housed in the newly completed Roosevelt Hospital in August 1954. Purges of the officers' corps in the next couple of years culled the most progressive from its ranks and made it a much more conservative institution than it had been under Arbenz.

Even so, friction remained within the military. This tension helped prompt the military to force the Liberation party to allow another conservative ex-officer, General Ydígoras Fuentes, to take the presidency in 1958. But during Ydígoras' administration, incompetence and corruption led to continual minor military revolts. Since army officers increasingly administered the Ydígoras government, these revolts pitted members of the military against each other and one uprising led to the bulk of the air force opposing the army command. Most importantly, a failed military coup in 1962 grew into a serious rural guerrilla war, a challenge the Ydígoras regime was unable to face. Thus in 1963, the majority of the senior officers, most of whom already held administrative posts in the government, once again agreed on the need to dismiss the president and forced Ydígoras from office.

In the following five years, the militia unleashed a vicious counterinsurgency campaign, primarily in the department of Zacapa, headed by Colonel Arana. By 1969, this campaign had killed perhaps as many as 8,000 people and had effectively silenced rural protest. In addition, it had once again expanded the presence and power of the military in rural areas through an aggressive military/civic action programme assisted by U.S. advisers. Popular organization in the countryside, slowly beginning to resurface after the post-1954 "liberation," was effectively stifled once again.[8]

Nevertheless, rural popular organizations reemerged in the 1970s. Stimulated by the spread of Catholic Action, liberation theology, increased literacy, and a rural cooperative movement, peasants and rural workers in Guatemala developed an array of organizations that pressured for change and policies to benefit them. Their demands met with sporadic and usually selective violence fostered by a particular sector of the military—those officers closest to the Institutional Democratic Party (PID), established by a few officers in 1964.[9]

By the late 1970s and early 1980s this violence had prompted increasing numbers of peasants, especially in the largely Indian highlands, to support revolutionary organizations. The government of General Romeo Lucas García and the PID officers that clustered around it, mired in incredible corruption, failed to confront effectively either the growing demand for new rural policies or the guerrilla organizations that grew up promising such policies. In March 1982, both the government and the military high command were swept aside by a coup of junior officers, those most intimately familiar with the dismal state of the military's campaign in the countryside.

The counterinsurgency that followed was in many ways an extension of the campaign in the 1960s. It sought to restructure highland Guatemala, destroying the basis of local government and organizations and rebuilding them with almost complete military control. It began with killing, or otherwise silencing, village leaders or potential leaders, but quickly moved on to a forced relocation of a substantial proportion of the highland population. Isolated *aldeas* were depopulated and their inhabitants either resettled in military controlled "strategic hamlets" or forced into refugee camps in Mexico. It was intensely brutal, resulting in thousands of deaths and the destruction of whole villages. It was also, at least in the short term, remarkably effective. Guerrilla organizations that in 1982 looked poised to take power from an ineffective and splintered military, were drained of support, and although they suffered few outright military defeats, gradually restricted their activities to tiny pockets of the countryside.

In the process, the military reinforced its dominance over rural Guatemala. The National Plan for Security and Development submitted to the top officers of the Ríos Montt government in April 1982, called for the destruction of traditional village government and culture and their replacement with institutions controlled by the military. This plan, which proposed "to structure and regulate nationalism . . . and to propagate it in rural areas," linked an intense pro-army propaganda campaign to the creation of civil guards (a revival of the rural militia disbanded in 1944) and strategic hamlets—all jealously controlled by the military.

As the danger of guerrilla victory faded, however, internal splits increasingly threatened the army. In 1983 a revolt of senior officers dismissed the administration of General Efraín Ríos Montt. They acted primarily because the Ríos Montt government had sidestepped traditional avenues of promotion and command. Thus, one of the first statements made by General Mejía Victores, Ríos Montt's Minister of Defense and head of the new military government, was that the military command was "aware of the need to preserve and strengthen the unity of the army, upholding the principle of hierarchy and subordination, to frustrate the attempts of some elements to fracture and confuse the armed institution." The new army code that quickly followed reaffirmed the fundamental importance of discipline and obedience.[10]

Two years later, relatively free elections were held and in January 1986, the Christian Democratic administration of Vinicio Cerezo was inaugurated. The military acquiesced in holding elections in 1985 because the main reasons for its direct intervention in the political process had been removed. The army exercised effective control of the countryside and had reduced dangerous schisms within the military institution. It was in a more powerful position relative to the other political actors in Guatemala than ever before. Formal political power was neither necessary nor probably even desirable in maintaining that dominance.

AGRARIAN REFORM AND POPULAR ORGANIZATION

The overthrow of Arbenz marked the end of the last serious attempt to alter land tenure in Guatemala. Nevertheless, from that point agrarian reform has been the preeminent economic and social question in Guatemala, and control over peasants and rural workers has been the dominant military concern.

The Agrarian Reform Law of 1952 was never officially abandoned and the leader of the Liberation, Carlos Castillo Armas, passed an Agrarian Statute in 1956 that promised, "Every Guatemalan has a right that land, necessary to insure his economic subsistence and that of his family, be given to him and fully guaranteed as his private property."[11] Nevertheless, more than 90 percent of the land expropriated under the 1952 law was returned to its previous owners. The new "agrarian reform," which centered on colonization and unrealistically large landholdings, was totally ineffectual either in bettering the lot of the rural poor or in altering the land tenure system. Only slightly more than 15,000 families received land under the Liberation government, while hundreds of thousands were deprived of land they had received under the 1952 agrarian reform law.

Governments in the 1954–64 decade concentrated on stifling the demands of the rural poor rather than any significant distribution of land. Even the limited reforms undertaken by the Liberation government slowly withered away under succeeding administrations. By 1970, the electoral winner, Colonel Carlos Arana Osorio, announced during his campaign that agrarian reform was "incompatible with the existence of a constitutional state." Arana's government abandoned even rhetorical support for agrarian reform. Land distribution became almost as inequitable as it had been in 1950. In that year, slightly more than 2 percent of the farm units controlled 72 percent of the arable land in Guatemala, and 88 percent of the farming units had access to only 14 percent of the land. Some 165,850 families had less than the bare minimum of two *manzanas* deemed essential for subsistence. By 1979, slightly over 2 percent of the farming units controlled 65 percent of the arable land, and almost 90 percent of the farming units had access to 16 percent of the land. Two million more people relied upon agriculture for a living, the vast majority of whom entered the ranks of the landless or near-landless rural poor.[12]

Nevertheless, the agrarian reform issue did not simply fade away, nor did popular organization in the countryside remain moribund. Part of the tension that existed under Ríos Montt during 1983 was caused by the persistent rumor that he was planning to implement an agrarian reform. After Cerezo came to power, the issue surfaced once again. In a debate between representatives of all the political parties sponsored by the University of San Carlos and broadcast over Guatemalan television in 1986, attention focused for much of the time on the experience of "the ten years of spring (1944–54)", the agrarian reform and popular rural oganization that accompanied it. But only Mario Solórzano, the leader of the Social Democratic Party, openly demanded an extensive agrarian reform.[13]

The greatest pressure for land came from popular rural organizations (as it had over thirty years earlier when a petition from thousands of peasants finally prompted Arbenz to introduce the Agrarian Reform Law). In early 1986, Padre Andrés de Jesús Girón de León, a Catholic priest in Nueva Concepción, Escuintla formed the National Peasant Pro-land Association (commonly called the Asociación Pro-Tierra). It met with immediate, enthusiastic support. An initial gathering of less than 200 *campesinos,* was followed by a meeting of 5000 on Feb. 22, 1986 when the Asociación was officially formed. Less than two months later, 35,000 peasants attended yet another mass meeting to demand land. Since that date, the agitation for land and membership in the association have grown tremendously.

Padre Girón and the Asociación took a moderate course towards affecting a redistribution of land in Guatemala. As indicated by his sermon quoted above, Girón proposed working within the current laws of the Republic. He and the Asociación urged the president to purchase *fincas* to distribute among the members. The purchase cost would be considered a loan from the government to the peasants who would repay it, with interest, from the proceeds of crop sales. The Asociacíon pressured the government to initiate this programme by holding mass meetings, first throughout the south coast where the movement began and then spreading to other areas of the country, eventually into parts of the highlands as well. When the government responded slowly, peasants—some members of the Asociación and some not—began a series of minor land invasions, mostly of state-owned land. This prompted the Cerezo government, in the summer of 1986, to turn over the first state-owned *finca* to members of the Asociación. There was a promise of more to come.

The purchase of land for distribution among peasants did not begin in Guatemala in 1986. It has been the major focus of the Institute for National Agrarian Transformation (INTA) since its inception in 1962. At the time it was suggested that a small tax on idle land would prompt enough *finqueros* to sell their land to the government to allow at least a moderate redistribution. But actual land transfers have been few and INTA has been discredited by increasing levels of corruption among its top bureaucrats until the end of the Lucas García government in 1982.

For a number of years the Christian Democratic Party has also suggested distributing purchased land. In 1970, competing in its first presidential campaign, the party's candidate, Major Jorge Lucas Caballero, called for a vigorous program of land redistribution. He promised "a complete and rapid agrarian reform with the object of increasing the productivity of the peasant." Through the 1970s the party consistently argued for land redistribution. In January 1986, it published a study called

"The General Strategies in the Agricultural Sector of the First Christian Democratic Government in Guatemala." Based on the study, the Ministry of Agriculture called for "the democratization of land tenancy, by assisting the processes of voluntary sale and purchase."[14]

The conjuncture of the agrarian policy proposed by the Christian Democratic Party and that of the Asociación Pro-Tierra led by Padre Girón led to suggestions that Padre Girón was working in league with the Christian Democratic Party. It has been argued that Cerezo was using the popular pressure for reform fostered by the Asociación to justify the introduction of the Christian Democrats' "General Strategies." Indeed, the Christian Democratic Party has offered some encouragement to the movement. The President's wife, María Blandón de Cerezo, and other party members attended an Asociación meeting on July 12, 1986. She assured the peasants demanding land that she was with them. The president and the minister of agriculture, Rodolfo Estrada Hurtarte, have promised more land to peasants of the Asociación, and have also provided Padre Girón with money to assist in the agricultural diversification of land previously distributed.[15]

The Asociación and the government's apparent encouragement have sparked opposition from many sides. Following the June 12 Asociación meeting attended by the president's wife and party members, the powerful Coordinating Committee of Agricultural, Commercial, Industrial and Financial Institutions (CACIF) demanded a meeting with Cerezo in which they denounced the "intent to cut short our emerging democratic process, through its use by unscrupulous leaders threatening de facto expropriations of land." They protested the presence of members of the government at the meeting which "creates a lack of confidence and uncertainty in the whole country and especially in both foreign and national investors." The same day the Association of Guatemalan Agriculturalists (AGA, another large landowners' institution) demanded an audience declaring that it is "irresponsible and immoral to feed hopes without solid bases and legal rights" and suggesting that gatherings by "these self-named defenders of a sector of the population, proposing a battle between the classes and leading the country to a possible economic and social disaster" require firm action on the part of the government.[16]

Once again rumors circulated about government plans to tamper with land tenure. Opposition parties denounced agrarian reform, pointing to the supposed disastrous experience of the 1952 law and "unsuccessful" reforms implemented in neighboring El Salvador. The rumors became so widespread and criticisms of them so vehement that the Christian Democratic Party felt compelled to issue a number of statements, some in paid advertisements, assuring people that the government was not considering such legislation and that there "would be no agrarian reform in Guatemala."[17]

The president, at a meeting of representatives of the AGA and the

Ministers of Defense and Agriculture, assured them that the government would not decree an agrarian reform law. This promise prompted the directors of the landowners' association to call on its members to give their confidence to the government, army, courts and the congress. Nonetheless, on September 26, 1986, the government officially recognized the National Peasant Association Pro-Tierra, giving it legal existence.[18]

Cerezo and the Christian Democrats were walking a fine line. They were attempting to develop popular support in the countryside by not discouraging peasant organization and by cautiously promoting adherence to the Christian Democratic Party and the government. On the other hand, they did not want to alarm powerful groups that opposed peasant movements and land redistribution. This balancing act has become increasingly difficult. The central idea of the Asociación Pro-Tierra—to purchase *fincas* and distribute them among peasants—can do little to alter land distribution in Guatemala. Even if the government had unlimited funds to purchase this land, in May 1986 there were only 124 *fincas* on the market. These cost about forty-three million *quetzales* and accounted for slightly over 42,000 hectares, approximately 1 percent of the total land in production. A recent estimate suggests that giving land to only three percent of the economically active population who depend on agriculture and lack adequate land, would require purchasing over 100,000 hectares of land annually at a cost of over fifty million *quetzales*.[19] Clearly, the purchasing and distribution strategy cannot come close to meeting the demands of Guatemala's rural poor or achieving a sufficiently equitable land tenure system.

The clamor for land among Asociación peasants increased steadily through 1986 and early 1987. They invaded a number of state-owned *fincas* in the summer of 1986 to speed up the distribution process, a move which prompted the government almost immediately to divide up more land. The Cerezo administration realized the concern this was creating among other sectors of Guatemalan society and the major, if unwelcome, impetus the government was giving to both peasant organization and land invasions through its actions. In December 1986, Padre Girón threatened further land invasions. The minister of agriculture responded by requesting patience on the part of Asociación peasants, promising that the government had five or six *fincas* that it would hand over to them within two weeks. He warned, however, that the government would act against peasants who invaded *fincas*.[20]

But the impetus for the land distribution was becoming a movement that the government could neither control nor assuage with legal solutions; neither, it appears, could the Asociación Pro-Tierra. On January 4, 1987 a new organization of peasants and rural workers, the Civic Organization of Peasants, was born in Puerto San José, Escuintla. This organization demanded the partition of the state-owned *finca*, Santa Rosa.

To press their demands, they called for a mass meeting on the twenty-fifth of January in the central park of San José.[21]

Just as in the 1950s, pressures by some peasants for land distribution met forceful denunciations from other peasants and workers. In some villages peasants demanded that neighboring *fincas*, whether state-owned or not, be distributed. This caused an expected clamor among the landowners' associations but also prompted opposition from workers on these *fincas* who feared for their jobs. The kettle of rural unrest is threatening to boil over, and the Cerezo government has shown it can do little to reduce the heat.

THE CEREZO GOVERNMENT AND THE MILITARY

Rural unrest is the greatest danger to the continuation of the Cerezo government. Military dominance severely restricts presidential power in Guatemala. Cerezo relies on the "good will" of sectors of the military to disband the various repressive apparatuses set up by the military and the National Police during the administrations of Generals Kjell Laugerud and Lucas García. Continuing denunciations from the Mutual Aid Group (GAM), and other human rights organizations, or even a quick read through any Guatemalan paper for a few days, make glaringly clear that the government has only been partially successful in dismantling such structures. It managed to destroy the Technical Investigation Department (DIT), considered to have been responsible for much of the repression during preceding regimes, but this occurred largely because of the military's desire to see DIT disbanded. Cerezo has suggested that he has less than the full range of powers that usually accompany a presidency and the military clearly keeps a close eye on government policies.

This scrutiny appeared to increase in early 1987. Cerezo began the year with an impassioned rejection of a military coup in his New Year's address to congress, denouncing the political parties that were embracing the army and trying to inspire the military to stage a coup. But in January, the military showed signs of instability as the minister of defense attempted to prolong his appointment, while the minister-designate, General Héctor Gramajo Morales, was not well respected. Gramajo's appointment led to a state of alert being called at the end of January and much speculation that the army was preparing to stage a coup. It was suggested that the military was upset not only at the Gramajo appointment but also at the government's policies towards Nicaragua and Belize.

The key to military restlessness, however, again lies in the Guatemalan countryside. The army has maintained its dominance over the structures of local government and continued to monopolize the provision of relief and services to most of the rural highlands. By early 1987, there were increasing signs that the military was becoming more unsure of its position in the highlands. Guerrilla activity increased in the departments of Huehuetenango and Quiché and the army again found itself in regular combat with guerrilla forces.[22]

The military's major concern, and the real limits to the prospects for "democracy" in Guatemala, are most clearly demonstrated in the appeals for agrarian reform. The similarities with the administration of Jacobo Arbenz are striking. Between 1952 and 1954, Guatemala was shaken by extreme conflict over land. A land reform that was envisioned to be moderate and which sought allies from most sectors of Guatemalan society, led to the organization of peasants and rural workers. In turn, this led to intense rural conflict that engulfed much of Guatemala. The government, at least briefly, proved unable to control this conflict, and the military responded, first demanding that peasant organization be curtailed and then overthrowing the president. Edelberto Torres-Rivas has suggested that the overthrow came primarily because the Arbenz government attempted to implement a moderate programme through immoderate means: the mobilization of the peasantry.[23]

This is the central dilemma that Guatemala faces at present. The limited alterations in the distribution of land envisioned by Cerezo and Padre Girón, can neither significantly alter the land tenure system, nor can they for long assuage a peasantry organized and clamoring for change. A true agrarian reform must do a number of things: it must redistribute land on a large scale, altering the land tenure system fundamentally; it must be prepared to spend the resources necessary to supply the beneficiaries of land redistribution with technical services, credit, marketing opportunities and transportation infrastructure; and it must entail a realignment of political power. In short, it must shift political power to the rural poor. Many would argue that this is the first step in an agrarian reform: true redistribution of the material resources of a society occurs only after those demanding the realignment have the political clout necessary to impose the transfer.[24]

The military has shown time and time again that it will not countenance such a transfer of political power. Over the last several years, the military has carefully planted its tentacles deep in the crevices of highland society and it will not permit autonomous organization among the peasantry. The rural poor of Guatemala, however, will continue to demand structural changes that even the sincerely reformist administration of Vinicio Cerezo is neither willing nor able to support. Consequently, peasant organization in the countryside—if allowed—will quickly outstrip the moderate Asociación Pro-Tierra. Or they will drag it along behind them, with its religious directors trying frantically but futilely to ride herd on the demands of its members. In 1986, when General Mejía Victores presided over the inauguration of Vinicio Cerezo, he made it clear that the military was handing power to a civilian government on probation, with unspoken but completely understood limits to the extent of that civilian power.[25] The likely spread of the Asociación Pro-Tierra, or organizations like it, to the highlands and its necessary radicalization, will lead to a quick end to Guatemala's short-lived democracy.

NOTES

1. *Excélsior* (Mexico City), 21 and 22 January 1986; *Unomasuno* (Mexico City), 22 January 1986.

2. See, for example, Paul Knox, *Globe and Mail* (Toronto), 2 November 1985; George Black, "El Señor Presidente," *NACLA*, no. 19 (November/December 1985); and Council of Hemispheric Affairs, *News and Analysis*, 30 October 1985. The first of these arguments has been applied to other countries in Latin America as well. See James Petras and Edward S. Herman, "Resurgent Democracy: Rhetoric and Reality," *New Left Review* 154 (November/December 1985): 83–98.

3. For a discussion of the Ubico administration, see K. Grieb, *Guatemalan Caudillo: The Regime of Jorge Ubico, Guatemala, 1931–1944* (Athens, Ohio, 1979); W. Krehm, *Democracia y tiranías en el Caribe* (Mexico City, 1949). For a discussion of the militia in one highland town, see R. Carmack, "Spanish-Indian Relations in Highland Guatemala, 1800–1944," in *Spaniards and Indians in Southeastern Mesoamerica*, ed. Murdo MacLeod and Robert Wasserstrom (Lincoln, Nebr.: University of Nebraska Press, 1983).

4. For a fuller discussion see J. Handy, "Revolution and Reaction: National Policy and Rural Politics in Guatemala, 1944–1954" (Ph.D. diss., University of Toronto, 1985), 359–415; J. Handy, "Resurgent Democracy and the Guatemalan Military," *Journal of Latin American Studies* 18 (November 1986).

5. For a more complete discussion of the Arbenz administration see J. Handy, *Gift of the Devil: A History of Guatemala* (Toronto, Between the Lines, 1985): 123–47.

6. The best known of these works are S. Kinzer and S. Schlesinger, *Bitter Fruit: The Untold Story of the American Coup in Guatemala* (New York: Doubleday, 1983); Susanne Jonas Bodenheimer, *Plan piloto para el continente* (San José, Costa Rica: Editorial Universitaria Centroamericana, 1981); and José Aybar de Soto, *Dependency and Intervention: The Case of Guatemala in 1954* (Boulder, Colo.: Westview Press, 1978).

7. Plan presented by Consejo Superior de la Defensa Nacional, 19 May 1954, Box 1, Guatemalan Documents.

8. Milton Jamail, "Guatemala 1944–1972: The Politics of Aborted Revolution" (Ph.D. diss., University of Arizona, 1972), 84–85; B. Jenkins and C. D. Sereseres, "United States Military Assistance and the Guatemalan Armed Forces," *Armed Forces and Society* (Winter 1977): 576.

9. For further discussion see J. Handy, *Gift*, 165–84; and S. Davis and J. Hodson, *Witness to Political Violence in Guatemala: The Suppression of a Rural Development Movement* (Oxfam America Impact Audit 2, 1982); *Amnesty International Guatemala*

Campaign Circulars, nos.1–9 (1979); *Guatemala: A Government Program of Political Murder* (London: Amnesty International, 1981).

10. Cited in *Latin American Regional Reports: Mexico and Central America*, 19 August 1983; see also ibid. 13 January 1984.

11. *Estatuto agrario, decreto* número 31 (Guatemala City, 1954): 5–6; *Estatuto agrario, decreto* número 559 (Guatemala City, 1956).

12. Arana cited in M. Monteforte Toledo, *Centroamérica: subdesarrollo y dependencia* 1 (Mexico City, 1972): 20. Land tenure data comes from the *Censo agropecuaria* (Guatemala City) 1 (1950): 17–34; and Isaac Cohen and Gert Rosenthal, "The Dimensions of Economic Policy Space in Central America," in *The Future of Central America: Policy Choices for the U.S. and Mexico*, eds. R. Fagen and O. Pellicer (Stanford, Calif.: Stanford University Press, 1983), 15–34.

13. "Foco apertura política," Television Broadcast Channel 11, 11 December 1986.

14. Cited in T. and M. Melville, *Guatemala: The Politics of Land Ownership* (New York: Free Press, 1971): 209.

15. *La Hora* (Guatemala City), 17 January 1987.

16. J. C. Cambranes, *Agrarismo en Guatemala* (Guatemala City, 1986): 237–42.

17. The government's promise was carried on "Guatemala Flash," Radio San Pedro Carcha, 16 July 1986.

18. Cambranes, *Agrarismo*, 243–54.

19. Ibid. 230–31.

20. *La Hora*, 5 January 1987.

21. *La Hora*, 14 January 1987.

22. While it is still difficult to get a true idea of the extent of guerrilla activity in the highlands, a trip through parts of the departments of Huehuetenango and El Quiché in December 1986 readily confirmed reports received from other investigators.

23. Edelberto Torres-Rivas, "Crisis y conjuntura crítica: la caída de Arbenz y los contratiempos de la revolución burguesa," *Revista Mexicana de Sociología* 41 (1979): 297–323.

24. J. Chonchol, "Eight Fundamental Conditions of Agrarian Reform in Latin America," in *Agrarian Problems and Peasant Movements in Latin America*, ed. Rodolfo Stavenhagen (Garden City, N.Y.: Doubleday, 1970), 159–72.

25. Mejía's speech was reprinted in *Excélsior*, 21 January 1986.

4

Consolidating Democracy Under Fire

H. E. Sergio Lacayo

INTRODUCTION

Few words are used, abused or misused more often than the term "democracy." Nations throughout the world describe themselves as democracies; yet many would fail to withstand the most basic scrutiny. Moreover, in all countries laws or practices exist which appear to contradict democratic principles.

Ancient Athens gave birth to the concept of government of the people, by the people, and for the people. Yet, the exercise of Athenian democracy never transcended the confinement of a small Greek agora. The Athenians perceived democracy as a restrictive political institution, applicable only for a few male citizens of high economic and social standing. Moreover, the prosperity of democratic Athens rested on slavery.

Despite shortcomings in practice, the idea of democracy continues to influence political thought. The communion of *demos* and *krateein*, unperturbed by the flow of history, still symbolizes the aspiration of most nations to assert the logic of the majority as the basic rule of government. On the other hand, if one examines democracy within a given society, we discover that democratic principles only flourish when they are constantly recreated within each nation, continuously revitalized by social practice.

In this latter sense, democracy becomes a vital process, a political institution that constantly changes, striving to reflect the complex social relations from which the principles and values of a nation's government are derived. Thus two contradictory aspects characterize democracy. As a principle, it is permanently and formally cast as a fundamental pillar of social justice and peace. Yet as a political institution, it registers the perpetual transformation and reorganization of social order. This apparently contradictory nature of democracy is central to understanding the process of democratization in Nicaragua.

In Nicaragua, democracy as a political institution had no history. In July of 1979, Nicaraguans ousted the Somoza dictatorship and discovered that they lacked the democratic tradition upon which to rebuild their society. For centuries, political, economic, and social power had been concentrated in the hands of the few. A ruling elite tightly controlled ownership of lands, the distribution of labor and capital, and access to services and opportunity. Competing factions within this group maintained the pretext of democratic rule through periodic sham elections and a self-interested application of law.

Nevertheless, the power of this elite was not absolute. The constraint on its authority, however, was not exercised by the majority of Nicaraguans. It was an external force, the government of the United States, which held a veto over the Nicaraguan leadership. Whatever the Americans lacked in legal authority, they made up in force, both economic and military.

Thus in the summer of 1979, revolutionary Nicaragua embarked on an uncharted course to build democracy. Three fundamental concepts undergirded the process: political pluralism, mixed economy, and popular participation.

The idea of *political pluralism* is straightforward. As a Nicaraguan reality, it is more complex. It includes twelve political parties: seven have elected members in the National Assembly (Parliament), three are extraparliamentary parties which boycotted the 1984 general elections, and two are new parties, constituted after the elections had taken place. With only 3,000,000 Nicaraguans, this explosion of political pluralism could perhaps be construed as a liability to the functioning of a democratic system.

The concept of a *mixed economy* is more arduous to define and even more difficult to comprehend as a complex reality in Nicaragua. It involves the coexistence of three types of properties, private, state and cooperative, with private sector production accounting for about 60 percent of Nicaragua's GNP.

Popular participation is essential to democratization in Nicaragua. Political theorists often have viewed society as comprised of two groups or classes: the workers and the elite; the proletariat and the bourgeoisie. In Nicaragua, these categories fail to reflect all of the forces interacting in the collective quest for democracy. A third force, crucial to the triumph of the revolution, plays a decisive role in the development of Nicaraguan democracy. It includes elements of both historic classes and is reflected in social groupings linked by a common belief in the principles that form the basis of the Sandinista Revolution.

In Nicaragua this third force, popular participation, expresses itself in a diversity of groups—Christians, women, students, artisans, professionals, youth, intellectuals, artists—and plays a key role in ensuring that the tension between government and the governed is sustained in a fruitful and creative way. Without the leadership of these groups, Nicaragua's revolution could not have succeeded. Without their continued participation, its goals cannot be realized.

In today's Nicaragua, a strategic alliance exists among the business community, workers, peasants, and this third force. In concert, they are asserting their collective power. Moreover, their control—and responsibility—is not restricted to electoral power. Rather, they are achieving dominion over all facets of their lives.

CONSTRAINTS ON THE DEVELOPMENT OF DEMOCRACY

Despite the achievements of Nicaragua's revolution, severe constraints inhibit the progress of democracy. Nicaragua's lack of democratic experience fosters skepticism about the possibilities for change and uncertainty about how to strengthen accountability. One still encounters cynicism about elections and a wary attitude toward dissent.

The Somoza legacy was underdevelopment: serious deficiencies in the country's literacy, communications, and organizational infrastructure. Nicaraguans have been denied the access to education, public services, and economic security which would allow them something more than subsistence. Consequently, there are too few skilled or educated women and men able to assume positions of authority and responsibility.

Economic constraints aggravate this heritage of underdevelopment. Unfavorable terms of exchange, a crippling debt load, barriers to trade, and inadequate economic cooperation undermine the social and economic progress upon which democratization relies.

The greatest constraint upon Nicaragua's democratic process, however, is the war of attrition waged by the government of the United States. In contempt of the World Court and in defiance of world opinion, the American government has trained and armed a proxy force that seeks to destabilize the government, exacerbate internal divisions and forestall the very development of democracy.

While death and destruction exact a daily toll, the war also has a more insidious impact on the emergence of a strong democracy within Nicaragua. American aggression obliges Nicaragua to defend itself. The population lives in a constant state of alert, aware that this is a war of life or death, of self-determination or extinction as a sovereign nation.

All Nicaraguans, military and civilian, have the obligation to defend their country and therefore the right to be armed and prepared to safeguard militarily their homeland. Yet even in the extraordinary circumstances of war, the principle of popular participation prevails, easily detectable within an armed nation literally twinned with its armed forces.

Many observers have cited this unity as confirmation of the popular support for the Revolution. Yet paradoxically, this telling evidence of the democratic nature of Nicaragua's revolution contains a challenge to its fulfillment. For with the mobilization of Nicaraguan society comes its militarization. Despite its defensive character, this tendency works against democratic pluralism. By its very nature, the military is hierarchical. One does not question a command in the trenches, one obeys. There is little room for doubt; no room for disobedience. Such attitudes are contrary to the development of a critical consciousness, the promotion of creativity and the fostering of dissent, each of which is central to revolutionary change and democratic development.

SOCIAL PRACTICE

Notwithstanding such constraints, democratic practice is flowering in Nicaragua. Over the past eight years, the country has achieved significant social progress. Public resources have been redirected to meet the needs of the poor and disadvantaged who comprise the majority of the Nicaraguan population.

Recognizing the critical importance of literacy to political participation, the Sandinista government launched a massive campaign to teach basic reading and writing skills within months of the revolution. Access to basic commodities has been improved, security of land tenure assured and public health promoted. An ambitious program of agrarian reform has provided thousands of rural workers with land and agricultural materials. Investments in infrastructure—potable water, energy, roads, and communications—have improved the quality of life, particularly in the rural areas, while breaking down the isolation of much of the country.

The growth of popular organizations has paralleled social development: labor unions, women's associations, youth and student organizations, producers' groups, church and community committees. These groups represent the third force mentioned earlier, the first line of democratization. They serve to build a new political culture within Nicaragua by encouraging participation, debate, dissent, and a general increase in political consciousness and commitment.

These popular organizations involve a broad range of individuals from all backgrounds and play a key role in advocating the interests of their constituencies. Most importantly, they heighten awareness of the diversity of social interests, while addressing the tensions among the various components of Nicaraguan society. And indirectly, they ensure that a new and critical generation of political leaders will be spawned.

POLITICAL INSTITUTIONS

In the initial stages of the Revolution, up to and including the general elections in November of 1984, the social practice of democracy massively outpaced the growth of its political institutions. In the second stage, Nicaragua's democratic advances were consolidated and finally consecrated in a political constitution, the supreme law of the land.

In the aftermath of the Revolution, Nicaragua strove to ensure the participation of all the political, economic, and social forces that had contributed to the overthrow of the Somoza dictatorship. The Junta of the Government of National Reconstruction constituted the executive branch of government. The Council of State, which served the role of an assembly, included representation from almost all organized groups and all regions of the country. A seven-member Supreme Court headed the judicial system, acting as a third independent branch of government.

One of the most important tasks of the Council of State was to lay the groundwork for Nicaragua's first national elections. The Council established a commission to seek input from all sectors of Nicaraguan society, to study the experience of other nations and to recommend an electoral system which would ensure, among others, the principles of individual vote, secret ballot, and universal participation. In August 1983, the Political Parties Law was approved and ten political parties applied for, and received, legal certification.

The Electoral Law, approved in March 1984, outlined the structure of the National Assembly and established the Supreme Electoral Council as an autonomous, fourth branch of government. Composed of five members from various political parties, the Electoral Council directed the massive educational and organizational efforts which were required to undertake elections in a country with no tradition of democracy. Hundreds of thousands of pamphlets, posters and newspaper advertisements instructed voters on registration and voting procedures and on the rights and responsibilities of voters. Citizens were required to register to vote but voting, being a right, was optional. All persons over the age of sixteen were eligible to vote, the age having been revised down from eighteen after students organized a massive protest.

The Electoral Law guaranteed political parties equal rights to compete for power, to organize, and to hold public meetings. Each party running a full slate of candidates was granted an equal amount of public subsidy and provided free access to radio and television publicity over the three-month campaign. No censorship of campaign material was ever imposed on the thirty-nine private radio stations or the three national newspapers. There were no restrictions on foreign donations to any parties.

As the election day approached, the efforts of the United States government to disrupt the elections and undermine their legitimacy intensified. Contras attacked election officials, leaving twelve dead and forcing the closure of eleven polling stations. An American-orchestrated boycott of the elections by three of the ten parties participating distracted international attention from the electoral process and the political debate within Nicaragua. Yet on November 4, 1984, seventy-five percent of the registered voters ignored the Contra intimidation and the U.S. call for a boycott. Of valid votes cast, the Sandinista National Liberation Front (FSLN) garnered 67 percent of the vote, 29 percent voted for the three parties to the right of the FSLN and 4 percent voted for the three parties to the left. These elections were internationally monitored and accredited, with official delegations from a range of nations attesting to the fair, honest, and responsible manner in which the elections were conducted.

Equally important for the long-term development of democracy and pluralism within Nicaragua, is the manner in which election results translated into legislative representation. In many countries, such a sweeping electoral victory would have resulted in only minimal opposition representation within the Assembly. In Nicaragua, however, proportional representation favors smaller parties, with support evenly distributed across the country, by ensuring their continuing participation in the National Assembly. The balance of support was accorded thirty-five representatives divided among the six other parties, including two members for each of the Communist, Socialist and Marxist-Leninist parties.

Within five years of the Revolution, a short time compared with other countries experiencing revolutionary change, the Nicaraguan people had their first elected government. In January 1985, the elected president was sworn into office and the National Assembly inaugurated its first legislative period.

The new government turned immediately to the task of forging a constitution. The constitutional process was as important as the final product. Given the constraints noted earlier—the lack of a democratic tradition, underdevelopment and the economic crisis, the war—postponing the drafting of a political constitution, or assigning this responsibility to a group of 'experts', working quietly and efficiently behind closed doors, might have been understandable.

But the Revolution's participatory values, and the goal of transforming the country's political, social and economic reality, meant involving all Nicaraguans in the constitutional process, both directly and through their political parties and popular organizations. Using public meetings, the media and open debates, the issues and the choices were widely disseminated and discussed. As a consequence, there is an awareness and understanding of the Constitution and its provisions among our citizens which we believe is unmatched. Most important, there is a sense of ownership of the Constitution and a commitment to its fulfillment.

The development of the Constitution reflects the importance accorded it. Within months of the 1984 elections, the National Assembly named a Special Constitutional Commission which organized a process for consultation, solicited international cooperation, and prepared a draft for discussion. The first phase of consultation involved the National Assembly itself with each of the seven participating parties contributing ideas and ideals. Popular organizations representing women, organized workers, students, journalists, religious groups, and others, made submissions on a wide range of concerns. A multiparty parliamentary committee examined and evaluated the constitutions of countries in Latin America, North America, Europe, and Asia. For each provision of the draft, Commission representatives sought consensus, recognizing the importance of the Constitution as a unifying document for all Nicaraguans.

In February 1986, the Draft Constitution was then disseminated widely throughout the country, as part of a constitutional literacy campaign. Despite the paper shortage, every effort was made to provide each citizen with a copy of the Draft. Extensive media coverage, including radio broadcasts, phone-in shows, and weekly televised debates among representatives of various parties, exposed Nicaraguans to a wide range of views, supporting and opposing the Constitution's provisions. To ensure direct participation, open forums were held throughout the country. More than 100,000 Nicaraguan citizens attended the seventy-three forums, representing all classes and social sectors of the country. Two thousand five hundred persons spoke out on the Constitution and more than 1,800 written submissions were received.

Citizen comments ranged from the particular to the general, from observations on social reform, the scope of executive power, and judicial independence to the nature of the army and the role of private enterprise. Suggestions were received to strengthen the provisions affirming women's rights, the multi-ethnic nature of Nicaraguan society, industrial democracy, and a just distribution of land. Commentators vehemently debated many of these issues. Based on this input, the Constitutional Commission made significant amendments to the Draft. Months of debate followed in the National Assembly, article by article, clause by clause, word by word.

On November 19, the National Assembly approved the Constitution. Despite renewed efforts by the government of the United States to organize a boycott, the final document won overwhelming support from the political parties represented in the National Assembly. On January 9, 1987 the Constitution was officially proclaimed and celebrated throughout Nicaragua as a critical step towards democracy.

The Nicaraguan Constitution invokes the spirit of the country's forefathers, its historic struggle for self-determination, and Central American unity. It sets out the individual and collective rights and obligations of Nicaraguans, the principles, nature and structures of government, and the powers and responsibilities of the state. To counter any tendency toward autocracy, the Constitution rejects the notion of a vanguard party or the supremacy of any social class. Rather, it recognizes the people as the forgers of their own destiny and assigns equal value to participatory democracy and representative democracy. In this way, popular mobilization is acknowledged as both the guarantor and the counterweight to one-party rule.

The Constitution commits Nicaragua to support a just international order and the struggle for peace among nations, referring as well to the solidarity of Nicaraguans with people around the world who struggle against oppression and discrimination. It reaffirms Nicaragua's commitment to political pluralism, a mixed economy, and nonalignment internationally.

The Constitution does not just protect Nicaraguans from state interference. It also requires the state to press for justice, to remove obstacles to political participation and economic equality, and to promote the fair distribution of the nation's resources and earnings. In other words, the state must work toward the goal of a life with dignity for all Nicaraguans.

More than one-third of the 202 articles deal with the rights of Nicaraguans. They affirm an ambitious range of individual, political, social, family, and labor rights. The Constitution guarantees the protection and promotion of all rights set out in the Universal Declaration of Human Rights; the American Declaration of the Rights of Man; the International Pact of Economic, Social and Cultural Rights and the International Pact of Civil and Political Rights of the United Nations, and the American Convention of Human Rights of the Organization of American States. Moreover, the Constitution stipulates that the full exercise of these rights cannot be suspended.

The Constitution acknowledges the historic claim of the indigenous peoples and communities of Nicaragua's Atlantic Coast, guaranteeing the right to preserve and develop their cultures, to use their languages and to organize themselves according to their values and traditions. Provisions on national defense affirm the national character of the army and its loyalty to the Constitution, arising from the mobilization and organized participation of the people. Despite the problems of militarization, such an approach reduces the distance between the army and the people and neutralizes the possible coercive effects of a state on society.

The Constitution also protects the basic framework of the economy, emphasizing the diversity of forms of ownership, the heterogeneity of economic actors, and the goals of agrarian reform. It acknowledges the state's responsibility to provide universal education and to promote "the participation of the family, community and people" in the education system. The Constitution describes education as a democratic, creative, participatory, dynamic and permanent process "which links theory with practice, manual with intellectual labor."

The Constitution also embodies checks and balances within the formal structures of government. The Assembly approves budgets, makes appointments to the Supreme Court and the Electoral Council, ratifies treaties, and reviews executive actions. It can override a presidential veto with the support of 60 percent of its members, and it must approve, within sixty days, the declaration of a state of emergency. Nevertheless, the president functions as head of government, head of state, and commander-in-chief of the defense forces, making Nicaragua a strong presidential republic. The independence of the judiciary and the electoral branch is guaranteed as is the supremacy of the Constitution.

The durability and effectiveness of a constitution depend largely upon its acceptance as a legal framework for government. The Nicaraguan Constitution, developed in consultation with our citizenry, is both comprehensible and understood. It will not be consigned to the archives and forgotten. It reflects the collective aspirations of Nicaragua. It is a living document with a moral and political force which extends far beyond its legal import.

The enactment of the Constitution by no means concludes Nicaragua's process of democratization. The next important step is to implement autonomy for the peoples and communities of the Atlantic coast. Home to the vast majority of Nicaragua's indigenous peoples and separated by history, geography, language and culture, the Atlantic coast is different and has different needs from the rest of the country. Having recognized the need for Atlantic coast inhabitants to define their priorities, enhance their cultures and direct their own development, the government established a regional commission to recommend how best to achieve these goals. The Constitution guarantees regional autonomy for the Atlantic coast; Nicaragua's ethnic minorities must now elaborate specific arrangements to exercise that autonomy.

Local government is crucial to democratization in Nicaragua. As in any country, there are a wide range of issues and services which are best dealt with at a municipal or regional level. More immediate access by citizenry facilitates direct participation in decision making, increasing the accountability and responsiveness of government. Planning is underway for municipal elections across Nicaragua in 1988. The exact form and powers of municipalities have yet to be confirmed, although the Constitution entrenches the autonomy of municipal governments without diminishing the authority of the central government.

Nicaragua must also establish a body of legislation and legal precedence that gives credence to the principles and goals cited within the Constitution. This is an awesome task at any time but all the more so for a government still organizing itself while attempting to transform a society, defend the country from external aggression, and correct shortcomings under the harsh glare of world-wide publicity. Three tasks are paramount: (1) the human and civil rights guaranteed in the Constitution must be translated into specific legislation, regulations and procedures; (2) the governmental process must be elaborated and fully implemented; (3) the ambitious yet fundamental goals which constitute a social contract among Nicaraguans must be achieved.

CONCLUSION

Each of these developments concludes a stage and constitutes a springboard for further advances in the process of democratization within Nicaragua. And each remains severely hampered by the constraints outlined earlier. Because of the experience of the past seven years—the tremendous progress Nicaraguans have made in political participation, in building their experience and confidence in assuming power, individually and collectively, and in acquiring a sense of control over their destiny—the country has made significant strides in overcoming its cultural and political legacy. The lessons must never end, however.

Moreover, Nicaragua's underdevelopment, compounded by its current woes, obstructs the social and economic progress which is integral to the emergence of a strong democracy. It is easier to increase opportunity and to redistribute wealth from an ever-expanding economic pie. In the absence of growth and development, the prospects for cordial relations among the various segments of Nicaraguan society grow bleak.

Most importantly, the war of aggression by proxy, perpetrated by the government of the United States, must stop if democracy is to flourish. Their intervention has forced Nicaragua to maintain a state of emergency, curtailing certain rights provided within the Constitution and diverting precious resources from production to defense.

Some observers cite this curtailment as evidence of a lack of good faith by the Nicaraguan government in pursuing democracy. Yet democracy can only be practiced by a sovereign nation, whose independence and right to self-determination is respected. As long as the war of aggression persists, Nicaraguans will assert their right to defend themselves, however regrettable the limitations which that defense imposes.

It is difficult to communicate the sense of destiny that Nicaraguans feel; the affirmation of the newly literate that they will never again be deceived; the confidence of women, of workers, of students who for the first time begin to understand their power. Nicaraguans are proud of the progress they have made in building democracy. They are not willing to short-circuit the process by accepting the past disguised as the future from those who held power and seek to reclaim it. In sum, despite the suffering, destruction and devastation, our response is not one of despair, but rather resolve. The greater the obstacles, the stronger the will of the Nicaraguan people to defend our sovereignty, to pursue our goals and to build our own democracy.

5
Honduras: National Identity, Repression, and Popular Response

Judith A. Weiss

Honduras is often considered a typical "banana republic," dominated first by U.S. fruit companies and now overwhelmed by massive U.S. militarism. With a few notable exceptions,[1] there is little published research on the country although its history is both complex and straightforward. The ups and downs of competing forces, few of them inherently strong and independent, form fairly clear lines of development, conflict, and styles of resolution. The present juncture in Honduras reflects decades of a sui generis development, a unique balance of competing social and political forces, and a "grooming" by the United States for what has become one of the largest networks of foreign military bases in the western hemisphere.

Understanding the historical connections between the Honduran economy, its class structure, and foreign corporate and strategic interests illuminates the 1981–87 period, when the Reagan administration made Honduras the linchpin of its regional policies. The contemporary situation results from Honduras' long experience as a divided nation controlled by foreign interests, whose hegemony is challenged increasingly by a variety of popular forces.

The United States has long influenced and controlled Honduras but its current involvement is unmatched anywhere in the Americas, except perhaps in Puerto Rico. The Sandinista revolution in Nicaragua, the stalemate in El Salvador, and the unreliability of Panama as a U.S. ally since the 1981 death of President Omar Torrijos, made Honduras a logical military base to support President Ronald Reagan's policy to "roll back" communism. The economic and political deterioration of an already desperate society, and the growing power of U.S.-backed Contras in Honduras, are paralleled, however, by the rise, fall, and rebirth of popular organizations there—making Honduras a far more complex situation than is widely thought.

SETTING THE STAGE: INTERNAL DEVELOPMENT AND U.S. INFLUENCE

Foreign interests have played a key role in the economic and political development of Honduras. The United States, in particular, has exploited or even engineered systemic weaknesses in Honduras' economy and society, beginning with the establishment of the banana companies early in the twentieth century, and, since the 1950s, through control of the military and major labor groups.

Infrastructural deficiencies are a major cause of Honduras' uneven development. The lack of roads, and transportation and marketing systems is rooted in the neglect of Honduras during the colonial period and in the chaotic and violent politics of the nineteenth century. In the 1870s the Liberals attempted to create a coffee oligarchy comparable to those of El Salvador and Guatemala but failed, largely due to an inadequate infrastructure for the efficient, large-scale development of an export product. Economic weaknesses, low export revenues, and a disastrous British loan, on which Honduras defaulted in 1873, left the country without the means to build the infrastructure necessary to exploit its resources. It was developed ultimately by subsidiaries of the major banana companies to serve their own needs.

U.S. fruit companies acquired land in Honduras toward the turn of the century, competing with local growers or buying them out. By 1918, United Fruit and Standard Fruit held 75 percent of the banana lands. The plantations functioned as relatively autonomous territories, employing nearly 45,000 by the 1940s—the largest segment of the Honduran workforce. During the 1950s, however, the fruit companies mechanized and diversified production to include hemp and cacao; they sold or abandoned large tracts of land, and laid off up to 50 percent of their laborers. By the late 1960s, they shifted some of their production risks to Honduran growers, taking advantage of the cooperatives formed with government assistance, and concentrated mainly on marketing and distribution of Honduran products.

In the early stages of their control of Honduran resources, the companies also exercised sweeping political control. During the 1920s, groups backed by the two main banana companies unleashed a divisive and weakening conflict—almost a civil war—that ended with United Fruit virtually controlling the national economy. For over three decades, U.S. interests dominated the limited economic development of Honduras. But that arrogant and unrestricted exploitation also produced the seeds of today's popular resistance to foreign occupation: the first militant labor unions, with the first strike (1916), the first general strike (1954) and, beginning in the 1950s, the struggle to maintain independent and progressive labor organizations in the face of U.S. penetration.

Concentrated political power matched concentrated economic power. Tiburcio Carías Andino, a dictator in the tradition of Estrada Cabrera of Guatemala and Machado of Cuba, ruled Honduras with an iron fist from 1932 to 1948. Carías crushed the Liberal revolt of 1932 with planes and troops and exiled or killed political opponents and labor organizers. His rule saw the consolidation and growth of the United Fruit Company; the repression of strong labor unions; and the emergence of a national coffee oligarchy.

With the modernization and economic liberalization that followed World War II, Honduras returned to an electoral political system that allowed increased diversification and expansion in a growing world market. A three-way rivalry for organized political influence emerged in the 1950s among coffee producers, cattle ranchers, and a growing mercantile and professional class. Meanwhile, the fruit companies began phasing out much of their own production and developing new relations with Honduran growers but maintaining significant economic power. By 1980, seven multinationals controlled 80 percent of the economy, and Standard Fruit and United Fruit headed the list. The armed forces, labor organizations and peasant groups remained largely outside the political parties. Instead, these dynamic sectors entered into varying patterns of open conflict and alliances during the 1960s and 1970s, becoming the most influential players in Honduran politics, although on the margins of the electoral process. Most recently, human rights organizations and small left-wing parties have emerged as a significant conscientizing and mobilizing force.

THE MILITARY

The armed forces, which became the most powerful single sector in Honduras by the 1970s and played a crucial role in the U.S. military penetration in the 1980s, form a relatively recent institution. The first national officer training school was founded toward the end of the Carías presidency and was strengthened after 1952 by U.S. instructors and financing. A modern army, no longer dominated by regional allegiances, emerged following the 1947 Treaty of Rio de Janeiro (the Treaty of Inter-American Reciprocal Assistance). The U.S.-Honduras military treaty signed on May 25, 1954 established the formal framework for one of the most consistent relationships of dependence between a Latin American military and the United States.

The Honduran armed forces first intervened in politics in 1956, ostensibly to uphold electoral democracy. The military's right to intervene and its virtual autonomy were then codified in a series of constitutional amendments introduced in 1957. These amendments reduced the powers and responsibilities of the defense minister appointed by an elected president, established the right of the armed forces to disobey presidential orders that they considered unconstitutional, and made the military formally independent of the elected government by having the high command name the chief of the armed forces.

A military coup in 1963 overthrew the reformist president Ramón Villeda. General Oswaldo López Arellano held power until 1971, retired briefly, and then returned in a second coup in 1972. López Arellano attempted to project a populist image through moderate agrarian reform programs, but only after repressing rural workers' organizations and the Standard Fruit union, and opening the country to new penetration by foreign capital when Honduras joined the Central American Common Market. It was under López Arellano that Honduras fought the so-called "Soccer War" against El Salvador (1969), after the latter invaded deep into Honduran territory.

The second López presidency brought two phases of agrarian reform (1972 and 1975), designed to defuse peasant militancy and bring more land into production. This, however, was largely a hollow reform since the Agrarian Institute (INA), to avoid antagonizing large landowners, distributed only unused, poorer quality land owned by the government. López also introduced a minimum wage, set up agencies to control forestry and grain distribution, and set up the National Investment Corporation (CONADI) to finance industrial development. These mild reforms antagonized Honduran conservatives: right-wing elements of the army, the Liberal and National Parties, and the National Federation of Farmers and Cattle-Raisers (FENAGH), which had organized into a strong reactionary force, largely because of the 1975 Agrarian Reform Law. Violent incidents marked the end of López' rule, including a massacre at Los Horcones in which seven peasant organizers and two foreign priests were burned to death in a bread oven. This was not the first violent reaction in Honduran history, but FENAGH's involvement and the anticommunist tenor of the violence foreshadowed the ideologically motivated, paramilitary violence of the early eighties.

Military-led governments continued in Honduras until 1982 but regional events triggered change. In 1979–80 the Sandinista victory, the U.S. desire to contain the guerrilla movement in El Salvador, and the Carter administration's concern to restore a semblance of democracy in Honduras (and thus limit opposition to U.S. plans for Honduras to replace Somoza's Nicaragua), all created pressure to call elections. In the two years prior to the 1982 election the Liberal and the National Parties competed furiously for military support.

In 1981, with the support of the new Reagan administration, General Gustavo Alvarez, chief of the National Intelligence Department (DNI) and of the Public Security Forces (FUSEP), became head of the Armed Forces Superior Council (COSUFA). Alvarez represented the most extreme right-wing ideological tendency in the army and had proven his anticommunism in a vicious campaign against Salvadorean exiles, Farabundo Martí Liberation Front (FMLN) representatives, and Honduran left-wing activists.[2] His appointment to COSUFA ushered in right-wing policies, disappearances, and torture, within the framework of a larger-scale repression that was unusual for Honduras.

The constitutional independence of the armed forces enabled the United States to bypass Honduran congressional authority for the construction of bases and to avoid any accountability for foreign assistance funds sent directly to the Honduran military. From the very outset, U.S. military connections with Honduras were largely outside civilian controls. With Alvarez heading the armed forces, two foreign armies virtually occupied Honduras: the United States and the Contras. The Contra force, aided initially by Honduran and Argentine advisers, grew with direct U.S. support after 1982–83, occupying a strip of southern Honduras which has become popularly known as "nueva Nicaragua." The United States has constructed ten bases throughout Honduras, many with permanent cement and concrete structures. Neither the U.S. nor Honduran legislatures directly approved the first bases although some have been used to train, supply and even house the Contras. The Contras' primary goal is to destroy economic and human targets in Nicaragua, to weaken the Sandinista government and force its collapse. The massive concentration of U.S. troops and materiel in what appear to be permanent bases may indicate that Honduras has replaced Panama, and to some extent Somoza's Nicaragua, as a reliable launching point for direct U.S. intervention in the region.

General Alvarez served Reagan well. But apparently his megalomania and desire for absolute power drove a group of officers to expel him from Honduras in March 1984. He left under a cloud of corruption and embezzlement, compounded by conservative Catholic mistrust of his links to fundamentalist Protestants. If his departure was a minor setback for the U.S. right, Alvarez had already fulfilled his main function. The civilian presidencies of Suazo Córdova (1982–1985) and José Azcona (1986–present) have neither restrained nor controlled the military. Suazo Córdova collaborated with the armed forces and the right in their persecution of Salvadoreans and the Honduran left.

The Honduran military participates in almost continual joint maneuvers with the United States and serves as a conduit for Contra aid. Individual officers profit as middlemen for arms and supplies, and internal divisions result from rivalry and greed as much as from tactical or ideological differences. News reports and analyses of the Honduran military over the past fifteen years read like a tangle of corruption, graft, equivocation, and inconsistencies. Yet two consistent patterns remain: (1) the Honduran military overrides the civilian sector in matters of defense policy; and (2) the U.S. military presence and its diplomatic support of Honduran military policies favor the continued militarization of the country.

In May 1987, President Azcona and Carlos Montoya, President of the National Congress, defended the acquisition of F-5E jets and the army's participation in U.S. military exercises on the grounds that Honduras needs stronger and more independent defenses should the peace talks and any subsequent negotiations fail. Montoya suggested that Honduras could not count on U.S. support, and had to increase the size of its air force because it could not afford to expand the army. The real implications of these statements are unclear but the Honduran air force might become a proxy for the United States in an attack on Nicaragua. Conservative sectors continue to back military initiatives, but the Contra presence has generated widespread opposition (even among reactionary circles) to U.S. policy in Honduras. Some centrists have become increasingly upset with the U.S. bases and militarization of Honduras, and these issues, in turn, are the main rallying points for labor, peasant, women's and human rights organizations.

LABOR AND PEASANT ORGANIZATIONS

Popular militancy in Honduras is rooted in the labor unions and *campesino* movements. The union movement cut its teeth in the early days of the banana companies but soon split between communists and socialists. Throughout the 1920s and 1930s, Honduran governments expressed class-based anti-union sentiment as much as anticommunism, although under Carías vicious attacks on the unions usually singled out the communists. By the early 1950s, the unions became the target of attacks by a new coalition: the antilabor, anticommunist Hondurans and the imported anticommunist labor organizing of the Inter-American Regional Labor Organization (ORIT) and the U.S.-based American Federation of Labor (AFL). Subsequently the American Institute of Free Labor Development (AIFLD) became the chief U.S. labor organization seeking to influence the Latin American labor movement.

The Gálvez administration (1949–54) permitted the establishment of some urban unions, but opposed the unionization of banana workers. Communist labor organizers were the special target of repression but a semiclandestine, progressive organization remained active: the Confederation of Union Unity (CUS). In May 1954 CUS, aided by Guatemalan communists, organized a general strike of 50,000 workers—35,000 of them at the banana companies and their railway subsidiaries. Despite widespread popular support, the strike dissipated within two months, largely the result of economic pressure, combined with the government strategy of cooptation and repression.

The United States contributed both money and training to strengthen Honduras' anticommunist unions and keep them firmly within the ORIT and later the AIFLD. Honduras' Christian Democrats fought hard to organize reformist unions which, in the early seventies, constituted the General Confederation of Workers. The United Fruit Workers Union became an important battleground for right-wing activity in the early 1980s. As in 1954, the rightists used selective repression and a combination of bribery and intimidation instead of massive police or military actions against the rank-and-file. Since 1980, the AIFLD and Honduras' paramilitary right, with its death squads, have alternated negotiations and repression throughout the trade union movement. The goal is to regain control of organizations that moved to the left in the 1970s, but their efforts proved only temporarily successful. As in El Salvador, the AIFLD's Honduran unions eventually rejected the constraints imposed upon them and became more militant. Left-wing unions have gained considerable strength since 1984–85, resulting in the targeting of their leaders by death squads and right-wing groups.

The struggle to control mass organizations extended to the Honduran countryside. In August 1962 the National Federation of Honduran Campesinos (FENACH) was founded, primarily to mobilize peasants seeking redress against land grabs by the United Fruit Company. One month later, the administration of President Ramón Villeda formed the National Association of Honduran Campesinos (ANACH), as a pro-U.S., anticommunist association. Like its labor union counterpart, the Confederation of Honduran Workers, ANACH came under the tutelage of ORIT-AFL. Between 1964 and the early 1970s, its U.S.-affiliated leaders kept ANACH under close control through financial assistance and advisers. The more militant National Federation of Honduran Campesinos was isolated; several of its members joined the short-lived guerrilla movement around Yoro (1963–65) and others joined ANACH, to work from within against its policies of neutralizing the militancy of rural workers.

In the mid-sixties, the Social Christian Peasant Association grew as a third force in the countryside, boosted in part by the community organizing work of the Catholic church in northern Honduras. The Association became the National Federation of Rural Workers in 1968, and the National Peasants Union (UNC) in 1970. The UNC is the most progressive rural organization in Honduras, spearheading land recoveries, marches and hunger strikes, and it is the most outspoken opponent of antisquatter legislation and police repression. The militancy of the UNC and its predecessors reflects the rural workers' dissatisfaction with the slow progress of agrarian reform. The price its members pay for seeking redistributive justice includes disappearances, detentions, and murder.

By 1974, independent co-ops within the pro-U.S. National Association of Honduran Campesinos came under direct attack by conservatives. Honduran cattlemen forced a number of these co-ops to disband through harassment and murder as evidenced by the massacre at Los Horcones. Despite these setbacks, many small rural organizations evolved into fairly democratic entities with the assistance of progressive elements within the National Agrarian Institute, and the 1975 Agrarian Reform Law which limited the maximum size of individual landholdings to 350 hectares. Catholic lay workers—"Delegates of the Word"—and progressive members of the Christian Democratic Party have been active participants in the conflicts generated by *campesino* demands for change. Despite opposition from conservatives and the anticommunist Catholic hierarchy, more than 1,000 lay workers work in remote areas of the countryside. Their presence reflects the variety of social forces at work in both rural and urban Honduras. Democratic impulses from below, reformism from above, and conservative reaction produce rising tensions throughout the country.

THE ORGANIZED RIGHT AND HUMAN RIGHTS

Political persecution usually targets those persons most committed to addressing the fundamental grievances. In Honduras, as in most of the Third World, these involve gross inequality of land tenure, and the right to a decent livelihood. These conditions have existed since colonial times, but events in Nicaragua and El Salvador have demonstrated the possibility of change. Many workers and peasants will no longer passively tolerate widespread (and worsening) deprivation.

Living conditions in rural Honduras have improved little since the promise of agrarian reform twenty years ago. There are more landless peasants now than in 1970. Of farms under ten hectares (four acres), 68 percent occupy only 13 percent of arable land. In 1985 the government renewed a land-distribution program, but—significantly—the first recipients could not take possession of their plots because the area was occupied by Contras.[3] The Contras, the U.S. military, and vastly increased U.S. aid were welcomed in the early 1980s but remarkably few benefits have "trickled down" to either rural or urban Hondurans. Nationally, unemployment hovers around 20 percent and inflation is at 50 percent. Annual per capita income remains below $900. The terms imposed by the International Monetary Fund as a condition for loans forced the government to cut over forty of the subsidies on basic goods, which sharply increased their cost to the poor. In 1984, 210 of the country's 362 rural health centers shut down for lack of staff, equipment and supplies. Infant mortality is over 13 percent. Thirty percent of the 1985 national budget was allocated to security and defense, and only 7 percent to health and education. During the 1970s, a period of moderate reforms, per capita food consumption declined 20 percent. Poverty is increasing, particularly among the rural poor displaced by the U.S. and Contra bases. Because of the rise in consumer prices, one can assume that nutrition throughout Honduras has not improved in the past decade. The massive U.S. military presence and the Contras have produced a sordid by-product: shoeshine boys, young prostitutes, and homeless street children are now far more numerous in Honduran towns, while drugs and sexually transmitted diseases, including AIDS, have become a serious concern.

Much of Honduras' social and economic decline followed the right-dominated years of the first Reagan administration (1980–84). Unusually harsh repression characterized these years, including systematic violations of human rights and the unleashing of a "dirty war" based on the Argentine model. Military and police personnel engaged in these activities with the support of U.S., Argentine, and reputedly, Contra, Chilean and Cuban exile advisers. They operated with the tacit approval of an organized Honduran right. The Association for the Progress of Honduras (APROH) heads the right-wing groups that emerged in Honduras during the last decade. Incorporated in 1983, APROH is a coalition of conservatives: businessmen, landowners, military officers, and peasant and union leaders. The president of the right-dominated Autonomous University was also a member, and APROH has had links to the most reactionary sectors of the Catholic church. In a few words, Honduras formalized the consolidation of its oligarchical forces under the leadership of the right.

The three de facto rulers of Honduras fostered the climate for the creation of APROH: Armed Forces head Gustavo Alvarez, President Suazo Córdova representing the right wing of the Liberal party, and U.S. Ambassador John Negroponte, the proconsul of Ronald Reagan's "New Beginning." Even before the Alvarez-Reagan era, conservative Hondurans responded to the perceived threat of reform with the resurgence of officially constituted organizations like FENAGH, the cattle-owners federation. But it was APROH that, according to reliable sources, sponsored and even funded the "dirty war" of the early eighties—the disappearances, tortures in safe houses, firebombings and murders—that bore the mark of its Argentine advisers.[4]

Through General Alvarez, APROH also received support from another source: CAUSA, the anticommunist, quasi-fascist political section of the Unification Church. Colonel Bo Hi Pak, the Reverend Moon's deputy, was a guest at APROH's opening meeting. He actively courted APROH, and the Unification Church is reported to have acquired interests in Honduran banks and businesses during 1983–84, when CAUSA was fundraising for the Contras and supporting highly publicized programs for Nicaraguan refugees in Honduras. Alvarez's flirting with the Moonies, however, disturbed many APROH members and his departure from power is said to have curtailed CAUSA's influence.

The Honduran extreme right was not the sole violator of human rights. Refugee agencies and nongovernmental organizations such as Oxfam and Americas Watch have repeatedly blamed military actions for such violations. During the early eighties Honduran forces, possibly with U.S. assistance, cooperated with Salvadorean troops to attack FMLN guerrilla pockets just inside the Honduran border with El Salvador, to attack refugees fleeing the Salvadorean military and others in Honduran camps, and to crush the few Honduran guerrilla movements that have arisen since 1963.

Protests against human rights violations have come from various organizations including, in the past four years, the Committee for the Defense of Human Rights in Honduras, the Committee of Relatives of the Disappeared, and most recently, the Visitación Padilla Committee of Women for Peace. The women's peace committee, whose slogan is "La Patria: no se vende, no se alquila, no se presta" ("our country is not for sale; it cannot be rented or loaned out"), focuses primarily on education and the mobilization of women around the issues of peace and self-determination. Such committees have undoubtly been inspired by the actions of similar groups in Guatemala, Argentina, El Salvador and other countries. Their Honduran roots, however, are in the peasant and labor unions and in the teachings of the progressive religious leaders. These labor and peasant organizations and leaders have been historically weaker than their U.S.-influenced counterparts, yet they persist.

National sovereignty and self-determination are becoming visible issues in Honduras. Potentially, these issues are strategic bridges to less progressive sectors that nevertheless share a concern with militarization and with U.S. and Contra bases. Human rights groups have exposed and protested the psychological war that President Azcona's administration wages against the left through unfounded stories of urban guerrillas, kidnapping and terrorism. Human rights workers also expose terrorist tactics of the pro-Contra factions, such as the 1986 car-bombing death of journalist Rodrigo Wong Arévalo.

The Honduran aboriginal peoples, now emerging as a new opposition force, have broached the issue of self-determination. Indigenous groups in the central regions are reclaiming communal lands guaranteed in the nineteenth century and currently occupied by outsiders. There are rumblings from the Atlantic coast that Miskito and other groups, heartened by the Nicaraguan example, are interested in pursuing demands of autonomy.

PROSPECTS

Two forces have boosted grassroots support for popular organizations: the widespread sentiment against the occupation of large areas of Honduras by U.S. and Contra irregulars; and the activity of the extreme right, particularly its terrorism. The growth in size and frequency of mass demonstrations and marches suggests effective conscientization on an ever-increasing scale.

By and large, the Honduran state has thus far allowed popular organizations to carry on their activities. But this tolerance has been hard-won, and it is assured only as long as the ruling sectors judge that popular protests do not threaten "national security." The extremism that characterized General Alvarez' tenure receded after 1983, but it would be naive to assume that it was an abnormal hiatus in an otherwise pragmatic pattern of control. A close reading of Honduran history indicates that the type, degree and extent of repression is associated with three main factors: the strength of the popular organizations; the government's ability to control them through selective intimidation and nonviolent means such as co-optation; and the particular juncture of U.S. interests in the region.

There are other secondary variables: the degree of unity within the ruling sectors and armed forces, and the interests shared between them; the success of limited reform as a self-regulating aspect of the system, and the ruling sector's perception of the threat posed by the opposition. These factors could determine the dominant sectors' response to the demands of the popular organizations and, possibly, the extent of Honduran compliance with U.S. demands.

There have been heartening developments. In January 1987, a petition presented to the Honduran Congress demanded the expulsion of the Contras from Honduran territory.[5] Displaced coffee growers have brought a lawsuit against the United States, protesting the Contra presence in southern Honduras. These cases have served to establish temporary alliances with more progressive sectors, but they should probably be interpreted primarily as indicators of acute grievances caused by the transient, semipermanent presence of 10,000 to 50,000 foreign military and irregular forces.[6]

Many Hondurans agree on the social cost of the military situation: unemployment, loss of productive land, economic chaos, the rise in prostitution and drug trafficking, and the climate of violence that permeates the country. Popular organizations expose these ills as a direct consequence of the sell-out of Honduras and thus strengthen a growing nationalist spirit based on the right to self-determination. Fed by the efforts of the peasant and labor movements and their counterparts among students, women's groups and human rights activists, Honduras seems to be on the verge of a major struggle for national liberation.

The key to Central America lies in Honduras, as the Reagan administration so astutely calculated. But as Hondurans emerge from a century of division, degradation and control imposed by U.S. interests and Honduran oligarchies, their country becomes a linchpin for regional liberation. Until U.S. bases are out of Honduras, there can be no genuine peace in Central America. Until U.S. economic interests and their collaborators are removed, there can be no economic and social progress in the region. Honduras was the first secure and peaceful base for U.S. *economic* hegemony. And it has now become the last secure and peaceful base for U.S. *military* hegemony. While every effort will be made to exploit Honduras as the "spoiler" in any regional peace negotiations, and to maintain the status quo, it is clear that a growing national frustration with these policies is in the air. It is still too early to assess the importance of the country in post-Reagan policy for the region, but it is increasingly obvious that the people of Honduras desire change—and are prepared to struggle toward that end.

NOTES

1. Among the best sources on Honduras are: *Honduras, State for Sale* (London: Latin American Bureau, 1985); Victor Meza, *Historia del movimiento obrero hondureño* (Tegucigalpa, Honduras: Ediciones Guaymuras, 1980); Mario Posas, *El movimiento campesino hondureño* (Tegucigalpa, Honduras: Ediciones Guaymuras, 1981); Juan Arancibia, *Honduras: ¿un estrado nacional?* (Tegucigalpa, Honduras: Ediciones, Guaymuras, 1984); Gregorio Selser, *Honduras, república alquilada* (Mexico: Mex-Sur Editorial, 1983); Steven Volk, "Honduras: On the Border of War," *NACLA Report* (November/December 1981); Father J. Guadalupe Carney, *To Be a Revolutionary* (New York: Harper and Row, 1984); Philip E. Wheaton, *Inside Honduras: Regional Counterinsurgency Base* (Washington, D.C.: EPICA Task Force, 1982). Three important periodicals/newsletters that contain up to date material are: CEDOH, Centro de Documentacion de Honduras, *Boletín Informativo* (Tegucigalpa) Apartado Postal 1882; Central America Information Service, *Honduras Briefing* (1 Amwell Street, London EC1R 1UL); and Honduras Information Center, *Honduras Update* (1 Summer Street, Sommerville, Mass. 01243). Also important is the special issue, "Honduras: The War Comes Home," *NACLA Report on the Americas* 22, no. 1 (1988).

2. Alvarez, whose favorite readings included Pinochet's *Geopolítica*, had close links to the Argentine military dictatorships. He maintained ties with his former classmates of the Argentine military school, and General Videla sent military advisers to Honduras between 1980 and 1982. Alvarez also trained in Panama and the United States (in Georgia and at the Office of Public Safety Program). He had led army attacks against cooperatives (La Isleta, 1977) and against striking factory workers (San Pedro Sula, 1979). He was also known to have a good working relationship with foreign agribusiness.

3. The Contra forces, numbering between 8,000 and 15,000 over the past five years, have attacked and captured at least three small towns and over 200 private farms in southern Honduras. A number of Hondurans have been killed by Contras and over 5,000 inhabitants evicted and forced out of the region as refugees. By the spring of 1988 it was estimated that there were 12,000 displaced farmers forcibly pushed from the border area. As recently as July 1987, the Tegucigalpa daily carried a report of attempts by the Contras to recruit local residents, a practice that has allegedly been widespread, and has sometimes included forced recruitment or the enlisting of unemployed youths through promises of regular salaries.

4. Scott Anderson and Jon Lee Anderson, *Inside the League* (New York: Dodd, Mead & Co., 1986), 217–241, quote several firsthand reports on the links between the organized right and the "dirty war."

5. This was, in part, an attempt to force an open discussion with the vice-president, the president and other civilian and military officials, who claim that there are no Contras in Honduras.

6. This assumes that the continuous joint exercises involve between 5,000 and 10,000 United States personnel and that the Contra forces in Honduras number between 5,000 and 10,000, not including Honduran nationals recruited by the Contras.

PART II
DEVELOPMENT

6

Central America: Dependent–Welfare, Authoritarian, and Revolutionary Conceptions of Development

James Petras and Morris H. Morley

INTRODUCTION

From the 1950s to the late 1970s two models of development emerged in Central America—the dependent, democratic-welfare approach in Costa Rica and the authoritarian-free market conception in Guatemala. Since both nations were "dependent" on their export sector, both experienced substantial growth based on their outward orientation, and the explanations for their difference could not be located in their external economic relations. The key factor was found in the political spheres—in the political organs of the regimes, in the political structures, in the social alliances which shaped policy. In brief, Costa Rica experienced an indigenous political revolution (1948) that dismantled the army and created a social bloc that included labor and small farmers (with local business); in Guatemala, the accumulation model was anchored in a foreign-orchestrated coup that strengthened the repressive arms of the state and concentrated power in a military-multinational-landowner complex.

The divergence between democratic welfare and authoritarian-free market models is rooted in the manner in which the state mediates between the local class structure and external dependence. It is not the world market that shaped the politico-social structure in Costa Rica and Guatemala; rather, their political-class structures determined the manner in which dependence would affect their social-economic systems. These differences and similarities highlighted the possibility of diverse roads of development within the dependent capitalist mode of production.

Common external dependency and divergent internal socio-political patterns assumed a constantly expanding world economy—an assumption taken as given by most analysts and promoters of externally oriented growth, both democratic and authoritarian. The debt and trade crises during the past decade, however, have called into question this assumption.

Declining terms of trade, the near bankrupting of the state treasuries, and a massive flight of capital have undermined the economic pillars of both "authoritarian" and "democratic" development. The evolution of the two regimes from the 1950s to the 1980s and the changing patterns of development suggest the importance of examining development models in a framework of *long-term, large-scale* change. This is particularly important because large-scale crises, structural factors and class relations may not change in the short-term and thus are rarely taken into account by behavioral and other narrowly focused approaches. A broader historical framework provides us with an understanding of both the importance of the politico-social changes and how they produced middle-term "models" of growth—authoritarian and democratic—as well as how, over the long-term, the internal/external contradiction emerged and eroded the basis of those models.

The emergence of a revolutionary regime (the problem of treating it as a model will be discussed later) is thus no accident of history nor merely an idiosyncratic episode peculiar to Nicaraguan history. It represents the culmination of a set of regional experiences in which both liberal and authoritarian politics had exhausted their historical possibilities within the framework of dependent development. In Guatemala, the polarized class structure led to a massive popular challenge, which was accompanied by capital flight and a deteriorating economy. The strictly military regime was modified to include civilians and restricted electoral politics. In Costa Rica, the marriage between capitalism and welfare politics was ruptured: from the 1980s outward growth is premised on austerity. The dependent-welfare model could not sustain itself in either its democratic or authoritarian versions, neither with welfare or with growth statistics.

The Sandinista revolution was an eminently political event, made by people moved by a profound sense of nationalism and desire for democracy. But it was also a revolution that took place in a time of converging economic crises: declining prices and revenues that weakened the state and energized the mass of social forces who had been marginal actors during the expansion years.

In brief, our major hypothesis is that by examining the *long-term, large-scale* patterns, we will discover several sets of developments: (1) that dependent capitalism is neither inherently democratic or authoritarian and that, in the middle and short run, there are multiple paths of growth and politico-social patterns; (2) that implicit in dependent capitalist growth over the long run is a tendency toward prolonged crises that erode the basis for growth, reverse social advances, and homogenize economic/social patterns; (3) that the crises of externally based models of growth linked to authoritarian structures create the basis for social revolution; (4) that revolutionary societies cannot crystallize a model of development until they have secured their survival against external aggression; (5) that revolutionary defense is linked to the extension and deepening of the process of social transformation.

COSTA RICA: FROM DEPENDENT SOCIAL DEMOCRACY TO EXPORT-ORIENTED CLIENT STATE

The Costa Rican development model up to the 1970s shares features common to Central America's development experiences, as well as having very distinctive characteristics. Like its neighbors, Costa Rica depends on an agro-export sector based on a limited number of commodities to earn most of its foreign exchange. U.S. multinationals have penetrated both the industrialization and agro-industrial processes. There are significant disparities in income and landownership, and outside banking and financial institutions have financed a substantial portion of the country's growth. Costa Rica has generally supported and voted with other Central American clients against revolutionary and reform regimes—supporting the 1954 overthrow of a democratically elected government in Guatemala, the 1961 Bay of Pigs invasion against Cuba and the U.S.-organized invasion of the Dominican Republic in 1965.

Costa Rica differs from the rest of Central America in terms of internal class alliances that have shaped state policies regarding distribution of the economic surplus obtained through external exchanges. Three social factors define this internal pattern: the existence of a substantial and influential class of small and medium-size farmers; a substantial organized petit-bourgeoisie with welfare proclivities that influence the dominant National Liberation Party (PLN) and the state apparatus; and a national-capitalist class willing and able to capitalize on import-substitution strategy and Costa Rica's entry into the Central American Common Market.

These social forces, under the leadership of the PLN, gained political ascendancy in the context of two significant facts: they defeated the standing army in a conflict for political power (in 1948) and dismantled the army as a politico-military force, thus ensuring the relative stabilization of a new broad power bloc in which middle class welfarism was not under constant threat by the traditional oligarchy; secondly, the PLN's social-democratic regime was preceded by a conservative regime which had already established an extended welfare system and protective labor legislation . . . thus providing a broad political consensus on welfarism and labor union legitimacy.

A broad coalition of classes defined the PLN regime including small and large farmers, agro-exporters, labor unions, foreign capital, and state managers of public enterprises. The new regime did not displace old power centers but built its welfare programmes upon the property foundations of the existing elite structures. It combined free education and public health programmes with substantial concentration of landownership and inequalities in income. Expanding state ownership of public utilities provided substantial contracts for national private capital. PLN governments protected local capital but opened the agro-business, chemical, and food processing sectors to multinational investments. The social democratic regime harnessed welfare measures to dependent development through state intervention—mediating payoffs to competing classes during a particularly favorable period in the world economy, roughly between 1950 and 1978. The reliance of Costa Rica's dependent-welfare model on global capitalist expansion became evident with the worldwide crises of the late 1970s (see Table 6.1).

The deepening crisis in the dependent development-welfare model throughout the 1980s was evident in negative growth rates and the reversal of welfare conditions throughout the early to mid-1980s. The very forces which had propelled "growth" and financed welfare were the same factors undermining the process and the development model. The fundamental structures that underlie the process of chronic regression and previous growth include: (1) the extensive penetration of capital in the 1960s and 1970s; (2) the increasing linkage of Costa Rica to the international circuits of capital that facilitated the large scale inflow of capital; (3) the increasing capitalization of the economy and the dynamic growth of exports, based on a combination of growing wage relations in the city and the countryside and the introduction of new technologies. These dynamic changes in productive forces, and social relations, as well as the extension of welfare measures, occurred within the framework of dependent capitalist relations. They were fueled by external financial and investment forces which were subject to the cyclical patterns of crisis and overproduction—now transferred to Latin America and, in particular, to Costa Rica. The deepening pattern of Latin American integration into the circuit of international capital facilitated the flow of capital during the expansive period, but amplified the outflow of capital during the crisis, leaving in its wake a development structure incapable of adjusting its ties toward the market without a fundamental rupture in the organization of the state. The change forced by the crisis has led to a strengthening of the externally oriented classes, especially the export bourgeoisie, and a marginalizing of the lower middle class; the privatization of state enterprises; and the promotion of unrestricted foreign capital flows.

The crisis in Costa Rica's dependent-welfare model is clearly seen in

Table 6.1

COSTA RICA: ECONOMIC GROWTH 1950-1983

Years	Growth Rates
1950-60	6.4
1960-70	5.9
1970-78	6.3
1978-83	-.4

Source: *CEPAL Review* No. 28, April 28, 1986, p. 12.

the decline of real per capita income which by the end of 1984 was barely equal to the 1974 level.[1] The social democratic regime's acceptance of the International Monetary Fund (IMF) austerity prescriptions to secure external financing led to a precipitous decline in living standards. One study reports:

In 1977, 24.8% of Costa Rican families were living in poverty . . . By 1980 the number had climbed to 41.7% and in 1982, 70.7% were defined as poor. In 1983 the government reported a marked rise in third degree malnutrition among children . . . Infant mortality, previously on a level comparable to developed countries is climbing rapidly.[2]

The collapse of the dependent-welfare model produced a wave of labor and popular unrest and efforts by the Social Democrats to create a new model of accumulation. The first concern of the social democratic regime was to secure external finance in order to refloat the economy and meet interest payments which were in arrears. To secure external financial support, the Social Democrats had to accept a new hegemonic bloc with a new accumulation model on the one hand and a further deepening of Costa Rica's client state relationship to the United States.

The new model involved massive reduction in state spending, privatization of public enterprises, weakening of state control over banking, lowering wages, and elementary tariffs and controls on foreign capital inflows and outflows. As a result Costa Rica's manufacturing wages became among the lowest in the region (nineteen cents per hour) but its external balances improved: its deficit was reduced from 9.2 percent to 3.3 percent and by 1984 the economy showed a slight upturn.

The relationship between heightened exploitation and recovery was mediated, however, by a massive increase in U.S. aid in exchange for Costa Rica's surrender of its sovereignty. With the U.S. government becoming totally immersed in organizing a counterrevolutionary war against Nicaragua, it needed an ideological cover for its interventionist struggle. Imperial intervention which cloaked its purposes in the rhetoric of a struggle between democracy and communism, desperately needed the presence of a regime with credible democratic credentials—as virtually no one took the claims of El Salvador or Honduras seriously. A deal was struck between President Reagan and Costa Rican President Monge: Washington turned on the economic spigot and Monge turned on the anti-Sandinista rhetoric.

The relationship between Costa Rica's willingness to promote U.S. policy against Nicaragua and U.S. aid can be seen in Table 6.2.

Between 1962 and 1979 total U.S. economic assistance came to $198.9 million. In 1983 alone, U.S. economic aid totalled $214 million—nearly 10 percent of Costa Rica's gross domestic product (GDP) and almost 40 percent of its total budget. This does not include the loans for Costa Rica that the U.S. representatives supported in the International Monetary Fund (IMF), Inter-American Development Bank (BID), and World Bank. As a result of this avalanche of funding, Costa Rica turned a negative growth rate (-7 percent) in 1982 into a positive 2.9 percent in 1983 while paying out 44 percent of their export earnings for interest payments. With large infusions of external finance, the Monge regime contained the economy's downward slide, producing 7.5 percent growth in 1984 and 1.6 percent in 1985. All the structural weaknesses remain, however, and the new export model has yet to demonstrate its efficiency— merchandise exports in 1985 were still 10 percent below 1981.[3]

The cost of this "external aid" was extremely high: Costa Rica traded its political sovereignty, its "tradition" of neutrality and its image as a promoter of democracy. Costa Rica slavishly promoted U.S. policies aimed at destabilizing the Sandinista regime, and allowed Somocista terrorists to operate from Costa Rican territory. It is particularly useful to examine the relationship between the economic crisis, U.S. aid and the role of Costa Rica as a U.S. client state.

COSTA RICA: DEMOCRACY FOR RENT

Crucial to any explanation of Costa Rica's vulnerability to Washington's pressures is the severe economic crisis that has gripped the country over the past six years, forcing the Monge government (1982–86) to accommodate conditions for an economic bailout established by the United States and the Washington-dominated international banks. The Reagan administration's political price was Costa Rica's willingness to submit to each and every one of the former's policy dictates in Central America.

When Luis Alberto Monge became president of Costa Rica in May 1982, the country's economy was in a shambles. The gross domestic product slumped to -3.6 percent in 1981 and -6 percent in 1982 under

Table 6.2
U.S. AID TO COSTA RICA, 1946–1986 (U.S. FISCAL YEARS)
(MILLIONS OF $ U.S.)

	1946-61	1962-79	1980	1981	1982	1983	1984	1985	1986*
ECONOMIC ASSISTANCE									
1. AID & predecessors	20.10	136.80	13.60	11.50	11.50	28.47	22.72	16.75	
loans	10.90	107.80	12.00	10.00	9.70	20.20	17.10	5.20	
grants	9.20	29.00	1.60	1.50	1.80	8.27	5.62	11.55	
2. P.L. 480 Food for Peace	1.10	18.30	0.40	1.80	19.10	28.20	22.50	21.40	
loans	—	—	—	—	18.00	28.00	22.50	21.40	
grants	1.10	18.30	0.40	1.80	1.10	0.20	—	—	
3. Economic Support Funds	—	—	—	—	20.00	155.74	130.00	160.00	
loans	—	—	—	—	15.00	118.00	35.00	—	
grants	—	—	—	—	5.00	37.74	95.00	160.00	
4. Other**	31.00	43.80	2.00	2.00	1.10	1.70	3.70	—	
loans	—	11.80	—	—	—	—	—	—	
grants	31.00	32.00	2.00	2.00	1.10	1.70	3.70	—	
Total Economic Assistance	52.20	198.90	16.00	15.30	51.70	214.10	178.92	198.15	187.0
loans	10.90	119.60	12.00	10.00	42.70	166.20	74.60	26.60	
grants	42.60	79.30	4.00	5.30	9.00	47.90	104.32	177.55	
SECURITY ASSISTANCE									
Total	0.10	6.90	—	0.03	2.05	2.64	9.15	9.20	2.73+
loans	0.10	5.00	—	—	—	—	—	—	—
grants	—	1.90	—	0.03	2.05	2.64	9.15	9.20	2.73

* Requested.

** Peace Corp, Narcotics Programme and others.

+ Does not include a request of $9 million for "anti-terrorist" training.

Source: U.S. Department of State and "U.S. Overseas Loans and Grants and Assistance from International Organizations July 1, 1945–September 30, 1982."

Source: Cited from Marc Edelman "Back from the Brink," *NACLA*, Nov.-Dec. 1985, Vol. XIX, No. 6, p. 41.

the combined weight of a dramatic fall in world coffee prices (the country's major export earner), and equally striking increases in the costs of petroleum imports and interest rates on monies borrowed abroad. Monge also inherited the world's second highest per capita debt, an inflation rate hovering between 80–90 percent, large-scale unemployment and a debilitated currency. Its currency's value began to fall in September 1981 when the government of President Rodrigo Carazo declared a moratorium on debt-interest payments rather than accept IMF assistance contingent on the implementation of "austerity" measures. Loans from other sources automatically dried up and currency devaluations resulted. Between September 1981 and mid-1983, the currency value plummeted by approximately 700 percent; between 1979 and 1984, the combined public and private debt rose from $3.7 billion to $8.3 billion. In 1983, debt payments accounted for over 55 percent of the country's total export earnings; by the end of 1984, Costa Rica was $180 million behind in its total debt payments.[4]

To the extent that Monge could pursue partial economic recovery, it was a function of his decision to reverse Carazo's attitude toward the IMF. During 1982 and 1983, Costa Rica received more than $100 million in Fund assistance, in return for which Monge began to cut back public spending, withdraw food subsidies, and instituted other austerity measures. The IMF "seal of approval" then opened the gates for hundreds of millions in new capital flows from private multinational banks and U.S. public and private sources. Washington also helped in other ways. When popular opposition forced Monge temporarily to halt his austerity programme in 1983, thus threatening future IMF loan installments, the problem was apparently solved by U.S. influence on the IMF. Following his visit to Washington, Monge was granted an IMF "special dispensation" that realized a threatened $20 million installment in December 1983.[5]

In return for its economic largess, the Reagan administration expected, pressured for, and increasingly received, Monge's support for its aggressive military policies in Central America, particularly its opposition to the Sandinistas. Washington's role in keeping the Costa Rican economy afloat was a powerful lever in eroding the country's traditional neutrality in regional affairs. Within a short time, this country without a standing army experienced an unprecedented military buildup under Pentagon auspices.

During 1982 and 1983, thousands of Judicial Police, Rural Guards, and Civil Guards received counterinsurgency training at U.S. military facilities in the Panama Canal Zone; teams of Green Berets and other U.S. Defense Department experts were transferred to Costa Rica to help establish and train a new 10,000-strong paramilitary force; and the Contras were allowed to establish military bases close to the Nicaraguan border—from which they launched repeated air, sea, and land attacks against Nicaraguan ports, cities, economic installations and public buildings, using bomber aircraft and naval vessels provided by the CIA.

This growing militarization of civil society did not lessen Reagan administration efforts to aggressively exploit Costa Rica's debtor status and dependence on access to lines of credit from U.S. public agencies and the so-called international banks in order to elicit a binding commitment by Monge to Washington's Central America policy. In early 1984, for instance, U.S. Ambassador Curtis Winsor, Jr., held a series of private meetings with Monge during which he raised the spectre of a decline in American economic assistance in order to push Monge toward a more public display of Costa Rican support for U.S. regional initiatives, especially its war against Nicaragua.[6] The pressures brought immediate results. In April, Monge denounced the Sandinistas as "(a) regime embedded in the scheme for world domination that attempts to destroy western democracy. . ."[7] Only days later, his foreign minister, Carlos José Gutiérrez, accused Nicaragua of "blocking the search for peace in Central America."[8]

In early May, a secret State Department report urged quick administration approval of a Costa Rican request for $7.6 million in increased military aid in 1984, bringing the total request to $9.6 million. This was almost double U.S. military assistance to Costa Rica in the previous three years. The report argued for swift action on the grounds that it offered an unexpected opportunity to openly draw Costa Rica into the anti-Sandinista struggle:

It provides an opportunity to help shift the political balance in our favor on Nicaragua's southern flank. . . . It could lead to a significant shift from (Costa Rica's) neutralist tightrope act and push it more explicitly and publicly into the anti-Sandinista camp. This could pay important political and diplomatic dividends for us.[9]

By mid-1984, four teams of U.S. military advisers were training the Civil Guard in counterinsurgency techniques. These Pentagon officers also set up radio communications antennae and relay stations along the border with Nicaragua. However, popular opposition forced Monge to reject an American plan for so-called "combat engineers" to build a network of roads to the Costa Rican-Nicaraguan border. Then, in November, a meeting between Monge and General Paul Gorman, head of the U.S. Southern Command, produced plans "to provide U.S. assistance for the formation of a new Costa Rican antiterrorist security force."[10] In efforts to further cement Costa Rica's support for, and participation in, U.S.

regional strategies, Monge and his senior officials were inundated with invitations to observe U.S. military maneuvers in Honduras and to participate in regional military exercises.

Meanwhile, the Contra forces in Costa Rica stepped up their attacks against government and industrial installations in Nicaragua from their training camps in the southern border regions—often with the active support of the Civil Guard. Foreign mercenaries who fought with the Contras in Costa Rica speak of the Guard's regular involvement, especially in the area of intelligence gathering. The Monge government also allowed the United States to expand the propaganda war against Nicaragua from locations inside Costa Rica. For example, it allowed Washington to circumvent a local law prohibiting foreigners from owning broadcast facilities by forming a secret contract that allowed the United States Information Agency to use a privately owned radio station that could broadcast into Nicaragua.[11]

Through 1985, the Monge administration expanded and deepened its military and political commitment to Reagan's policy in Central America. U.S. military assistance totalled between $9 and $11 million, including thousands of M-16 rifles and large numbers of machine guns, mortars, recoilless rifles and grenade launchers; American advisers continued to provide counterinsurgency training to the Civil Guard in Costa Rica and Honduras; and U.S. and Israeli intelligence and security agencies, operating in Costa Rica since 1982, increased their cooperation with the Monge regime.[12] In the political sphere, Monge began to identify himself publicly with Reagan's efforts to pressure Congress for new Contra appropriations. At the time of an April 1985 heads-of-state meeting in Washington, the Costa Rican president announced his support for the White House campaign to force Congress to pass a $14 million Contra aid bill.

Costa Rica's growing involvement in Washington's military policies in Central America has had two important consequences. Domestically, the militarization of a society without a standing army has been accompanied by the proliferation of right-wing paramilitary groups, a rising level of police brutality, and an increase in the level of human rights violations perpetrated by the state's coercive forces.[13] Externally, Costa Rica has been a major beneficiary of U.S. economic assistance. During the three-year period 1981–84, American economic aid totalled $50.1 million; in 1984 it skyrocketed to $152.6 million; for 1985, it amounted to $137.7 million. The Reagan White House 1986 request was for just under $188 million. In other words, U.S. economic assistance to Costa Rica between 1984 and 1986—the period of greatest support for Washington's Central American policy—increased tenfold over the first three years of the Reagan administration. The rise in multinational development bank and private multinational bank loans and credits has been almost as striking, reaching $205 million in 1985.[14]

CONCLUSION

The rise and demise of the welfare-dependent development model suggests several conclusions. Welfare and dependency are possibilities in the short and even middle range in Central America in the context of several internal and external circumstances: first, the reformists must be in a position to restructure the state apparatus making it congruent with their political project and the class alliance in the regime; secondly, dependent growth in order to finance internal reforms depends on an expanding world capitalist market; thirdly, the regime must be willing to conform to the global politics of the hegemonic power in the region.

In the long-term, however, the structural weaknesses inherent in the dependent development model undermine the social consensus by depleting the regime's capacity to promote capitalist growth and social welfare. The tendency is for the regime to restructure the alliance favoring a social bloc of externally oriented classes (exporters, agro-business, overseas banks), thus reversing the welfare gains of the previous period and deepening the client-state role of nation in the international system.

The peculiar role of Costa Rica as a client state that "rents" its legitimacy to the efforts of the dominant power to reestablish repressive regimes suggests that contemporary Costa Rican democracy does not promote democratic regimes, but rather is an active agent undermining them. By taking advantage of its own special status as a democratic ally of imperial interests, it contributes to the demise of democratic aspirations of its neighbors.

Finally, the Costa Rican case suggests that when social democracy is in government during a period of capitalist crisis and has to choose among its coalition constituents, between deepening its reliance on labor/ small farmer base or creating incentives for the capitalist-landowning-banking groups at the expense of the former—it will choose the latter. In the final analysis, Costa Rican social democracy is more committed to the dependent-capital side of its welfare-capital model. In these times of declining external opportunities in the world market, the prospects for creating new Costa Rica style welfare states are very unlikely, since even the original model itself has come under severe strain. A thorough-going welfare system requires the creation of a productive system, class structure, and new international linkages compatible with and capable of anchoring these welfare changes over the long run. Clearly, a set of welfare measures derived from a dependent capitalist system increasingly dependent on austerity, downward pressures on income, and high external payments is not such a system.

GUATEMALA: DICTATORSHIP AND DEPENDENT DEVELOPMENT

The origins of dictatorial-dependent capitalist models of development are political—the imposition by force of arms of a regime, and a state apparatus capable of defending and promoting private investments and management-dominant labor relations.

In the case of Guatemala and Nicaragua, the decisive political intervention was organized and initiated by the external hegemonic state. The subsequent dependent form of capitalist development reflected the nature of its origin. In Nicaragua, U.S. military intervention in the 1930s led to the creation of the National Guard; and the promotion of Somoza created the dependent-dynastic capitalist framework, within which politics evolved. In Guatemala, the CIA's organization and direction of the 1954 Castillo Armas coup created the basis for the long-term, military controlled-dependent capitalist system. Recognizing the violent, illegitimate, external sources of the police-state apparatus that sustained the economic process is essential in understanding the social, economic and political issues that ensued over the next thirty years.

In nineteenth-century France, Balzac said that "behind every great fortune there is a great theft." In present-day Central America we say that "behind every great fortune there is violent U.S. military action." The autocratic-dependent capitalist model, however, did not dispense with violence once the economic mechanisms were in place; violence was a continued aspect for the renewal and reproduction of the system. Indeed, the expanded reproduction of capital was matched by the escalation and multiplication of mass violence. As new space—land and resources—was required, the "primitive" or original forms of capital appropriation, namely violent coercion by the state, became a central feature of the model. Hence the violent methods of original accumulation—associated in the West with the first period of capitalism and the separation of producers from the means of production—were replicated in Central America throughout the stages of normal and extended reproduction of capital. Accumulation through terror was directed at displacing subsistence Indian communities and incorporating their labor into capitalist production. But violence was also central to the appropriation of labor within established capitalist production: the power of capital in the market place could not sustain the subordination of labor; hence the continued use of force to ensure the subordination of labor to capital on terms socially and politically acceptable for the accumulation of Guatemalan capital. The illegitimate and dictatorial nature of the state after

1954 conditioned capital to seek to maximize control and exploitation of labor which, in turn, required continued use of state terror. The politically determined basis of capital accumulation is central to understanding the enduring relationship between dictatorial and police state rulership and economic expansion—and the unwillingness of elected civilian regimes to tamper with the institutions of the state apparatus or to reform the property bases of accumulation.

In order to best understand the dictatorial-dependent model in Guatemala it is useful to outline its different phases and then proceed to analyze the underlying sociopolitical conflicts. There are essentially four phases in the Guatemalan politicoeconomic development:

1. Foundation of the dictatorial-dependent model, 1954–56
2. Capitalist expansion from above and from outside and a polarized class structure, 1957–77
3. Rising popular and guerrilla movements, crisis of the dependent model and mass state terror, 1978–85
4. Electoral-terror regimes, continued crisis of dependent-capitalist model and disarticulated social movements.

FOUNDATION OF STATE POWER: 1954–56

The foundations of the contemporary Guatemalan state emerged under joint U.S.-Guatemalan military/elite supervision following the coup of 1954. The new regime stifled land reform and social legislation, and purged progressive nationalist military and civilian employees from the state apparatus. The homogenized state apparatus was centralized and placed under the control of a client group of military officials. Employer organizations were strengthened and labor and peasant groups were dismantled or put under state supervision. More important, the legal system was subordinated to the power of the military and the exigencies of local and foreign investors . . . opening the door to the regime of arbitrary terror from the 1960s onward. The consolidation of the power of other new ruling classes and the legal-military apparatus sustaining them were the sine qua non for the elaboration of the economic development that followed.

CAPITALIST EXPANSION AND POLARIZED CLASS STRUCTURE: 1957–77

Large-scale flows of international capital followed the consolidation of the military-elite state. The international banks and the U.S. government provided large-scale, long-term funding creating the infrastructure

for the expansion of large-scale commercial agriculture, export industrialization, and the massive entry of multinational capital. Between 1953
and 1979 the Guatemalan oligarchy received $526 million in U.S. eco-
nomic aid and $41.9 million in military aid in addition to some $593
million from the international financial institutions.[15] By 1976, $260 million
in U.S. private capital dominated the high growth sectors of the economy.
Guatemala's GDP grew by 5.2 percent between 1960 and 1970 and 6
percent between 1970 and 1978. Industry grew by 7.8 percent and 7.6
percent during the same two decades, while agriculture expanded by
4.3 percent and 5.3 percent. The growth was accompanied by the transformation of land use through irrigation and transport networks and
increasing mechanization. Tractors increased from 2,250 in 1961–65 to
3,750 in 1976, and irrigated land almost doubled from thirty-eight to
sixty-two thousand hectares. Growth was largely tied to overseas markets
with foreign trade growing 9 percent during 1960–70 and 3.4 percent in
1970–78.[16]

Concentrated political power and the elite character of the economic
development model has created a polarized class structure in Guatemala.
Rapid capitalist growth has occurred in a framework which includes: (1)
the continuity of the traditional ruling class which has increasingly diversified its holdings from agriculture to commerce and industry while
retaining its family-based source of political and economic power; (2) a
new class of military and security elites who have carved out economic
empires through the violent appropriation of wealth and foreign aid while
retaining ties to the traditional economic elite and the military-political
agencies of the U.S. state; (3) multinational corporations and banks with
links to internal security/economic elite and imperial state agencies. This
triumvirate has provided the framework for growth in Guatemala—and
in most other nations in the region.

The growth of production and use of technology in Guatemala did
not alter, but reinforced, the concentration of landownership: in 1980,
2 percent of the landowners owned 70 percent of the land. Mechanization
accelerated the displacement of peasants and swelled the ranks of the
unemployed and underemployed. Polarized growth is evident in the
structure of income where the poorest 50 percent of the population receive 19.8 percent of income and the richest 20 percent receive 54 percent.[17] The tendency toward greater inequality within this development
process is seen in the evolution of family income (see Table 6.3).

Using 1980 as a base year, a United Nations study found that 71 percent
of the Guatemalan people were in a state of poverty with 39.6 percent
in a state of extreme poverty. Clearly, growth depended on deepening
the levels of exploitation and poverty and increasing the inflows of capital
from abroad. Public and publicly guaranteed medium- and long-term
loans increased from $37 million in 1970 to $107 million in 1978. Foreign

Table 6.3

EVOLUTION OF GUATEMALA FAMILY INCOME DISTRIBUTION
DURING THE 1970s
(IN 1970 DOLLARS)

Strata	1970	1980	Growth Rates (Annual Average)
Poorest 20%	1,088	996	- .9%
30% below the mean	2,014	1,962	- .3%
Richest 10%	12,081	12,970	+4%

Source: *CEPAL* No. 28, p. 20.

export and import coefficients rose from 18.6 percent and 16.3 percent in 1950 to 30.4 percent and 33.6 percent in 1978.[18] In the meantime, the tax coefficient remained unchanged, hovering around 8.5 percent between 1955 and 1980, indicating the power and opposition of the oligarchy to any fiscal reforms and its dependence on external sources of financing.

Economic changes transformed the class structure, which, in turn, facilitated class organization and class struggle. The displacement of Indian communities created a growing number of propertyless wage laborers—more amenable to union organization. The expansion of industry led to an increasing number of factory workers concentrated in urban factory belts and capable of being organized. The growth of cities and towns and the incapacity of industry to absorb the rural migrants has led to the swelling of the service sector and the growth of a large, volatile and unemployed youth component. Large-scale invasion of foreign capital has violated the sensibilities of both middle-class professionals and students.

In a word, the transformation of the class structure in the countryside and the city led to the wider and deeper involvement of the labor force in agrarian and social movements and the struggle for unionization.

RISING SOCIAL MOVEMENTS, CRISES OF THE DEPENDENT-AUTOCRATIC MODEL AND MASS TERROR: 1978–85

Nineteen seventy-eight witnessed Guatemala's biggest popular demonstration in history: 200,000 people from peasants to factory workers, to school teachers and students protesting socioeconomic inequalities, dictatorial rule, and foreign dependence. Between 1977 and 1980 scores of unions were organized, thousands of strikes erupted and tens of thousands of demonstrators challenged the regime in the name of social reforms and political democracy.

This massive upsurge coincided with the onset of the collapse of the economic model after the onset of the capitalist world recession. Because of the declining prices of Guatemalan exports and rising interest rates, the regime was no longer able to finance growth and the economy sank into chronic stagnation (see Table 6.4).

Debt payments have risen from $60 million in 1981 to $350 million in 1985, while the terms of trade deteriorated by almost 25 percent during this period.[19] In the face of chronic stagnation and rising social movements, Guatemalan capital began to flee to the United States—over a half billion dollars in bank deposits alone.[20]

The military regime responded toward the combined challenge of a faltering economy and democratic political movement by unleashing a savage reign of terror which led to the murder of over 40,000 people in five years. State-sponsored death squads, wholesale torture, decapitation, the disappearance of executive boards of trade unions and, in some cases, of whole villages were logical outgrowths of a foreign-imposed regime linked for a quarter of a century to the tasks of protecting property and repressing the populace. When human rights protests forced even the U.S. Congress to limit military aid, President Ronald Reagan thought that the state terrorist regime got a "raw deal." Mass terror was successful in killing or temporarily intimidating the majority of the citizen activists but it did not solve any of the continuing economic problems. Given the military and the oligarchy's unwillingness to sacrifice their income or budgets, the only possibility was to secure outside funding. Likewise, the capacity of the hegemonic power to finance a revival of the economy hinged on changing the image of the Guatemalan regime: the needs of the oligarchy, the military, and the United States coincided in promoting a new electoral-civilian regime to be superimposed upon the existing state apparatus and development model to secure external funding to refloat the model.

Table 6.4

GROWTH OF GUATEMALA'S GDP, 1981-1985 (PERCENT)

1981	1982	1983	1984	1985
.7	-3.6	-2.7	.7	-1.1

Source: *BID Yearly Report*, p. 276.

ELECTORAL-TERROR REGIME: REFLOATING THE DEPENDENT MODEL

Two features characterize the regime of President Vinicio Cerezo—its ability to project the image of a civilian-democratic regime abroad, eliciting financial and political support from western European liberal, conservative, and social democratic regimes; and its accommodation to the terrorist state apparatus, large landowners and foreign multinationals who oppose agrarian reform, investigation of human rights violations or even progressive income policies.

In September and October of 1986, President Cerezo traveled to the United States and western Europe "to overcome the isolation both political and economic to which Guatemala has been subjected in recent years . . . (to) consolidate confidence in Guatemala's process of democratization and enable us to secure resources—both donation and low interest loans—that will permit us to consolidate our economic reorganization program and initiate the powers of economic reactivization."[21] Cerezo succeeded, according to his claim, in obtaining more than one-quarter billion dollars.

The basic question is: "What kind of regime is in place?" Cerezo's assertion that political repression has ended since he took office is belied by Guatemala's human rights groups and union movements. The Mutual Support Group, using public newspaper reports, compiled the following data on disappeared people since Cerezo took office: 128 disappearances including twenty school teachers.[22] Cerezo has even refused to follow up his promise to create a human rights commission. Political assassinations continue unabated; in October 1986, of the 101 killings reported in the press only twenty-three were attributed to deliquents or family quarrels, two were attributed to the guerrillas . . . and most of the rest seem to be products of state terror. Instead of investigating the military's role in mass killings and disappearances, Cerezo has sought to exonerate the military, treating the disappeared persons as dead, thus closing the book on any prosecutions. The military's control over thousands of "model villages" remains intact and the military-organized "civilian self-defense" patrols continue to function. The government has foresworn any agrarian reform and has promoted an export growth strategy which has been favorably received by major traders and large commercial farmers.

Like the Duarte government in El Salvador, the Christian Democratic regime of Cerezo is essentially a mechanism for re-legitimizing the military to the outside world, re-financing the economic elites oriented toward the world market and coopting sectors of the middle strata and political class into collaboration with the preexisting power bloc.

CONCLUSION

The transfer of government from the Guatemalan military to an elected civilian regime did not result in any rupture with either the structure or operation of the state apparatus, or in the nature of the accumulation model. Electoral civilian regimes which fail to dismantle repressive institutions, eliminate the practice of state terror, or reform the rural structures of power are not part of, nor agencies of, a democratization process.

Democratization involves the extension of effective popular participation to the previously powerless, an effective articulation of basic interests, and a responsiveness of elected representatives to popular political and social initiatives. In Cerezo's Guatemala, there are anywhere from fifty to one hundred assassinations per month, effectively intimidating popular participation. The military occupy the countryside and repressive trade union legislation blocks effective articulation of interests. The close collaboration between Cerezo's economic team and the local entrepreneurial and commercial elite illustrates his regime's responsiveness to those in the higher circles and not to those below. His unwillingness to pursue the issue of the disappeared persons and human rights violations underlines his responsiveness to the military command and not to the demands of tens of thousands of victims and their families—Indians, peasants, trade unionists.

The Guatemalan electoral process responds to a different logic than that of a democratization process. The civilian regime is disassociated from the democratic process because it is the creature of a crisis-ridden military and oligarchy, and an internally divided hegemonic power. Its function is to mobilize external resources to revitalize existing institutions. The atomized populace that participates in the election is the product of the terror which preceded the elections. The destruction of civic society—the networks and local opinion leaders—creates a vulnerable mass with narrow choices: remaining with the terror state or a combined state terrorist-civilian regime. The incapacity of the civilian terror-state to reform itself, and the dependent-capitalist model's inability to alter deteriorating external conditions, decisively shape the possibilities for democracy and recovery—the crisis festers, the social movements reemerge, the struggle continues. The civilian electoral regime will be tolerated by the military as long as it is necessary to secure external funding and as long as it is able to secure it.

NICARAGUA: FROM RADICAL DEMOCRACY TO WAR ECONOMY

It is not possible to speak of a "revolutionary" or "radical model" in the case of Nicaragua today because of the overwhelming reality of war which threatens the very existence of the state and thus defines the nature and function of the political economy. The U.S. war against Nicaragua has forced the regime to reallocate labor, financial resources, and production toward sustaining the war effort. Thus the character of Nicaragua's social, political and economic structure is not shaped by its revolutionary ideology and programme but by necessities and demands of the military struggle. Insofar as the ideology is operative, it shapes the defense of the revolution. The nature and tasks of national defense, the scope, depth and duration of the war, the strategy and type of aggression launched by the United States—all influence the Sandinista government's allocation of human and material resources.

Within the framework of a war economy, the revolutionary nature of the regime is revealed in the measures taken to organize defense, allocate scarce economic resources and to balance security concerns with the process of institutionalizing political power. The forms of politicoeconomic organizations that are established for surviving a imperial war of aggression must be judged in terms of their efficacy in winning the war, and ensuring that the principal revolutionary classes will not be displaced from power in the postrevolutionary period. Judgments about the nature of the Nicaraguan political system that extrapolate from the real politics of military-political survival—that compare its institutions and current policies to abstract, ahistorical measures of "democracy" and welfare— are engaging in the worst kind of propagandizing, popularized by the lumpen intellectuals that preside in the Reagan White House.

There are, of course, some indications of the direction and process of the Nicaraguan revolution which were in place before the United States launched its full-scale military offensive (mid-1979 to the end of 1981). But even here, the Nicaraguan revolution faced the tasks of reconstructing the economy from the devastation resulting from Somoza's policy of rule or ruin as he was driven from power. Nevertheless, within the process of "national reconstruction" and preceding the full-blown mercenary war that the United States launched particularly after 1982, there are signs of the type of development which the revolution would promote.

The algebraic terms used to describe this process are a "socialist pluralist" state and "mixed economy." The content of these terms varies from context to context as different social actors provide a different balance of forces. In the case of Nicaragua, the notion of socialist pluralism involves political competition of all parties and interest groups within the framework of a popular state—the product of the revolutionary struggle. The hegemonic power of the "popular classes" (self-employed, workers, small farmers, unemployed, employees and professionals), was the keystone for the organization of the military and civil service, as well as the basis for the national defense of the country. Within these foundations all parties and social classes were free to exercise their democratic freedoms. The "mixed-economy" as originally envisioned involved the promotion of an active public sector in strategic sectors (power, utilities, foreign trade and finance) and a private sector in downstream industries, in medium and large size export farming, and in most of the retail trade. The revolutionary government also promoted a variety of cooperatives and forms of "popularly managed" firms, the former growing in importance until the war created operational problems.

If we were to sum up in a word the embryonic model which was emerging we could characterize it as a kind of "revolutionary social democracy" or "radical welfare state." "Social democratic" or "welfare" because its socioeconomic reforms redistributed income and increased social services, promoted popular participation and extended democratic rights without transforming the basic operation of capitalist social relation of production. "Revolutionary" or "radical" because the model shifted the balance of power within the state and civil society from propertied groups to the popular classes, anchoring the new political power in mobilized, organized social forces in civil society (neighborhood groups, trade unions, peasant and farmer organizations, women's movement) and within the state through the composition and ideological direction of the popular army. The time frame for evaluating this embryonic "model" is quite limited—before the onset of the large-scale U.S. military aggression and after the essential services destroyed in the wake of Somoza's defeat were put in place. In terms of GDP, the revolutionary regime successfully launched its reconstruction programme (see Table 6.5).

Modest progress was realized in the areas of agrarian reform affecting only about 93,000 hectares, expropriated by 1982—mostly Somoza-owned land. More significantly, a national literacy and health programme was launched with significantly reduced illiteracy, lowered infant mortality rates, and improved health and educational services. Nicaragua halved its unemployment rate—from over 30 percent to close to 15 percent. State planning and the development of diversified external trade exchanges were set in place.

Table 6.5

GROWTH OF NICARAGUA'S GDP 1980-1985 (PERCENT)

1980	1981	1982	1983	1984	1985
8.3	5.4	-.6	5.2	-1.5	2.6

Sources: ECLA, p. 12; *BID* p. 322.

The key weakness in the process was the minimal cooperation of significant sectors of private capital—who either openly supported the emerging counterrevolution or refused to invest in new productive forces, despite generous credits and state guarantees of profit. As one writer notes, "Production in the capitalist industrial sector has been irregular and in decline. . . . this is partly due to the reorganization of the sector . . . but it is also due to decapitalization on the part of many of these businesses."[23] The authors point to the same behavior among the agrarian bourgeoisie:

All in all, the capitalist sector is in a sense "on hold," producing with generous credit and little of their own working capital. It is neither investing nor augmenting the area under production (except for the single private sugar plantation). Its economic logic focuses on accumulating foreign currency and the subsequent deterioration of farm and plantation.[24]

Likewise, the promotion of social services, reactivization of the economy to provide employment, and the financing of agrarian changes led to a decline in wage levels in 1981 of 12 percent, particularly among urban wage workers.

At a more meaningful level, mass popular organizations were spreading. Peasant unions expanded to include 120,000 members by 1980. Cooperatives encompassed 60 percent of rural households while union, neighborhood, militia, women's and cultural groups mushroomed throughout the country. Civil society was coming into being and provided the bases for the creation of social consciousness, national identity and class politics. In this political-social sense the revolutionary regime was succeeding in laying the foundation for the realization of its larger version of a democratic socialist society. Apart from the unevenness in development and change, the direction and movement of the revolutionary regime (in this brief interlude) was toward the attainment of its promise.

Washington's launching of a large-scale military offensive, particularly from 1983, changed the context and internal conditions for the development of Nicaraguan society—and hence the criteria for evaluating the efficiency of the regime.

WAR ECONOMY: DEMOCRATIZATION, RADICALIZATION, AND ECONOMIC CRISES

The U.S.-sponsored invasion of 20,000 mercenaries, together with logistical and military support and CIA mining of harbors has forced Nicaragua to allocate over 50 percent of its budget to the war effort. The Sandinista government vastly increased its military forces through conscription, and allocated significant amounts of imports, foodstuffs and local manufactures to defense. Mercenary terrorism seriously affected agricultural production and transport networks in the northern and southern regions of the country. As a result of this aggression, growth in the GDP declined from −1.4 percent in 1984 to −2.6 percent in 1985 and by almost −5 percent in 1986. Hyperinflation also set in during 1986. Exports fell to $250 million in 1986—a third of prerevolutionary levels—and real money fell by 45 percent, with workers receiving payments in kind as a complement.

On the other side, however, as the war developed the democratization process deepened in two directions—one increasing the involvement of the popular classes and democratic political forces and the other excluding and constraining the enemies of democracy. In 1984, Nicaragua held national elections which compare favorably with elections held in the United States—involving proportionately more people, with a broader choice of parties, programmes and issues, and greater access to the mass media and campaign financing. Following the elections, a series of open town meetings discussed the major provisions of the new constitution and deepened democratic institution-building, reflecting the understanding of the Sandinistas that the war was not only a question of "arms" but of political consciousness and mobilization.

Parallel to increasing participation, the Sandinista regime acted to defend the democratic process by restricting the activities of sectors of the media, church, and business who were politically supporting the military invaders. These measures were essential to protecting the survival of the democratic process. The regime drew a clear line between legitimate dissent and subversion: between those who would defend the country and those who stood with the armed mercenaries and the imperial state security agencies. To secure peasant support for the war, the Sandinistas revised the agrarian reform law in January 1986, making it easier to redistribute land where it was most needed, not simply because it was "insufficiently exploited." The Ministry of Agricultural Development and Agrarian Reform (MIDINRA) projected plans to redistribute 105,000 hectares of land of which 55 percent would come from the private sector, 39 percent from the state and 6 percent from co-ops.[25] As the war continues, it thus deepens the process of social change; the regime is forced to channel scarce resources toward the principal social classes fighting to sustain the war effort.

At the same time, the war has shifted the relative balance between civilian mass organization and military in favor of the latter. As one writer notes ". . . the impact of the war of aggression has meant a gradual weakening of the popular organizations in comparison with the growth of state power and party organization, particularly in the military sphere."[26] As would be expected, the war effort has, of necessity, led to greater centralization and fusion between the state and the Sandinista political party, increasing the political centrality of the Ministry of Defense. Moreover, as in all revolutionary wars, the best and most dedicated cadres and activists take on the most challenging and dangerous positions—on the military front—depleting the civilian political structures of those forces with the strongest popular links.

The war and declining economic resources has forced a sharp cutback in social services and, in some cases, a reversal of the social progress (particularly in health) of earlier years. Likewise, unable to finance and provide technical assistance to successfully operate the cooperatives, the regime has acceded to popular pressure to subdivide and privatize holdings to retain peasant support. Austerity in state spending, an end to subsidies of basic food and increased farm prices are measures that the government hopes will increase production and exports and lower the state's budget deficit. Attempts by the Sandinistas to retain the confidence of the private sector have been met, however, by mounting popular discontent.

The revolutionary regime's project of a mixed economy and the internal relationship of forces have thus been shaken by the war and the resulting economic crisis. Sustaining the previous mix in present circumstances requires political choices which will have decisive consequences on the successful prosecution of the war. The Sandinistas depend heavily on the urban and rural poor. It is difficult to envision them pursuing a policy of supply side economics and at the same time eliciting the high level of popular participation necessary to win the war. Insofar as the war becomes a people's war it means that inequalities and exploitive interest in the control exercised by the private sector and state bureaucrats will have to be severely modified. Popular mobilization necessary for the successful transition to socialism is even more necessary to the successful struggle against a military offensive orchestrated by a superpower. Nothing dissolves popular enthusiasm more than the privileges and profits that accrue to market forces during wartime. Radical social democratic regimes will encounter serious problems sustaining a war in which the poor classes sacrifice their lives fighting while entrepreneurial classes increase their profits. As one wage worker said in the last days of the Allende government, "We don't have (cooking) oil or revolution; we can live without oil but not without revolution." Paradoxically, the U.S.-launched war raises the need to radicalize further the Sandinista revolution in order to successfully end the war.

If and when the war ends, the 'model' of the revolution will be a product of the new configuration of forces emerging from that struggle. A conflict is being played out at many levels by radicalizing and by privatizing forces. Which among them will ultimately define the strategic direction of the revolution, and in what global/regional context, remain issues for future analysis.

CONCLUSION

The existence of three models of development suggests possible alternative political, social and economic strategies. The two alternative possibilities present from the 1950s to 1970s (democratic and authoritarian) were anchored in a world-historic context in which several very specific sets of circumstances were present: (1) the expansion of the world economy; (2) a low debt/export ratio; and (3) hegemony or undisputed military-political dominance by the United States and its client regimes— i.e., the absence of any revolutionary alternative. The political-economic crises which affected both models in the late 1970s and 1980s show no sign of abating. While the forms of regime in Guatemala and Costa Rica seem to be converging (militarization and deteriorating welfare programmes in Costa Rica; elected civilian regimes under military tutelage in Guatemala), there is still a very substantial difference in the texture of political and social life. Nevertheless, in the current crisis both regimes have opted for modernization strategies which put a premium on promoting investor interests and restricting wages, salaries, and social services. In the present conjuncture and perhaps beyond, the economic imperatives of compliance with overseas lenders and investors has ruled out the possibility of a social pact between labor-capital and the state in which social welfare and reform accompanies capitalist growth. The absence of a social pact has been accompanied by two significant features that characterize the regimes: (1) in Guatemala the commitment to investors has led the civilian regime to maintain and support the continued military-controlled, forced-labor detention center "Gulags" (model villages) that contain tens of thousands of Indians uprooted from their communities by state violence; (2) in Costa Rica the new accumulation strategy has strengthened Costa Rica's client-role as a surrogate for U.S. policy in the region. The experience of both countries suggests that beneath the surface of civilian regimes the process of the militarization of politics has not been changed—indeed there are indications that it may be deepening. The revival of the Central American Defense Council CONDECA (supported by Guatemala and Costa Rica), the U.S.-sponsored Central American Defense Organization, is one indication.

The second reality in the region which has changed the basis of politics is the emergence of the Sandinista regime. It demonstrates the possibility of combining welfarism, independent economic policy and popular participation, without subordination to the dominant hegemonic power. The revolutionary example occurs, moreover, in a context in which both previous models are in deep crisis and are tending to converge in a repressive, elitist direction. This makes the Nicaraguan experience even more relevant, despite the wartime hardships. Going beyond Costa Rica's earlier consumption-based welfare style, the Sandinistas have redistributed the means of production, creating a new basis of class power. Under the pressures of the crisis and war, Central America witnesses the emergence of polarized conceptions of development: either the redistributive, participatory model based on popular politico-military power, or a model which reconcentrates income at the top, extends state control over civil society, and subordinates the nation to the hegemonic power.

NOTES

1. *CEPAL Review*, no. 28 (April 28, 1986): 23.

2. Marc Edelman and Jane Hutchcroft, "Costa Rica: Resisting Austerity," *NACLA* (January–February 1984): 38.

3. See "The Recent Evolution of the Costa Rican Economy," *Central America Report* 13, no. 34 (Sept. 5, 1986), special document.

4. See "In the Grip of Its Foreign Debt," *Central America Report* 12, no. 28 (July 26, 1985): 219; Richard Alan White, *The Morass: United States Intervention in Central America* (New York: Harper & Row, 1984), 215; "Back-Breaking Foreign Debt," *Central America Report* 12, no. 12 (March 9, 1985): 90. In 1985, debt servicing accounted for an astronomical 74 percent of export earnings. See "Arias Wins," *Washington Report on the Hemisphere* 6, no. 10 (February 19, 1986): 6.

5. See White, *The Morass*, 224.

6. See Richard J. Meislin, "U.S. Said to Seek Costa Rica Shift, " *New York Times*, 11 May 1984, 11.

7. Quoted in "A Peaceful Solution Unlikely," *Central America Report* 11, no. 17 (May 4, 1984): 129.

8. Quoted in "Looking Less Neutral Every Day," *Central America Report* 11, no. 18 (May 11, 1984): 137.

9. Quoted in Joanne Omang, "Secret Report Says Costa Rica Asks More Aid," *Washington Post*, 10 May 1984, A1. On U.S. military assistance between 1981 and 1983, see Christopher Madison, "Consensus Eludes Administration on Contra Aid," *National Journal* 17, no. 5 (February 2, 1985): 270.

10. "The 'Honduranization' of Costa Rica," *Central America Report* 11, no. 46 (November 23, 1984): 367.

11. See Walter Pincus, "U.S. Enhances VOA, Sets Pact in Costa Rica," *Washington Post*, 11 September 1984, A1, A4.

12. See "Upgrading Costa Rican Security," *Latin America Regional Reports; Mexico & Central America* Rm-85-06, (July 12, 1985): 5; "Increasing Concern over Militarization," *Central America Report* 12, no. 13 (April 12, 1985): 101.

13. See "Human Rights Violations Bad as Ever," *Central America Report* 12, no. 41 (Oct. 25, 1985): 326.

14. See "Consensus," 270; *Department of State Bulletin* 85, no. 2098 (May 1985):

83; Richard J. Walton, "How the U.S. Is Changing Costa Rica," *The Nation*, (October 5, 1985): 311.

15. U.S. Agency for International Development, *U.S. Overseas Loans and Grants and Assistance from International Institutions*, 1 July 1945–30 September 1976, 48, 184, and ibid. 1 July 1945–30 September 1979, 50, 220.

16. World Bank, *World Development Report 1980*, 112–13, 124–25; James W. Wilkie, ed., *Statistical Abstract of Latin America, 1979, Volume 20* (Los Angeles, Calif.: UCLA Latin American Center, 1980), 39.

17. *CEPAL*, no. 28, 19.

18. Ibid., 13.

19. *BID Yearly Report*, 276.

20. *CEPAL*, 28.

21. Americas Watch, *Guatemala News in Brief* (Oct. 1986): 9.

22. Ibid., 1.

23. Eduardo Baumeister and Oscar Neira Cuadra, "The Making of a Mixed Economy: Class Struggle and State Policy in the Nicaraguan Transition," in *Transition and Development: Problems of Third World Socialism*, eds. Richard Fagen et al. (New York: Monthly Review Press, 1986), 188.

24. Ibid., 186.

25. *LARR*, 6 June 1986, 3.

26. Peter E. Marchetti, "War, Popular Participation and Transition to Socialism: The Case of Nicaragua," in *Transition and Development*, eds. Fagen et al., 322.

7

One Road to Democracy With Development: José Figueres and the Social Democratic Project After 1948

Anthony Winson

INTRODUCTION

During the 1980s world attention has continuously focused on Central America. The Nicaraguan revolution initially sparked this interest, but in the last few years, concern with the region has been maintained largely because American foreign policy seeks to stem progressive change. Costa Rica is on the edge of the Central American cauldron, but not entirely out of the spotlight. Historically this republic has had much in common with its sister Central American republics, but in today's highly charged political climate, Costa Rica's peculiarities as a country stand out more than its shared heritage.

If Costa Rica is known to the student of contemporary Latin America it is probably for one specific reason. For nearly forty years this country has followed a political path that distinguishes it from both its other Central American neighbors, and from many South American republics. This path has entailed the successful transition from the kind of liberal oligarchic state still present elsewhere in Central America, to liberal democratic politics similar to that of the advanced capitalist economies. Although many observers point to Costa Rica as an alternative model to revolutionary change in the region, little attention has been given to the question of *how* liberal democratic politics emerged in Costa Rica. An answer to this latter point would seem to be essential before we can assess the possibilities of "transplanting" this model elsewhere. This chapter examines and evaluates the critical political conjuncture that set Costa Rica on the path of liberal democracy.

THE HISTORICAL BACKGROUND

Costa Rica witnessed the emergence of a class of agricultural estate owners in response to the demand for coffee in the European market during the latter half of the nineteenth century. It shared this experience with Nicaragua, El Salvador and Guatemala. The interests of this class, in conjunction with European merchants and commercial capital, shaped the structure of economic development. Coffee exports provided the primary impetus for the growth of infrastructure—railroads, communications, and port facilities. At the same time, the internal organization of estate agriculture and the exploitation of the small coffee growers by the coffee oligarchy blocked the development of local manufacturing and a more diversified economy. Given its economic strength relative to the other social classes, the coffee oligarchy also predominated in politics, with a virtual monopoly on the highest positions of state.

The economic damage done to the oligarchy during the Great Depression, however, had important repercussions for this political monopoly. In the early 1940s, the large coffee interests became "detached" from their traditional political party once its new leader and then president Rafael Calderón Guardia, formed an alliance with the Communist political party, *Vanguardia Popular,* to ensure his political future. This seemingly unlikely event must be seen in the light of a weakened export oligarchy and also the growing Communist influence among the small urban working class and the more numerous laborers on the coastal banana plantations. No longer a force that could be ignored politically, the Communists attracted Calderón's attention when his own government began to falter. The quid pro quo for their support included a commitment on Calderón's part to basic social legislation—legislation which the powerful coffee interests found very difficult to swallow.

In the following years, the Communist-supported Calderón government not only lost support within the coffee oligarchy, but also managed to alienate the middle class—professionals, entrepreneurs and intellectuals—through electoral and administrative irregularities, without satisfying in any substantial way the aspirations of this class. As time progressed, the Calderón government faced an increasingly well-organized opposition alliance. It included the more progressive sections of the petty bourgeoisie, now organized within the Partido Social Demócrata (PSD), and the traditional agro-export bourgeoisie, which by 1948 had begun to regroup under the banner of the Unión Nacional party led by Otilio Ulate.

By the late 1940s, the regime had become vulnerable to those types of political incidents that are capable, under favorable conditions, of provoking a "crisis of authority." The widespread irregularities in the elections of 1948 proved to be just the type of affair that would trigger such a crisis. In this context, an opening was created for a third force to emerge and decisively end the stalemated political struggle. The following discussion considers the factors that seem to account for the initial successes of those who struggled to begin a new political experiment in Costa Rica.

THE JUNTA OF 1948

By choosing to resolve the nation's political crisis by force of arms, José Figueres and his followers accomplished two things, in the short-term. First, and most obviously, they prevented the Calderonistas from using the ambiguous outcomes of the elections to prolong their government. Secondly, they took the initiative away from the new party of the traditional bourgeoisie—the Unión Nacional—and thereby forestalled, for a time at least, the return of the oligarchy to its former position of prominence. For if the anti-Calderón alliance had come to power through the normal electoral route, it is highly probable that the fundamental differences of the temporary allies soon would have surfaced. Given the superior financial resources of the forces represented by the Unión Nacional party, the social and economic aspirations represented by the PSD would likely have been thwarted, and the trajectory of national politics then would have conformed more to the rest of Central America.

On the other hand, it must be recognized that progressive nationalist movements in Central America, even those that have come to form governments, have, for the most part, been granted the same fate—annihilation. Until the Sandinista revolution in Nicaragua it was only in Costa Rica that an attempt to challenge the dominance of the landowning and commercial oligarchy has had any long-term success, and even here this process has had its limitations.

One important factor for the success of the Junta of 1948 was that it differed in its political composition from the ill-fated Guatemalan regime of Jacobo Arbenz a few years later. This situation made it politically possible for the Junta to proclaim openly what was already inherent in the political philosophy of many of its members: that is, though its orientation was reformist, it was also definitely anti-Communist. Given the role of the Vanguardia Popular in the nation's political life over the previous several years, the emergence of cold war politics at the international level, and the country's strategic position in geopolitical terms in the eyes of the United States, over the short-term it was most important for the survival of the Junta that it could make this claim. With American warships off the Costa Rican coast and Somoza's National Guard having intervened from the north, there seems little doubt that a victory of a broad coalition of popular forces, including the Vanguardia Popular, would have very quickly faced an armed force much superior to that which such a popular government might have mustered. In an interview many years later, Figueres made it clear that it was this party of the proletariat that was the chief obstacle to constituting a balance of forces favorable to himself and the Junta:

When we recovered popular sovereignty in 1948, and began the construction task, we did not feel, quite frankly, we had the capacity to carry on a free and open battle with international communism. The Communists had external support. We did not. They had the strength derived from fanaticism. We did not. We resolved to put them outside the law, as a political party. A sign of weakness, one would say—yes!—a sign of weakness. I admit it, when one is relatively weak before the force of the enemy, it is necessary to have the valour to recognize it.[1]

These conditions formed the backdrop to one of the darker episodes of the country's contemporary political history to which Figueres alludes—the incarceration of the leading members of the Vanguardia Popular, the repression of its members and the formal proclamation of this party's illegality. In essence, and in a most unequivocal fashion, Figueres and the Junta denied a substantial section of Costa Rican society the opportunity to struggle for political power, and for a very considerable period of time given that attempts in later years to constitute a workers' party "above ground" were also thwarted by the state. By so doing, they probably did more to tilt the scales in their favor in the short-term than with any other single act.

These initial internal and external threats, however (and among the latter should be included the attempted *putsch* in December 1949 by rightist elements of the Calderonistas, with the aid of Somoza), were only a preliminary to a struggle that was to be much more prolonged. Although this second struggle never took the more dramatic form of an armed conflict, it was central to the long term viability of the political goals favored by the Junta and the social forces they purported to represent. The chief antagonist was the landowning and commercial bourgeoisie (in particular, the *cafetaleros*) and their political representatives. While this was first and foremost a struggle for political power and ideological domination, it also concerned the distribution of the social surplus generated within the Costa Rican society.

THE JUNTA TAKES POWER: THE BIRTH OF THE INTERVENTIONIST STATE

The Costa Rican Social Democratic movement had incorporated, almost from its very beginnings in the early 1940s, a decidedly "developmentalist" approach. The model elaborated over the years linked basic

social reforms with economic transformation that went beyond the traditional framework of the agro-exporting economy. An integral part of
the Social Democrats' vision was the conception of the state as a driving
force that would channel part of the economic surplus of the wider society
towards planned investment to improve and expand "productive enterprises." Their position clearly differed from the economic liberalism
of the old landowning and commercial bourgeoisie. It also varied with
the essentially redistributionist social reformism that emerged out of the
fusion of Calderón's Social Christian doctrine and the political line of
the Vanguardia Popular in earlier years. Social democratic policies were
not ad hoc in their conception then, but rather corresponded to a well-
articulated analysis of what was required to overcome the long-term
stagnation of an economy dominated by the agro-exporting system of
the oligarchy.

In the initial months of the Junta, Figueres demonstrated his importance by giving concrete expression to the fundamental tenets of the
economic and political philosophy of the Social Democratic party. The
Junta quickly nationalized the banks and placed a 10 percent tax on
wealth. Bank nationalization was only the first step towards strengthening state power, but it was a key one. Figueres publicly argued on
behalf of the Junta that, through the control of credit, the banks decided
the fate of every enterprise, thereby reducing each business to a "trib-
utary" and determining the "economic progress" of the nation.[2] This
power, he said, did not belong in private hands. Nationalization of the
banks suggests that the Junta had no illusions about the minimal conditions needed to allow the state to play its necessary role in the economy.
In addition to giving the new state economic institutions more maneu-
verability, this move by the Junta likely had other objectives. A key one
would have been to deflate the representatives of financial capital who
had traditionally been a bulwark of reaction in national politics, and
thereby smooth the way for further interventionist policies in the future.

A nationalized banking system, moreover, gave to the state, for the
first time, a critical instrument for influencing a broad range of economic
activities. It was an important break with the past—a shift away from
liberal oligarchic state structures and an apparent move against those
class interests that had been the chief beneficiaries of the old political
scheme. Nevertheless, the relatively limited opposition to the nationalization suggests that this act did not contravene interests that were
particularly vital to the traditional bourgeoisie as a whole, even though
it ended a privileged monopoly within the class.

The importance of the bank nationalization for laying the groundwork
of a new economic and social order was soon demonstrated with the
establishment in 1949 of a cornerstone of state-sponsored infrastructural

development: the Costa Rican Institute of Electricity (ICE). ICE was designed to develop and control the production and distribution of electrical energy throughout the country and spearheaded the state's move into areas that were previously the domain of private capital. Together with water programs, it came to occupy almost a third of all public investments. Indeed, public investments in electricity and water programs jumped from a scant 500,000 *colones* in 1950 to over 88 million by 1965 and increased even more dramatically to 350 million in the ten years after. Meanwhile, the production of electricity expanded by a factor of ten over this period. ICE was only a first, albeit crucial, step towards the amplification of the state's presence in the national economy, and was a necessary outgrowth of the attempt to concretize the Junta's well-defined conceptions about the future direction of the Costa Rican economy.

Before further developments of this type could be undertaken, however, a number of serious problems confronted Figueres and the Junta. The success in handling these was to determine whether their initial attempts at economic reorganization would be continued and broadened, or terminated, either abruptly or through a process of prolonged strangulation. Indeed, the latter possibility seemed the more likely given the Junta's commitment to allow Ulate to constitute the government by the end of 1949.

The first matter that jeopardized the foundations laid by the Junta then, was precisely the problem of Ulate's claim to the presidency and a return to "normal" electoral practices. Furthermore, given the presence of powerful enemies, Figueres could not expect to push further ahead in the future without first locating new social bases of support. Finally, there was a critical need to establish a revenue base for the interventionist project favored by those forces grouped around Figueres. Ultimately, solutions had to be found before any substantial headway could be made in a state-sponsored reorganization of the economy.

PROTECTING THE CONTINUITY OF THE
INTERVENTIONIST PROJECT

Neither Costa Rica's political traditions nor the particular circumstances surrounding Figueres' coming to power favored a prolongation of the unchecked rule of the 1948 Junta. Historically electoral politics, even when accompanied by corruption and fraud, had a long history in Costa Rica, while the exercise of dictatorial powers over extended periods had never been as integral to oligarchic rule as elsewhere in the isthmus. "Figueres was the hero and he had the guns," Ulate was to have said, "but we had the legitimacy."[3] These conditions dictated the dissolution of a Junta ruling outside the constitution, even more perhaps than any desire of the PSD forces to close the gap between their earlier vigorous criticisms of the "undemocratic" actions of the Calderonista alliance, and their own political practice while in power.

The Junta, moreover, had quickly alienated a large part of the propertied elements of the old opposition alliance with its moves to regulate private capital and even restrict the latter's sphere of operation. It mistreated and exiled many of Calderón's supporters, not to mention many members of the Vanguardia Popular, and rapidly, to quote one observer, "used up much of its political capital."[4] The PSD's political position was further eroded by the success of Ulate's new National Union Party (PUN) in the 1948 elections for the Constituent Assembly.

The crisis tactics employed by Figueres indicated the vulnerability of the regime at a time when it was no longer armed and thus could not easily threaten to use force to push through its measures. Nor had it yet cultivated a social base with which to augment its political clout. Although Figueres' tactics were reasonably successful in the short term, there was little evidence to suggest that his power would long remain suspended in midair, bereft of some strong element of political support. The most pressing problem was to secure a slate of candidates for the 1949 election that would safeguard the Junta's program and keep it on course until it could be mounted on a firmer political base. The move by Ulate and the opposition to block Figueres' candidacy indicated their own astuteness in appreciating his importance as a motor force behind the program they sought to undermine. Their response to Figueres indicates the weakness of the propertied classes in protecting their perceived interests.

At this point, the Junta's options were few indeed. Nevertheless, Figueres showed an uncanny ability to perceive the true weakness of his opponents, deciding that the boldest route was the most likely to succeed. The threat of immediate resignation of the Junta, so that they could take their program to the people and thereby defend it "from above and below" proved sufficient to force Ulate, (whose forces were far superior in the Constituent Assembly) to renegotiate the question of the upcoming electoral slate. Once again the bourgeois opposition had shown its fear of extraparliamentary politics and their perception that their interests lay in the most rapid return to government under the constitution, which not only enshrined the basic rights of private property, but also guaranteed the primacy of electoral politics over which they would have some control.

By the end of 1949, then, as Ulate took over the presidency, Figueres and his forces had managed to minimize the opposition's capacity to undercut the new directions forged by the Junta. Through his showdown with Ulate, Figueres had ensured that a slate of candidates favorable to the Junta's position would be put forward in the elections of that year. Although Figueres had to acquiesce to Ulate's claim on the presidency by the end of 1949, much had been done to secure the Junta's political orientation until such time as he could return to office through legitimate means.

STATE AUTONOMY AND THE QUESTION OF A SOCIAL BASE

In previous decades, particularly prior to the Calderón years, the state rested significantly on the support of the oligarchy. Though not as exclusionist as elsewhere in Central America, the political process did not entail the interplay of parties with an organic relationship to the different social groups and classes. Rather, different political figures, typically having roots in the oligarchy itself and never fundamentally questioning the primacy of the agro-exporting scheme, occasionally sought to mobilize the largely agrarian population by means of platforms that incorporated some minor concessions for the popular classes.

As has already been argued, in the 1940s an unstable situation developed in which the state became clearly more autonomous from the large coffee and commercial interests than at any previous time, and the Partido Vanguardia Popular emerged as a salient political force through its contingent support of the governing party. But the relative autonomy of the state achieved at this time was inherently precarious. If the state was no longer simply an executive committee for managing the affairs of the oligarchy by the 1940s, what could be said about the relation between the state and the traditionally dominant class during the 1950s? In essence, a process of "autonomization" of the state continued and indeed was strengthened after 1948, although it came to rest on a different relation of forces in society than in the previous decade.

In 1950, Figueres began organizing a base of social support for the Social Democrats, to ensure continuity of the movement. A first important step was to create a political vehicle to gain Figueres the presidency in the 1953 elections and thereby strengthen further the Social Democratic influence in the General Assembly. The creation of the Partido Liberación Nacional in 1951 had this goal as its primordial purpose. Initially it did not function as a traditional parliamentary party; rather, Figueres' dominance was indicated by the fact that while he was to be the presidential candidate, the party did not nominate him in convention. The absence of forums for internal political discussions at any level, or of party congresses to debate fundamental policy issues, further suggests the nature of this political machine that dominated Costa Rican politics in the period when the relationship between the state and civil society was being restructured. Although the ideological roots of Liberación Nacional as articulated in its "Fundamental Charter," were basically those established years earlier, its raison d'être could not be separated from Figueres' political ambitions, immediate and long-term. Beyond the personal, these ambitions were basically those the Junta had attempted to put into concrete form during its brief tenure, many of which had yet to be realized.

Having established the requisite political vehicle, Figueres sought to maximize his chances of success and acquired financial interest in the newspaper *La República*. This shrewd move suggests that the Liberacionistas fully appreciated the importance of the press to liberal democratic political process and that to counter the influence of the traditional dominant groups, they would have to break the former's ideological monopoly.

The substantial majority won by Figueres in the 1953 elections showed that support for him and the PLN was particularly strong among the rural population of the *meseta central*, and considerably weaker among the banana workers on both coasts. In the latter areas, the rates of abstention in 1953 were approximately double the national average, at a time when both the Calderonista and the Communist parties were banned.[5] The political personality of Figueres clearly played a key role in bringing an important sector of the rural population to the PLN cause. It must be remembered, however, that the PLN counted among its top ranks some very influential members of this rural community, large coffee growers and processors well-connected to the rural middle class elements so crucial in molding political support. In 1953, then, there is some reason to believe that the success of Figueres and the PLN rested substantially with rural smallholders of the *meseta central*.

With an historical perspective, and looking specifically at governments in the 1980s, it is apparent that the domination of the Partido Liberación Nacional in Costa Rica's political life has been closely associated with the social consequences of its own program. Given its decidedly statist orientation, it is not surprising to find that public sector workers, as a proportion of all workers, increased by the end of the first terms of Liberación Nacional rule (1958). In fact, the increase was quite dramatic—from 6 percent of the active population in 1950 to 10 percent only eight years later. The further proliferation of the so-called "autonomous institutions" of the state were, of course, integral to this growth. The massive program of public works and the new state institutions spawned by the Liberación Nacional governments, and the Junta before it, did not guarantee the loyalty of state workers to Figueres. But he did not leave it to chance that this considerable and growing segment of society should make a connection between their own employment status and the fact that PLN formed the government. The history of the *aguinaldo*, in essence a bonus equivalent to one month's salary, is most interesting in this respect.

What we are speaking of, then, was a general increase in the level of salaries for a segment of the population that was becoming evermore important in social, and ultimately, political terms—a point which cannot have been lost on Figueres and the *Liberacionistas*. This whole episode has been viewed by some as a well intentioned proposal (i.e., an effort towards a more equitable distribution of social wealth) that subsequently got out of hand as the growing state machine acquired a political force that could not be controlled. However, the original proposal and its timing was surely no strictly spontaneous act, and neither could the government have been ignorant or totally unaware of its probable trajectory. In the end, the *aguinaldo* reminds one of a "grand gesture" which was not so much in accordance with the longstanding philosophy of the Social Democratic forces as it was the politic thing to do in order to build up a social base for the *Liberacionista* program in years to come.

Schemes such as that of the *aguinaldo*, however useful they may have been politically, were at best a tenuous basis upon which to build a base for a "movement" such as was being constituted by the PLN. In the long term, the inroads made in integrating the public sector workforce into labor organizations of *Liberacionista* doctrinal orientation were unquestionably a more significant factor in establishing the hegemony of Liberación Nacional over this expanding sector of the country's workforce.[6] In fact, the decade of the 1950s was a time of considerable change and reorganization of the unionized workforce involving a very substantial expansion of unionization amongst "service sector" workers. Moreover, data on the occupational bases of the major labor confederations in Costa Rica show the strength of the reformist Costa Rican Confederation of Democratic Workers (CCTD) to be strongest in the sector including state workers, while the strength of the other major labor federation, the one traditionally under Communist hegemony, is much stronger among the traditional working class and independent artisan population. As a result, as one observer of the country's labor scene has noted, "the obvious conclusion of this study is that unionization in Costa Rica is, fundamentally, a unionization of 'the middle class.' "[7] Despite the element of exaggeration here, it is apparent that those categorized as "employees," most of whom would be employees of the state, have been the subject of considerable organizational activity, especially since Liberación Nacional became the major force in national political life.

CONCLUSIONS

For Costa Ricans, 1948 marked a critical break from the Central American pattern—in the economic and, especially, the political realms. The unstable coalition of Calderón Guardia which had disrupted the traditional influence of the coffee oligarchy was replaced, after a brief armed struggle, by a new configuration of social forces. The latter inaugurated a program that sought to address the fundamental ills of this agro-export oriented economy. The successful implementation of this program would eventually remake the nation's political life and the oligarchy's role in it. The "midwife" of this program that would eventually set Costa Rica on the path to economic revitalization and liberal democracy was a regime without an organic relationship to either the traditionally dominant class, or the organized proletariat. Indeed, one of the accomplishments of the Junta led by Figueres was to end the stalemated political struggle between these two antagonistic forces in a decisive way.

Figueres played a most vital role in moving quickly against the party of the proletariat, on the one hand, later preventing the oligarchy from reestablishing the ancienne régime, through force of arms, or by electoral means, on the other. Moreover, Figueres moved fairly rapidly to solidify a social base upon which to build a sustained political movement—one that would guarantee economic and political reforms over the longer term. In establishing precedents for active state intervention, and in forcing through legislation such as the tax on wealth, the material pre-conditions for the revitalization of the economy under state tutelage were at least partially established. Further progress was made in this direction when, following a protracted struggle with the large coffee interests, the Figuerista forces pushed through a major tax on coffee in the early 1950s that would become a vital source of state revenues in the future.

Costa Rica's anomalous development after 1950 vis-à-vis the other Central American republics was not simply the product of its "natural" evolution out of an earlier and more traditional social order. It was, rather, the outcome of struggles within the confines of socioeconomic and political arrangements passed on from an earlier period. The peculiar configuration of social forces created in the time of Calderón Guardia was an especially important factor. We have to look beyond these structural arrangements, however, to come to a fuller understanding of the postwar trajectory of Costa Rica. The contingent role of individuals in making their own history must not be diminished, or overlooked entirely, as is often the case. We must not forget that those elements who were intent on promoting social change had thoughtfully analyzed the problems of the old order and worked out a plan of action that proved to be viable, given the conditions of that time. Finally, the role of the extraordinary personality of José Figueres in skillfully guiding this program past the barriers erected by internal and external enemies must figure into any serious account of Costa Rica's recent historical trajectory. The amalgam of these diverse currents continues to this day in what has become identified as the "Costa Rican model," one which is based on a poor economic base, and possesses all the disadvantages and advantages of liberal democracy—but one which is startlingly different from its Central American neighbors.

NOTES

1. Jaime G. Delgado, *El Partido Liberación Nacional* (Heredia, Costa Rica: Editorial de la Universidad Nacional, 1980), 123.

2. Speech by José Figueres, cited in Jorge Rovira M., *Estado y Política Económica en Costa Rica, 1948–1970* (San José, Costa Rica: Editorial Porvenir S.A., 1983), 48.

3. See John P. Bell, *Crisis in Costa Rica* (Austin, Tex.: University of Texas Press, 1971), 156.

4. Ibid., 158.

5. Jacobo Schifter, *La Fase Oculta de la Guerra Civil en Costa Rica* (San José, Costa Rica: Editorial Universitaria Centroamericano, 1979), 104. Schifter's study also shows that PLN support continued to be weak in the banana zones in subsequent elections (Schifter, 1979, 105, table 30).

6. Basically, we are speaking about an orientation towards so-called "free" unionism, meaning essentially the formal separation of unions from politics, although still open to the active promotion of labor's economic corporate interests within society by means of their respective labor organizations. See Ponciano Torales, *Reseña Historica del Sindicalismo en Costa Rica* (San José, Costa Rica: International Labour Organization, 1978), 23.

7. Roberto Salom E., *Estudio Sobre las Organizaciones Político-Partidistas de las Clases Dominantes en Costa Rica* (San José, Costa Rica: Instituto de Investigaciones Sociales, 1978), 23.

8

Resisting Conquest: Development and the Guatemalan Indian

W. George Lovell

Indian survival in Guatemala depends on how cultural resistance by twenty different Mayan peoples tempers the impact of conquest. The capacity to respond creatively to invasion and domination demands that Maya Indians be viewed not as vestiges or victims but, foremost of all, as actors, as folk who adapt to conquest in ways that ensure meaningful group preservation. Conquest, therefore, must be seen not as a remote, historical experience but as a visible, present condition. It did not begin and end, in 1524, with the *entrada* led by Pedro de Alvarado. Conquest in Guatemala is played out in the present tense, is suffered and endured, lived and survived as part of the daily round. The sixteenth century and the twentieth, looked at through Indian eyes, mesh and intertwine, collapse to become a single, oppressive flow of time. Thus conquest as a way of life remains *the* central fact of life for over four million Maya Indians who, to this day, comprise fully one-half of the national population of Guatemala.[1] The continuum of conquest may be broken down into three discernible cycles, the last of which ebbs and flows to this very day: conquest by imperial Spain, conquest by local and international capitalism, and conquest by state terror. This chapter examines the relationship between Indians and development during the three cycles of conquest that mark Guatemala's unfinished passage from Spanish colony through independent republic to modern nation.

We must first, of course, attempt to define "development." For this writer, development in the Guatemalan context is defined most meaningfully in relation to land and labor, specifically the right to deploy land and labor as one sees fit. But people think differently, people feel differently, about how land and labor should be deployed. They think and feel *so* differently that the right to deploy becomes a fight to deploy. The victor promotes an idea that, for the vanquished, invariably means the opposite of development, a condition we call "underdevelopment."

Development and underdevelopment are thus inextricably linked, are the heads and tails of the same fatal coin. In Guatemala, development "winners" in the colonial period collected tribute; underdeveloped "losers" paid it. During the nineteenth century, development "winners" deemed that coffee be planted; underdeveloped "losers" picked it on land that once was theirs. Today, development "winners" preside over a countryside where billboards and signposts celebrate their triumph over communism; underdeveloped "losers" dwell quiet and hushed in "model villages" or "strategic hamlets," not knowing still what communism really means. The "winners" have been, in cyclical chronology, Spanish *conquistadores,* foreign entrepreneurs working closely with local elites, and the Guatemalan military. The "losers," almost always, have been Maya Indians. Appreciation of how a culture on the losing side of history has managed to retain so much is our primary objective.

CYCLE ONE

The first cycle of conquest is one in which the reality of conquest is most generally acknowledged, even if, historically and psychologically, it is improperly understood. Imperial Spain invaded Guatemala in 1524 and governed it for three centuries thereafter as part of an American empire vast in size and complex in nature. What needs to be stressed about the Spanish conquest of Guatemala is that it was protracted and incomplete, *made* protracted and incomplete by Maya resistance. Several highland groups inflicted temporary defeat on Spanish forces while lowland groups stalled Spanish penetration of their Petén homeland for up to a century and a half following Alvarado's initial military thrusts. At least one Maya group, the Lacandones of the Usumacinta rainforest, were never brought to heel, and carried out troublesome raids on "pacified" highland communities throughout the colonial period, much to Spanish frustration and dismay. It is thus not an exaggeration to claim that parts of Guatemala witnessed more symbolic Spanish occupation than genuine Spanish conquest. That said, we must be careful not to obscure the essential meaning of the Spanish presence nor to mystify how Spaniards viewed and dealt with Indians.

In Mexico, Guatemala, and elsewhere, Spaniards exploited Indians and forced them into varying degrees of servitude. Maya submission, the efforts of Las Casas and others notwithstanding, was simply nonnegotiable. It was assumed, taken for granted, regarded as a privilege of victory, a natural fixture in the pursuit of empire. Under these terms, relations between Spaniards and Indians hardly fostered tolerance and respect. What it engendered was suspicion, distrust, hatred, and fear. Michael Taussig suggests how the Spanish maintained Indian subordination through widespread terror. Like torture and disappearance, terror is not a pleasant thing to contemplate, but any discussion of why Guatemala is the way it is would be perfunctory if we chose to ignore it. For Taussig, terror was not merely a physiological condition but rather a social means of ensuring hegemony.[2]

Terror and resistance, then, must be seen as omnipresent, as constructs that alter in form and rhythm but never disappear. Against their interplay other aspects of the colonial experience in Guatemala may be seen in a clearer light. Holding on to land, for example, was a crucial expression of resistance for Maya communities. Likewise, for Spaniards exploiting labor was the most overt way of wielding power; Indians furnished labor through fear of the consequences if they did not. The Spaniards regarded control of labor, at least at the outset, as more important than control of land. Thus, early on, an emphasis was placed on extractive devices such as the *encomienda* and the *repartimiento*, institutional mechanisms whereby the conquerors received from the conquered tribute in goods and services without actually being awarded seigneurial rights. Spaniards turned to the land as an alternative means of support and enrichment only after the exploitation of Indian labor proved to be an unpredictable source of wealth. Economic stability was undermined by outbreaks of disease that caused massive native depopulation during the first century and a half of colonial rule and that retarded demographic recovery for an equal length of time thereafter. Large estates certainly were carved out by seigneurially minded Spaniards, but one of the most striking features of the colonial experience in Guatemala was the extent to which land remained in Mayan hands, especially throughout the rugged northwestern highlands. Land retention by colonial Indian communities contributes to a fuller appreciation of Mayan resistance, whether fought for physically in mountains and forests or waged persistently through litigation in the courts.

Although the Spaniards eagerly sought to control labor, the resources of Guatemala, compared with those of Mexico and Peru, presented far less scope for entrepreneurial endeavor. Colonial Guatemala thus became something of an economic backwater, a rather sleepy place where only modest returns could be expected in terms of gold, silver, or commercial crops such as cacao, cochineal, indigo, and sugar. This gave the Mayas a breathing space not enjoyed by other Amerindian groups harder pressed and, consequently, more systematically assimilated to the ways of the conqueror. Despite the efforts of both church and crown, Indians created for themselves a culture of refuge that blended pre-Columbian and colonial Spanish mores. They sheltered themselves in this culture with long-term benefits for meaningful indigenous survival.

CYCLE TWO

The second cycle of conquest is by far the least generally recognized of the three under discussion. This epoch of conquest lasted about a century. It began in the early 1870s with policies promoted by President Justo Rufino Barrios and, by the late 1970s, had created the conditions that were to trigger the present cycle of conquest.

Independence from Spain, attained in 1821, was an event of little apparent consequence for Maya communities throughout Guatemala, most of which for the next fifty years effectively maintained the culture of refuge shaped during colonial times. Not until President Barrios enacted certain programs Liberal politicians had been prevented from implementing earlier, did the reality of being part of the Republic of Guatemala affect Indian life more visibly. The Liberal Reforms, embodying contemporary notions of progress and prosperity, were designed to develop Guatemala from a backward ex-colony into an outward-looking, modern nation. Their centerpiece was the promulgation of laws that entailed not just appropriation of native land but acquisition of native labor. This double plunder turned Guatemala into an export-oriented "coffee republic" as Indian lands were sold to enterprising, non-Indian planters who found the volcanic slopes of the Pacific piedmont and the sheltered valleys of the Verapaz highlands ideal for growing coffee. These same planters, among whose ranks figured German and Swiss as well as Guatemalan nationals, also found that Indian hands made ideal pickers. Very importantly, the Liberal Reforms did not register in a uniform way across the country. In locales especially suitable for the cultivation of coffee, the "Indianness" of some communities disappeared or was dissipated by the joint operation of land and labor encroachments. In other communities, expropriation was less pronounced due to land being situated at elevations beyond the upper limits of the zones where coffee grows best. Nevertheless, even a mountainous location in *tierra fría* was no guarantee against labor recruitment, whether by means of coercion, negotiated contracts, or the enforcement of vagrancy laws.

How much land was taken, how much labor was usurped cannot yet be ascertained. Given the political sensitivity of such inquiry it may never be possible to move beyond an approximation. The most accurate assessment is probably that of Carol Smith who reckons that Indian communities "lost about half of the lands they traditionally claimed during the colonial period."[3] Case studies like those undertaken by Shelton Davis for Santa Eulalia and Robert Carmack for Momostenango, when extended to scores of other communities, may lend greater validity to Smith's assessment.[4] What *is* becoming clearer is that Indian resistance to the Liberal Reforms—by flight, damage to property, acts of civil disobedience—was more intense and widespread than previously thought, even if it never assumed the dimension, as in nineteenth century Yucatán, of full-fledged insurrection.

The second cycle of conquest, then, transformed Guatemala quite radically. Coffee, moreover, set an important economic precedent, for its cultivation on former Indian lands was followed in the course of the twentieth century by the promotion of other cash crops (bananas, cardamom, cotton, sugar cane) for export abroad. None of these crops has ever matched the performance of coffee, which accounted for "50 percent of foreign exchange earnings by 1871, 92 percent by 1880, 77 percent in 1929, 78 percent in 1950, and 32 percent in 1970."[5] But, as the last statistic indicates, dependence on coffee as the predominant "development" commodity has lessened considerably, the result of cotton, sugar, and beef "booms" during the 1960s and early 1970s. Some would argue that this shift, and the impressive indexes of economic growth that accompanied it, reflect positively on such initiatives as the Alliance for Progress and the Central American Common Market. What tends to be overlooked, if not ignored, is that the economic gains of export agriculture in Guatemala benefit only a privileged, non-Indian minority. Most Guatemalans suffer, not prosper, because fertile lands are used to produce crops for consumption abroad while local populations go underfed or malnourished. Geographies of inequality that crystallized during the second cycle of conquest, especially those of skewed landholding and income distribution, linger and afflict Guatemala still. In 1979, for instance, over 60 percent of the best farmland was held by about one-tenth of all owners, and in 1986 only 13 percent of total government revenue came from an elite stridently opposed to higher taxation of their incomes. Such inequities are responsible for Guatemala, according to a recent UNICEF evaluation, having a "physical quality of life" that is the lowest in Central America and the third lowest in all Latin America.[6] They are also responsible for the challenge to the existing order that emerged in the 1970s, a challenge that precipitated, with a swiftness and brutality few foresaw, the third cycle of conquest.

CYCLE THREE

As a litany of atrocities that confounds our ability to relate and to comprehend—Panzos, 1978, Finca San Francisco, 1982—the third cycle of conquest is well-documented and commonly acknowledged, even if the word "conquest" is seldom used to characterize the events and circumstances of the past decade. Since the third cycle is a response to measures Indians took towards the end of the second cycle to change their lives, attention must focus on what these measures were and why they triggered the response they did.

The overthrow of Jacobo Arbenz in 1954 signalled unequivocally that alteration of the structures of political and economic domination in place since the time of President Barrios was something members of Guatemala's ruling elite would neither support nor tolerate. Clearly, however, an issue of some concern was the lot of poor Guatemalans, the numbers of whom were rapidly on the increase due to an acceleration in the rate of population growth. To ameliorate the situation, a development program known as *Acción Católica* was reinvigorated by inviting priests to work more closely with the rural poor. These priests soon became involved in projects that sought not just to illuminate questions of faith but to improve aspects of social and economic life as well. Schools were built, classes taught, and a spirit of collective endeavor promoted. Most important of all, priests helped to organize agricultural, consumer, and credit cooperatives that grew to become the cornerstone of *Acción Católica*. By 1967, 145 cooperatives had been formed, many of them in the predominantly Indian regions of El Quiché, Huehuetenango, San Marcos, and Sololá. Eight years later, the cooperative movement had expanded to include some 500 different associations, with a combined membership of more than 132,000 family representatives. According to Shelton Davis and Julie Hodson, over half of these cooperatives "were located in the western and central highlands where they were having a major impact on Indian political attitudes, marketing strategies, and agricultural techniques."[7] If the land base of Maya existence had been diminished in the course of the preceding century, a vibrant sense of community had not.

The cooperative movement, which actually received official government endorsement at the beginning of the presidential term (1974–78) of General Kjell Laugerud, eventually was perceived to pose a direct threat to the status quo. Especially undermined was Guatemala's plantation economy, which had experienced unprecedented expansion throughout the 1960s and early 1970s. Native labor, to be sure, helped develop this export potential. But, on returning to their highland communities, more and more Indians began to invest their plantation wages in ventures that generated local employment. What Indians ultimately achieved was to create for themselves practical alternatives to seasonal migration. Certainly Indian hands continued to cut sugar cane, to pick cotton, and to harvest coffee, but native pools of labor relied upon for decades began to evaporate. Matters reached a crisis shortly after the earthquake of February 4, 1976, when Indians chose to remain in their ruined settlements in order to rebuild them rather than hire themselves out as plantation labor. Tension between the state and Indian communities only increased after the latter sought reconstruction assistance directly from international agencies rather than go through government channels long recognized as unresponsive, inefficient, and corrupt.

Around this same time, left-wing insurgents committed to the revolutionary overthrow of a repressive state began to gain operational strength throughout the western highlands. By 1978, when General Romeo Lucas García assumed the presidency of Guatemala and events in Nicaragua and El Salvador heralded imminent regional conflagration, the stage was set for a major confrontation. In the name of "anticommunism," war was declared on the citizenry of Guatemala by its own government, a government controlled by an army whose two decades in political office saw generals and colonels become a powerful economic, as well as military, force. Especially targeted as "subversive" were communities where cooperatives had been successfully established or where guerrillas had enjoyed some success in winning Indian converts to their cause. Conquest by state terror, the third cycle of a continuum stretching back four and a half centuries, moved into high, lethal gear.

Little stands to be gained by reiteration of the chilling details of state terror when it is now apparent that Indians have survived another wave of subjugation, even if it is less apparent how conquest will continue to be resisted. In one sense, simply to exist as an Indian, to be Mayan in Guatemala today, is itself a supreme act of resistance. Meanwhile, the good intentions of civilian president Vinicio Cerezo grow more rhetorical by the day. Although his Christian Democrats took over the reigns of government from a military regime in January 1986, the latter still rule victorious from the sidelines. The conquest goes on. But so, too, does a distinctively Mayan way of life, fuelled by an inner, mystic combustion that, in the end, eludes conventional modes of analysis.

NOTES

1. John D. Early, *The Demographic Structure and Evolution of a Peasant System: The Guatemalan Population* (Boca Raton, Fla.: University Presses of Florida, 1982).

2. Michael Taussig, *Shamanism, Colonialism, and the Wild Man: A Study in Terror and Healing* (Chicago: University of Chicago Press, 1987).

3. Carol A. Smith, "Local History in Global Context," *Comparative Studies in Society and History* 26 no. 2, (1984): 204.

4. See Shelton H. Davis, "Land of Our Ancestors: A Study of Land Tenure and Inheritance in the Highlands of Guatemala" (Ph.D. diss., Harvard University, 1970); and Robert M. Carmack, "Spanish–Indian Relations in Highland Guatemala, 1800–1944," in *Spaniards and Indians in Southeastern Mesoamerica: Essays on the History of Ethnic Relations*, eds. Murdo J. MacLeod and Robert Wasserstrom, (Lincoln, Nebr.: University of Nebraska Press, 1983), 215–52.

5. Carol A. Smith, "Beyond Dependency Theory: National and Regional Patterns of Underdevelopment in Guatemala," *American Ethnologist* 5, no. 3 (1976): 589.

6. See James Painter, *Guatemala: False Hope—False Freedom* (London: Latin American Bureau, 1987), 3, 10, 33.

7. Shelton H. Davis and Julie Hodson. *Witnesses to Political Violence in Guatemala: The Suppression of a Rural Development Movement* (Boston: Oxfam America, 1982), 14.

9

Developing Democratic Education in Central America Means Revolution: The Nicaraguan Case

W. Gordon West

INTRODUCTION

Formal education systems have always sold themselves as enhancing (economic) development. The impact of rich nations on schooling in the third world is seldom questioned critically. Education is blithely assumed to be benign in civilizing the world, freeing people from past enslavements, offering hope for a future of development and democracy. Modernization theories, analyses, and prescriptions have seen education as crucial to development and, eventually, to democracy.

The crisis in Latin America today revolves in large part around this intimate relationship between democracy, development, and education: economic development requires schooling, but critical education almost inevitably challenges the dominant (capitalist) model of development. Education in Central America demands not only democracy, but change. When resistance makes peaceful change impossible, critical intelligence and the lived experience of exploitation have bred revolution. The experience of Nicaragua provides an alternative model of education's contribution to democratic development. This chapter focuses on popular education in the local Sandinista Defense Committees as well as on democracy in the schools.

This chapter is a greatly revised version of "Nicaragua es Una Escuela: Una Alternativa Educacional Progresista para la Juventud Latinoamericana en el Contexto de la Crisis" [Nicaragua is a School: A Progressive Educational Alternative for Latin American Youth in the Crisis]. In *Educacion y Trabajo: El Norte y El Sur* [Education and Work: North and South]. Santiago, Chile: CIDE/PIIE, 1988.

UNDERDEVELOPMENT, IGNORANCE, AND
DICTATORSHIP

Contemporary developments in Nicaragua spring from a particular historical context. Twentieth-century Nicaragua suffered under the Somoza family dictatorship (1933–79) for almost half a century, unusual from preceding governments only in its extreme brutality and its final overthrow. During the nineteenth century, the liberal ideals of Central America's revolt from Spanish rule in 1821 never moved beyond a formal commitment to the concept of the rule of law: the social and political realities were latifundism, dictatorships, interfamily rivalries and American occupation from 1911 to 1933.

On the eve of the 1979 revolution, more than half the land units in Nicaragua composed less than 4 percent of the total arable land; while less than 1 percent of the units made up 30 percent of the land area.[1] Nicaragua also experienced the rapid population growth rates typical of Latin America (over 3 percent) resulting in half the population being under age fifteen. At the same time, the Somozas kept Nicaraguans mired in underdevelopment: swollen cities, one of the world's lowest per capita income levels ($600 in 1979), a 20–45 percent unemployment rate, a population of whom more than half were illiterate, an infant mortality rate of 130 per 1000 live births, and a life expectancy of only 56 years. Malnutrition affected 50 percent of the children under five years of age. Half the homes of Nicaragua lacked toilets and 20 percent lacked water.

Education under the Somozas was disastrous. Of those who started elementary school, less than one-fifth reached the sixth grade.[2] Less than half of the school-aged population attended school at all. As Somoza stated: "I want oxen, not men, in my country."[3]

In 1976 only 68 percent of the 409,000 children in the 7–12 age group registered (there are no figures for attendance) and half of these dropped out within a year. Some 20 percent of the secondary school age group and only 5 percent of the postsecondary age group were formally enrolled in 1977. Education in rural Nicaragua barely existed. Two-thirds of all pupils registered were in urban areas. Ninety percent of rural schools had only one teacher who taught all the six primary grades. In rural areas, only one in twenty of those who started first grade finished all six grades; even in the urban areas the completion rate was under 50 percent.[4]

Paradoxically, the Somoza dictatorship's neglect of education stimulated new forms of popular education that emerged from a variety of social groups: Christian base communities, neighborhood improvement associations, social work and union programs, and spontaneous organizations of neighbors who needed and trusted each other for information, clearing blocked sewers, or providing "safe houses" for guerrillas. During the final offensive from April of 1979 onwards, such neighborhood organizations were often the only "government" operating, as services broke down and factories and businesses were struck, bombed or shut.

Neighborhood committees played a vital role in the final stage of the revolution. During the uprisings in 1978 and 1979, the Sandinista Front could not abandon the spontaneous insurgencies in the cities, but neither could its few hundred armed militants defeat the Guardia. The organization of these neighborhood committees through 1978–79 became the missing link in the strategy; without them, the Sandinista revolution might not have succeeded.

The committees not only supported the revolution, but also suggested: the possibility of changing the social and economic bases of politics; the reformulation of education; and an alternative strategy of social development. They exemplified a participatory, cooperative structure in which citizens taught each other, and provided the needed resources to develop their immediate social environment. The committees continue to operate as a core element in social defense, and as a key resource in popular development efforts.

DEMOCRACY AND EDUCATIONAL DEVELOPMENT IN NICARAGUA

The triumphant Nicaraguan revolution inherited all the problems of underdevelopment and poverty described above, plus the wanton destruction suffered in the overthrow of Somoza's Guardia. In a country of less than three million, some 50,000 were killed—almost all of whom were under age 25 (proportionately more than Britain lost in all of World War II). The armed struggle left 100,000 injured, 40,000 orphaned, 200,000 families homeless and 750,000 depending on food assistance. Somoza and his cronies inflicted half a billion dollars in damage, looted the national treasury, leaving only $3.5 million, and indebted the country to the tune of $1.6 billion (the highest per capita in Latin America), much of which they had also managed to siphon off for their personal use.[5]

In 1984, under war conditions, Nicaragua successfully held general elections, offering public financing and free media exposure to all interested political parties, and registering an extremely high voter turnout. In what international observers declared a fair and open election, opposition parties won a third of the seats in its legislative assembly.

Democracy in Nicaragua, however, has not remained within narrowly defined, parliamentary voting traditions accepted in the North. It has flowered to include the stimulation and development of alternative and participatory power structures through mass organizations of all sorts, from unions and professional associations to women, peasant, youth organizations, and especially, the neighborhood Sandinista Defense Committees (CDS). The neighborhood committees are in many senses quintessential examples of Sandinista democracy. They are the largest (with 600,000 members) and most powerful mass organization, with the largest number of seats on the Council of State. Organized territorially, the committees cover the country; they have been central in various government campaigns, from real income maintenance to health and education; and they retain their status as crucial partners with the Sandinista Front in making the revolution.

There are over 15,000 committees operating, varying from a handful to dozens of members. Anyone, regardless of age (above 14), sex, race, religion, or politics can join as long as they support the goals of the revolution. The committees meet approximately once a week. Decisions are carried out by executive members in charge of the task areas, working with citizen volunteers. Both incorporation to membership/participation and decisions are made democratically by argument, discussion and persuasion. Each local CDS elects representatives to the Barrio or rural community committees which in turn elect zonal, regional and national committees in a democratic pyramid structure. The original CDS representatives to the governmental Council of State included a spectrum of students, accountants, peasants, and various small tradespersons. Suggesting, stimulating, administering, and criticizing almost the entire range of programmes normally carried out only by government agencies in the liberal-democratic North, the CDS have proposed new legislation, sent representatives to commissions, and worked closely with government ministries. Their provision of *"vigilancia revolucionaria"* (nightwatch) is crucial in public safety. There have been changes in the operations of the CDS since 1979, as the economy has been restored, governmental services began to operate, and policing and other services were established. The CDS have identified their specific objectives and tasks in defending the revolution as: organization maintenance, provision of information and education, economic defense, community development, and social defense.

Nicaragua's right-wing opposition has launched fierce attacks on the CDS. The Comisión Permanente de Derechos Humanos (CPDH), the newspaper *La Prensa* and the Consejo Superior de Las Empresas Privadas (COSEP) are the principal critics—all of which have received U.S. government funds. Nonetheless, almost all investigating commissions from without as well as within Nicaragua (e.g., Pax Christi, 1981; Americas Watch, 1985), have found such charges to be exaggerated, unsubstantiated, or relatively isolated cases (many of which occurred immediately after the revolutionary victory) rather than systematic government or CDS policy.

The CDS developed under Somocista oppression. Civil war shaped them and the threat of invasion continues to animate them. In that eventuality, intimate knowledge of friends and enemies of the revolution would be crucial to any orchestrated defense. It is also very clear that the committees have been very much "in process," constantly learning, and that they have never been "standardized".[6] The CDS thus continue to exemplify the liveliness of popular education and democratic debate within Nicaragua. The local committees offer a model of community self-development and learning far beyond any experiments in the north. Let us now examine how they relate to more formal attempts at a democratic education.

EDUCATIONAL DEVELOPMENT

There is an ironic hubris over the past century of schooling in North America and Western Europe. We have cut young people off from full participation in society, especially through compulsory, prolonged schooling which we too easily assumed automatically promoted social development. Our frustrated belief is that this will somehow better prepare them to develop our society. In dramatic contrast, the new Nicaraguan government has clearly enunciated an alternative educational policy:

To shape students in and for creative work, and to develop in them an awareness of the economic, social and cultural value of productive labor, and of the fundamental role of the working class in the formation of the new society.[7]

The expansion of education since 1979 is remarkable. The basic figures speak for themselves: in a time of extreme scarcity and demand, public resources for schooling have soared from 1.41 to 5.00 percent of the Gross Internal Product from 1978 to 1983. Education accounts for some 11 percent of government expenditures,[8] during a time when government costs have rapidly increased their predominance in the economy:

This huge investment has resulted in the construction of over 3,700 new classrooms and 1,400 new elementary schools, plus 48 new high schools. The number of primary and secondary school teachers has approximately doubled.[9]

This expansion can also be seen most clearly in comparative registration statistics (see Table 9.1)[10].

Especially noteworthy are the expansions of preschool education, primary schooling, and technical areas (most notably in agriculture), clearly showing a decided attempt to target the most destitute population sectors. Furthermore, within these figures are major qualitative shifts: post-secondary level scholarships have shifted from bachelor's programmes to locally relevant agricultural and teacher training ones while agricultural

Table 9.1
NICARAGUA: COMPARATIVE REGISTRATION IN
SCHOOL COURSES, 1978–1983

Levels	1978	1979-80	1980-81	1981-82	1982-83
Preschool	9,000	18,292	30,542	38,534	61,495
Primary	369,640	431,164	503,497	534,996	579,261
Middle/Sec	98,874	110,726	139,743	139,957	161,680
Higher	23,791	29,173	34,710	33,838	39,765
Special	355	—	1,430	1,591	1,800
Adult	—	—	167,852	148,369	161,317
Total	501,660	589,355	877,756	897,285	1,005,318

Source: MINED: 1984, p. 15.

programmes have been dispersed from two universities to twelve local regional colleges.

Nicaragua's school curriculum has been entirely revamped to try to address needs felt by the popular sectors. It stresses subjects of relevance to rural life, combined with useful school-work cooperative projects. Rural Work-Study Schools (ERETs) are attempting to become full-fledged production centers. Furthermore, "nuclearization" plans are underway to group local schools into educational and productive strategies with territorial/community relevance.

Students participate in work projects within the school and the surrounding community during the regular terms (e.g., manufacturing clothes and tools, local sanitation, clearing land, and harvesting crops). In addition, all schools organize Student Production Brigades (BEPs) in the vacation months to help harvest the agro-export crops that earn Nicaragua foreign exchange. Besides their immediate economic value, these activities also provide an effective substitute for the socially disruptive mass peasant family migrations of the past—and help retain students in school, especially in rural areas. Finally, the brigades have proven to be enormously educative regarding the regions of the country, urban-rural differences, and modes of social organization.

The new educational programmes are not without criticisms and problems. Conservatives charge that the new school system is a totalitarian project, politicized to destroy the family and religion. The Contras' war of attrition reduces the resources available for education, and teachers and schools are high priority targets for terrorist attacks. Attempts are underway to address real problems of overcentralization, and bureaucratization. Many teachers were schooled in traditional pedagogies, and lack flexibility to adapt to the new circumstances while younger teachers often lack formal training. Many university-level technical courses continue to demand formal training and lack coordination with the more popularly oriented elementary and secondary systems.

Regular school participation depends upon a populace providing students/itself with a satisfactory minimum base of subsistence, welfare, and preparation. Immediately after the insurrection, and now again as the Contra war has orphaned tens of thousands, the Nicaraguan Institute for Social Services and Welfare (INSSBI) has experimented with very innovative programmes: for instance, allowing single parent adoptions in a country where many marriages have not been formally legalized. INSSBI has also established a network of child development centers which not only provide direct medical and nutritional aid, but also run extensive education programmes. Special education programmes have been established for the most severely handicapped.

Nicaragua has also experimented with model programmes for the thousands of street urchins in its large cities, an endemic problem in all Latin American countries except Cuba. Under the dictatorship, until 1974, there was neither juvenile delinquents legislation nor welfare legislation. The 1974 Code continues in force, administered by the police and Institute of Social Services and Welfare. The majority of youngsters recently taken into care are usually homeless, drug abusers, or prostitutes. Upon completion of 6–12 month rehabilitation programmes, they are usually paired with young police officers, who continue to supervise them in a "big brother" role.

The new government has not seen its task as simply the reconstruction of war-damaged schools, nor the expansion of the previously existing education system: it seeks an entirely new direction for schooling, aimed at development rather than the maintenance of underdevelopment. The Nicaraguan Literacy Crusade typified this process of education for democracy. It sought to liberate people to become fulfilled human beings, aware and empowered to build their own futures. The Nicaraguans understood that creating a literate person is a political, as much as an educational, activity. Without a conscious, committed people, there could be no revolution:

The attainment of literacy was not simply the gaining of an academic skill, but the empowerment of a people who became aware of their reality and gained the tools, reading and writing, to affect and determine their future. The Literacy Crusade was not a pedagogical undertaking without political effects, it was a political undertaking with pedagogical effects. It was a political mobilization with political goals.[11]

Instituted shortly after the July 1979 triumph, the enormously successful literacy crusade resulted in illiteracy rates falling from 62 to 12 percent within a year.[12] Using a modified Freirian approach, supported by censuses and mass media, the campaign mobilized some 100,000 volunteer instructors, many of them high school students who left their city homes for billets in the country with poverty-stricken peasant families.

The campaign was not without problems and criticisms. Paulo Freire himself provocatively questioned the balance between domestication and liberation; others felt that it was too centralized; that it was propagandizing; that there have been great difficulties in maintaining high levels of literacy. But more than half the adult population did learn to read, and expert observers have depicted it as the fundamental first step of Nicaragua "to free itself from cultural backwardness and dependence."[13] The goals of the literacy campaign were far broader than just "readin' 'n' 'ritin' " and included the following:

1. to eradicate illiteracy;
2. to encourage integration and understanding between Nicaragua's different social classes;
3. to nurture attitudes and skills related to creativity, production, cooperation, discipline and analytic thinking;
4. to support national cohesion and consensus;
5. to strengthen the channels for economic and political participation.[14]

No education can simply be politically neutral. In support of the literacy campaign and to allow entrance to technical programmes, adult popular education programmes have continued on an unprecedented scale, supported by every government ministry, touching every neighborhood and hamlet, and covering topics from mixed crop farming and civil defense to husband-wife relations, social theory and popular theatre. The techniques are similarly innovative, ranging from newspaper cartoons, neighborhood slide and film talks, to popularly produced posters, song, and drama:

. . . in a revolutionary process, the communications media should serve the interests of the great majority of the people. . . . if people are to be the protagonists of information, then it's necessary that among other things they produce their own informational and training materials. This means that people should directly produce their own news and educational materials; in other words, they should be their own media producers.[15]

THE DANGERS TO DEMOCRATIC EDUCATIONAL DEVELOPMENT

External forces increasingly threaten the educational successes of the revolution. Since 1981, the administration of President Ronald Reagan has waged a so-called "low-intensity" war of attrition against social development in Nicaragua led by former officers of Somoza's National Guard.

But a "low-intensity" war from Washington's viewpoint means terror in the Nicaraguan countryside. Between 1982 and 1985, the American-supported mercenaries murdered 3,346 children and adolescents. Another 6,236 children lost one or both parents. On average, there have been more than four deaths per day; by March 1985 there were 170,000 displaced persons within Nicaragua. Education suffers heavy losses. In 1984, the Contras killed ninety-eight adult education teachers and kidnapped 171; killed fifteen primary school teachers and kidnapped sixteen and destroyed 14 schools. Because of the threat to life and the scarcity of resources, the government has closed 840 adult education centers and 354 schools.[16] Since 1983, few new schools have been built. The budget for education was frozen, no new teachers hired, and no new texts published.[17] In modern history, each and every progressive revolutionary movement towards education and democracy has brought with it not only the promise of liberty, but also the burden of avoiding, controlling, and defeating a counterrevolution. The costs of any progressive revolution that challenges the U.S. empire must be so high that no other peoples will be tempted to imitate the offending client state in its opposition to imperial domination. A militarily-successful revolution must be bled economically so severely that it cannot fulfil its promise, and cannot be a model of alternative development.

CONCLUSION: EDUCATION MEANS REVOLUTION, AND THE REVOLUTION IS EDUCATION

Nicaragua has opted for novel educational development. The Nicaraguan transformation has scored spectacular successes in democratic development that have an educational impact. Health clinics, the literacy crusade and the extension of schooling, participation in the electoral process, representation through mass community organizations, and unions all indicate important developments. In a fundamental sense, many of these measures can be understood as relevant education, broadly construed.

Of course, the Sandinista government's clear "option for the poor" has not immediately changed economic reality: Nicaragua is still small, poor, economically dependent, and has a huge marginal class dependent upon petty commodity production and service industry trades. But along with better housing, nutrition, health, and social services, this country also has an explosion of learning, of arts, of culture—of hope. Its people can feel, taste, and see that if the problems are not yet solved, they are at least being addressed. This unique programme of radical restructuring poses a highly pertinent question for us: just what can we learn from the Nicaraguan experiment and the bloody resistance financed by the United States?

First, one must recognize that in Nicaragua, educational change comes with critical differences: it emphasizes informal, community-relevant programmes and deemphasizes unthinking adoption of universal secondary schooling: and it combines liberation theology, a conception of "the new person" ("el hombre nuevo"), community service, and relevant vocational education. It sees democratic development as dependent upon social justice: basic rights to food, shelter, health, education and employment are fundamental. The Sandinista Revolution has integrated education into all aspects of life. Nicaragua has become a "school" from which others can learn.

Education in Nicaragua thus prepares people for a new relationship with their government, a new civil society that is democratic, popular, and progressive:

The task of the people, more than commenting on the state, is to act within it in a way that serves both them and their functionaries. . . . a civilian society-state takes shape, a people-state in which society and people do not merely have opinions, do not merely vote and have representation; in addition, they become integrated into, joined with, and form part of that emergency state, that state-nation or that nation-state, in which curiously, one can find the extreme discipline implied by liberation combined with the most diverse moral, religious, popular and civilian currents of a war that involves the civil population.[18]

Serious educational development not only challenges the traditional school curriculum, pedagogy, and organization. It also questions priorities that are taken for granted throughout the globe. Consequently, the Nicaraguan education experiment is resisted not only directly and militarily by the United States through their Contra mercenaries, but also by seemingly "objective" and "politically neutral" international agencies, such as the International Monetary Fund and the World Bank which demand cuts in social development programmes as a condition for further international loans required to maintain payments on foreign debts.

Democracy depends upon education—upon an informed electorate, able to assess issues, debate, defend their interests, and call leaders to account. It depends upon information and knowledge about such issues upon which debate can be based. Conversely, real education implies democracy. It makes learners aware of their world, not simply to remember and regurgitate "facts," but aware in the sense of contacting, embracing, contesting—engaging their world. If education is not liberating, it is domesticating: in either case, it is inevitably political. Such active engagement of the world challenges hierarchies and taken-for-granted situations, including authoritarian declarations of what constitutes truth, right, or justice.

The Nicaraguan revolution has enormously wider implications beyond Nicaragua, beyond Central and Latin America: it touches even our relatively safe, northern, liberal democracies. Vice President Sergio Ramírez has perhaps best expressed the educational (in the broadest sense of the term) threat that Nicaragua represents:

For us, the efficacy of a political model depends on its capacity to resolve the problem of democracy and the problem of justice. . . . We are not a people chosen by God to accomplish any Manifest Destiny; we have no capital to export, nor any transnational enterprises to defend beyond our borders. Our dreams are not of dominion, nor of expansion nor of conquest, but they are the humble dreams of a humble people who aspire to full-fledged justice and to full-fledged independence.[19]

NOTES

1. Jaime Wheelock Román, *Nicaragua: imperialismo y dictadura* (Havana, Cuba: Ciencias Sociales, 1974–79), 203.

2. A. R. Tefel, *El infierno de los pobres* (Managua, Nicaragua: Universidad Centroamericana, 1972), 35–37, 93ff.

3. J. Maine, "The 'New Education': The Revolutionary Education Project of Sandinista Nicaragua," (unpub. mss., Toronto, OISE, 1985), 67.

4. George Black and J. Bevan, *The Loss of Fear: Education in Nicaragua Before and After the Revolution* (London: World University Service, 1980), 18.

5. EPICA (Ecumenical Program for Interamerican Communication and Action), *Nicaragua: A People's Revolution* (Washington, D.C.: EPICA, 1980).

6. CIERA (Centro de Investigaciones y Estudios de la Reforma Agraria), *La democracia participativa en Nicaragua* (Managua, Nicaragua: CIERA, 1984), 56.

7. IHCA (Instituto Histórico Centroamericano), *ENVIO*, 11 June 1985.

8. MINED (Ministerio de Educación), *Educación en cuatro años de revolución* (Managua, Nicaragua: MINED, 1984), 64.

9. Maine, "New Education," 15.

10. MINED, *Educación*, 15.

11. Carlos Tunnerman, "Educating the People," in *Nicaragua: A New Kind of Revolution. 45 Key Spokespeople*, eds. P. Zwerling and C. Martin (Westport, Conn.: Lawrence Hill, 1983), 67.

12. See Valerie Miller, *Between Struggle and Hope: The Nicaraguan Literacy Crusade* (Boulder, Colo.: Westview Press, 1985); S. Hirshon and Judy Butler, *And Also Teach Them to Read* (Westport, Conn.: Lawrence Hill, 1983).

13. C. Gander, "New Forms for a New Nicaragua," *Media in Education*, December (1983).

14. Fernando Cardenal and Valerie Miller, "Nicaragua in 1980: The Battle of the ABC's," *Harvard Educational Review*, 51 (1981): 5.

15. Debra Brandt, ed. *Popular Education in Nicaragua* (Toronto: Participatory Research Group, 1983), pp. 24–25.

16. D. Melrose, *Nicaragua: The Threat of a Good Example?* (London: Oxfam, 1985), 37.

17. Maine, "New Education," 25.

18. P. González Casanova, "Intervention and Negotiation in Central America," *Contemporary Marxism*, no. 8 (1984): 220–21.

19. Sergio Ramírez Mercado, "Countering American Propaganda," *This Magazine* (Toronto 1983): 11–13.

10

Militarization, U.S. Aid, and the Failure of Development in El Salvador

Charles Clements

No one seems certain how long it will take to win in El Salvador. Various predictions suggest decades rather than years:

> We may not know whether this experiment will succeed for another ten years.
> —Edwin Corr, U.S. Ambassador to El Salvador

> The guerrillas may be able to maintain the struggle until the turn of the century.
> —U.S. Embassy Official

> . . . Central America is not Southeast Asia. The U.S. by supplying treasure, training, and technology can aid its allies conducting a protracted war of perhaps decades duration.
> —Senior U.S. Military Official

Whether it takes ten, twenty, or thirty years to win the war in El Salvador, the critical question is: How much will it cost to win? Already the United States has sent over $2.5 billion in economic and military assistance to El Salvador, but the Reagan administration apparently is not too concerned, at least publicly, about being able to sustain this financial commitment. It took the State Department almost two years to respond to a 1985 request by this committee for a three-year cost projection. The reply, a pathetic ten-page, double-spaced memorandum, was as evasive as "winning" seems to be in El Salvador.

In 1985, about the same time the Congress requested a cost projection from the State Department, United States military advisers were talking to a delegation of Vietnam veterans visiting El Salvador, vowing "We're going to win this time!" Unfortunately, who pays the price of pursuing this elusive victory is not discussed openly for reasons recent history makes clear. The principal lesson that our government learned in Vietnam is that America does not tolerate her sons coming home in body bags. The result, in military terms, is called "low-intensity conflict," which permits us to fight communism in the third world without expending American lives. Put more bluntly, it means that in the case of El Salvador, we provide the training, we provide the logistics, we provide the intelligence, we provide the command and control, and they—the Salvadoreans—provide the dying. Obviously, an administration that is especially sensitive to its public image would not admit this distasteful fact to the American people, who desire some semblance of morality in the conduct of our foreign policy.

Consequently, when casualty figures were released several months ago indicating that thousands of Salvadoreans—civilians, soldiers, guerrillas—had been killed and wounded last year, hardly an eyebrow was raised in this country. However, the recent death in El Salvador of Army Staff Sergeant Gregory Fronius, an American military advisor, prompted a spate of editorials wondering if all was well in El Salvador.

It is important to understand that guerrilla warfare is nothing but an appendage of a far vaster political contest and that, no matter how expertly it is fought by competent and dedicated professionals, it cannot make up for the absence of a political rationale. A dead Special Force sergeant is not spontaneously replaced by his own social environment. A dead revolutionary usually is.

These words are relevant to Sgt. Fonius' death but they are not excerpted from any news commentary on the killing. Rather, they are taken from a book entitled *Street Without Joy*, a classic work on Vietnam written in the early sixties by a Frenchman, Bernard Fall. I first read the book at the Air Force Academy almost twenty-five years ago. I did not understand what Fall meant then, but I do now and I hope his views can help us realize that the policy Sgt. Fronius died for is failing.

Sgt. Fronius was one of the "competent and dedicated professionals" fighting the war in El Salvador. He was slain in the early morning hours of April 1, 1987 at the heavily-fortified El Paraíso garrison. Of the 250 Salvadorean soldiers stationed there that night, there were at least 200 casualties. Yet not a single officer was reported killed or wounded. Survivors told journalists that the officers had locked themselves in a bunker, which says little about the professionalism of the Salvadorean officer corps that the United States has spent so much money to improve. It is a tribute to the courage and dedication of Sgt. Fronius that he chose to lead the enlisted men rather than join the officers.

In the wake of the assault, it is important to ask, using Fall's words, what "social environment" will produce replacements for the 200 Salvadorean soldiers who were killed or wounded. The streets of poor neighborhoods to the north of San Salvador and the villages of Chalatenango near El Paraíso will be empty the next few weeks except for cruising military vehicles that, resembling dog catchers here in America, seek young men to press-gang into military service. Mothers will attempt to hide their sons, but with little success. However, these trucks will not cruise the Zona Rosa, where the sons of the well-to-do will dine and drink every night in outdoor cafes while their parents declare unconstitutional a tax hike aimed at helping defray a small portion of the cost of the war. The recruiters will catch some men in the dark as they come out of a movie theatre. Perhaps a few unsuspecting ones, who thought that the Christmas draft quota was filled, will be grabbed in the early morning on their way to the fields, and still a couple of others appearing to be drunk will allow themselves to be picked up because they are guerrillas who want to infiltrate El Paraíso and sabotage it yet a third time.

In attempting to determine why the El Paraíso garrison was so easily overtaken that night, it is not certain if the "absence of a political rationale" might have contributed to poor morale or a breach of discipline. But we do know about the technology the Salvadorean armed forces had at their disposal to ward off a guerrilla assault.

The garrison, built in 1982, was designed by United States advisers. Once thought to be impregnable, it was overrun in a similar incident on New Years Day, 1984. No officers were wounded or killed then either, but not because they were in a bunker—later it was discovered that they were all celebrating in the capital. To prevent another such occurrence, the perimeter of the garrison was reinforced with a mine field. These garrisons also are equipped with sophisticated vision devices that permit nighttime surveillance. To top it off, El Paraíso had electronic monitoring devices, capable of eavesdropping on guerrilla communications. Indeed, intelligence reports made the day before the April 1 raid noted the presence of several hundred guerrillas in the vicinity.

In the event that garrisons like El Paraíso come under siege, the Salvadorean Air Force is capable of flying close support missions in AC-47 gunships armed with infrared fire support systems and parachute flares. This enables their three .50 caliber machine guns to concentrate some 2,700 rounds per minute on a single target in daylight or darkness. Further early warning capability, which could prevent such a siege, can be provided to the Salvadorean armed forces by U.S.-piloted, Panama-based AC-130s, which have infrared scopes capable of detecting the heat of an infant from 10,000 feet. A classmate of mine from the Air Force Academy, who piloted one over El Salvador for several months, described its considerable technical capabilities more quaintly saying, "When our scopes are hot, we can watch a guerrilla take a leak and follow his stream."

Though their primary mission is to help the Salvadoreans interdict arms traffic, they have supplied battlefield intelligence support in violation of the War Powers Act.

Similarly, the El Paraíso garrison did not lack the assistance of outside personnel. U.S. advisers officially are forbidden from entering zones of conflict. Instead, American mercenaries like Robert Brown of Omega Group Ltd. furnish invaluable service on combat reconnaissance missions, introducing new, aggressive tactics to the Salvadorean army such as small-unit long-range patrols and multiple small-team ambushes. By denying the guerrillas the capability to operate near garrisons like El Paraíso, these tactics are supposed to provide yet another layer of defense.

Civic-military actions form still another perimeter of defense for the Salvadorean armed forces. The *Wall Street Journal* described one such action as "clowns, a mariachi band, and skimpily-clad dancers performing between speeches by Salvadorean army officers and social workers . . . while army barbers cut hair, and soldiers pass out rice, dresses and medicine."[1] This is "winning the hearts and minds of the peasants," according to a CIA agent clad in battle fatigues and toting an M-16 rifle. Out of appreciation for the army's beneficence, their hearts and minds won over, the peasants around El Paraíso were supposed to warn the military at the first sign of subversives.

None of these defenses protect El Paraíso or other outposts from attack. Before the El Paraíso attack, the nation's largest barracks at San Miguel had been attacked. Before San Miguel, the country's largest training center at La Unión was a target. The State Department projection of long-term policy towards El Salvador describes these as "occasional large-unit military actions," but says "the current military situation is promising," citing as evidence the inability of the guerrillas to operate at battalion strength, and their drop in field strength to between 4,500 and 6,000. Promising or not, these garrisons are not likely to be saved from such assaults in the future.

After seven years of war, there is no reason to believe that more money and more troops will markedly improve the Salvadorean government's chances of winning this war. After all, it already has received virtually all the money that it has asked for, spending over $2 million for each dead guerrilla. A quick summary shows that at the peak of their strength in late 1980, the guerrillas of the Farabundo Martí National Liberation Front (FMLN) numbered no more than 10,000 combatants. The $5 million worth of emergency military aid that the Carter administration authorized in its final days in office enabled the Salvadorean armed forces to stymie what the guerrillas had heralded as their "final offensive." By 1981, estimates indicated that if the Salvadorean armed forces could only double their own strength to 24,000 they could control the insurgency. The guerrillas still numbered 10,000, but some estimates put them at 12,000.

Likewise, by 1982, it was said that if the Salvadorean armed forces were equipped with sophisticated weaponry such as A-37 fighter bombers, the insurgency could be quelled. The guerrillas still totaled only 10,000 to 12,000. By 1983, it was said that if the Salvadorean military doubled their troop strength to 40,000 for a force ratio of 4:1, they would be able to keep the insurgency in check. The guerrillas still only numbered 10,000 to 12,000. By 1984, it was said that if the Salvadorean armed forces could achieve rapid air mobility with an expanded helicopter fleet and with close air support provided by gunships, the insurgency could be curbed. The guerrillas still numbered 10,000 to 12,000. By 1985, estimates were that if the Salvadorean armed forces could expand to 50,000 for a force ratio of 5:1, the insurgency could be controlled. In 1987, the Salvadorean armed forces number 55,000 strong.

The guerrillas operate at a tremendous military disadvantage. They have no close air support and no rapid air mobility, moving instead by foot like soldiers during the American Civil War. They have no indirect fire support except weapons such as hand-carried 90 mm recoilless rifles and 81 mm mortars. They have little support from the peasants, who either have been driven off their land by massive search-and-destroy maneuvers such as Operation Phoenix in Guazapa or because their hearts and minds have been wooed by government largesse such as free haircuts, dresses, and rice. The guerrillas have obtained their weapons via land routes from Honduras (closed off by thousands of Contras), via sea routes in the Gulf of Fonseca (sealed off by heavily armed navy patrol vessels) and via air routes (closely monitored by CIA overflights). Their ranks have been reduced by half, according to State Department estimates.

Despite these disadvantages, in each of the last two years they appear to have inflicted 20 percent more casualties than the year before. I am not talking about the exaggerated claims made by the guerrillas, but rather indications by Armed Forces Chief of Staff Blandón and other military sources. Similar estimates for 1985 showed an increase of almost 20 percent over 1984 losses. These statistics do not depict a guerrilla force on the verge of defeat.

Tactically, although it has been outspent, outgunned and outnumbered, the FMLN has shown remarkable resilience. For example, in 1984 the guerrillas were fighting in battalion-size units and defending large fixed positions such as Guazapa, giving the conflict many characteristics of a conventional war. Then, the government stepped up the air war and started conducting prolonged search-and-destroy operations. This had two consequences. First, it forced a significant portion of the guerrillas' civilian supporters to flee to the cities. Contrary to public opinion, in El Salvador there is very little jungle; the people are the jungle in which the guerrillas take refuge. Ironically, in purging these people from the rebels' northern strongholds of Chalatenango, Cuscatlán, Cabañas and Morazán, government forces have spread this conflict to all parts of the country.

Second, the guerrillas responded to the significant escalation of the war simply by changing the terms of military engagement. No longer able or constrained to defend territory, the battalion-size units of 1,000 combatants were divided into fifty units of twenty guerrillas each. The insurgents also began the extensive use of mines—or what they called "meeting high technology with low technology"—with devastating effect on the Salvadorean military. The guerrillas would survey a scene of confrontation to determine the likely sites where soldiers would take cover when receiving hostile fire and mine them. A few guerrillas would thus engage a much larger military force.

During Operation Phoenix, an almost year-long confrontation on the Guazapa volcano, military sources indicate there were 397 government soldiers wounded by land mines alone. When I visited the military hospital in San Salvador last July, the surgeon general confirmed that there had already been more than 600 amputations since the beginning of the year. The Salvadorean military has a fierce and admirable loyalty to these crippled young men. It does not discharge them, but rather absorbs them back into their units where they learn new administrative or communication skills. In the barracks their presence serves as a constant and grim reminder of what may befall other soldiers, with predictable consequences on morale.

In a conflict in which the civilian casualties resulting from death squads, the air war, and military confrontations have dropped significantly, the guerrilla use of land mines has become another alarming source of morbidity and mortality. Contrary to what the U.S. State Department says, the military situation today holds little promise for either side and only continued suffering for the people of El Salvador.

In 1963, Bernard Fall wrote that there would be no light at the end of the tunnel in Vietnam as long as the "vaster political contest" remained subordinate to the armed conflict. The same is true in El Salvador today, where all civilian institutions are now subordinate to the military. An example of excessive military influence is the highly touted, comprehensive counterinsurgency campaign "United to Reconstruct" (Unidos Para Reconstruir or UPR), which was launched in mid-1986. The overall objective of the campaign is to neutralize civilian support for the guerrillas and to win active support for the armed forces and the government. Initiated and coordinated by the Salvadorean armed forces, UPR reflects their determination to control all relief, resettlement, and reconstruction activities.

The UPR campaign is heavily endorsed by United States military advisors and the Agency for International Development (AID). The current $16.4 million price tag, paid for with economic support funds (ESF) and

PL480 (Food for Peace) money, will quadruple next year, according to General Blandón. Decisions about what kind of activities to undertake, where and to whom aid should be provided, and how it is to be administered, are all based on military considerations. A key component calls for civil defense patrols. AID considers this "humanitarian assistance." But United States funding and endorsement of such a counterinsurgency campaign, which subordinates civilian ministers and private aid efforts to the prerogatives of the military high command, undermines civilian control over the armed forces.

Indeed, it is doubtful that AID really will control these funds. Douglas Blaufarb, the former CIA station chief in Saigon, commenting on the similar programs under his supervision in Vietnam, said: "All of this was done under the formal rubric of refugee emergency assistance and resettlement, and of rural development, in order to conform to AID categories of approved activity. In actual fact, it constituted the civilian front of an unconventional war which could not have been prosecuted without the aid program." He is describing the infamous CORDS program, one component of which was the assassination program known as "Phoenix." A heinous episode in history may be about to repeat itself.

The Catholic church and most Protestant churches have refused to participate in the UPR program, seeing it as primarily an effort to advance the military's war efforts. A recent *Miami Herald* article described the coercion that follows the subordination of humanitarian assistance to military priorities. In Jacoatique, a half-destroyed, weed-infested village in Morazán, emaciated farmers were quoted as saying that they live on the edge of starvation because Captain "Long Knife" García Grande intermittently refuses to permit the passage of supply trucks boasting, "We let them suffer a little to wake them up." Such military-supervised relief and reconstruction activities, which General Blandón described as "conquering the minds and will of the people," can hardly be construed as "development" as understood in the Foreign Assistance Act.

The Salvadorean armed forces also hold the judicial system hostage, blatantly blocking any prosecution of men within their own ranks who are suspected of committing human rights abuses. Despite testimony in 1982 by then-Assistant Secretary of State for Human Rights and Humanitarian Affairs Elliott Abrams, that "several hundred officers have been dismissed from the armed forces or jailed," and despite testimony by former Assistant Secretary of State for Inter-American Affairs Thomas Enders, that the Salvadorean military had "transferred, retired, cashiered, or punished a thousand officers and men for various abuses of authority," the truth is that no Salvadorean officer has ever been tried or convicted for a human rights abuse. Punishment has often meant a cushy posting as an embassy attache.

General Blandón once told me that he had lists of officers who had committed rapes, robberies, and even murders. Asked why he could not discipline the perpetrators, he explained that legally, he was obliged to turn them over to civilian judges for trial because the Uniform Code of Military Justice did not give him jurisdiction over crimes committed against civilians.

What about the judges? I asked the former attorney general, a Christian Democrat, why charges were dropped even in such cases as the massacre at Las Hojas, where there were numerous witnesses. He replied that judges who were not bought off were receiving death threats from those who had committed the crimes.

President José Napoleón Duarte has backed off, too. During his presidential campaign, Duarte pledged to bring to justice Colonel Araujo, whom the U.S. Embassy accused of ordering the murder of over seventy Indians at Las Hojas, and more recently, of pocketing $250,000 in an ammunition scam. His alleged partner is now serving a jail sentence in Virginia for the scam. Nevertheless, Duarte appointed the colonel to the board of the National Port Authority, a lucrative post. At least two other officers, Major Pozo and Lieutenant Colonel Moran, were included on the list of Salvadoreans involved in death squad activity that U.S. Vice President Bush took to El Salvador in 1983. They also received promotions.

Still another instance of the Salvadorean military's corruption of law enforcement is the case of Colonel Roberto Staben. A secret investigation headed by Colonel López-Nuila, Vice Minister of Public Security, uncovered a massive kidnapping ring run by several rightist army officers and businessmen who form the core of ultraconservative opposition to President Duarte. Despite strong evidence implicating him, including eyewitnesses, Colonel Staben has been allowed to resume his command. Other accused officers were warned in time to escape arrest.

Counterinsurgency succeeds only when it is combined with "nation-building," which means strengthening civilian institutions and controlling corruption and abuse. This simply is not happening in El Salvador. To the contrary, the military is extending its influence over key civilian institutions. The Reagan administration has requested funds for police aid to El Salvador but a recent study completed by the Unitarian Universalist Service Committee and the El Rescate Human Rights Department in Los Angeles documents continuing military authority over what should be civilian law enforcement operations, a complete breakdown of the Salvadorean judicial system, and brutal investigation and interrogation techniques which routinely involve torture. Without accountability to a strong civilian government, no amount of aid to the police will help "professionalize" it.

There is little pressure on the U.S. Congress to do anything about the seven-year-old war in El Salvador. Few constituents stand in congressional waiting rooms or district offices clamoring for a cut-off of aid or attaching conditions to it. Members of Congress who fought against aid to the Nicaraguan Contras have little energy or political capital left to expend on what undoubtedly would be a bitter fight with the Reagan administration if they tampered with its aid request for El Salvador.

Similarly, in El Salvador it is business as usual. An economic crisis is only simmering and a political crisis is yet far off. More importantly, for us, news of more killings in El Salvador has become banal, so banal that it is tempting to write off the country as just another Northern Ireland or Lebanon, the scenes of other fratricidal conflicts, where whole societies seem hopelessly bent on devouring themselves. After all, the reasoning goes, both sides perpetuate violence. Both sides claim to be fighting—and dying—for freedom. Each can cite the death toll of 62,000 as 62,000 vainglorious reasons to continue fighting.

This cynicism has no place in the debate about United States foreign policy towards El Salvador, particularly since the United States has funded one party to the conflict to the tune of over $2.5 billion. Members of Congress, as legislators, bear an especially heavy burden of responsibility for ending the war in El Salvador—the administration can be expected to act as it has in the past and continue to dissemble and prevaricate about the reality of what we are doing there. While there may not be a political, economic, or military crisis to deal with at the moment in El Salvador, there is a moral one. It is summed up in the question: Will Congress continue to vote aid to fuel a war for which the Reagan administration envisions no end? Pressure from Congress has worked before. Its effort to attach conditions to aid and its threat to cut off aid forced Vice President Bush to go to El Salvador and to confront government officials with a list of alleged death squad members.

But why take the risk? The trouble with those who actually do something with their moral choices is that they could, in the end, be proved wrong. It is safer to state ultimate principles and then allow the interested parties to apply them to the specific issue.

We must take the risk to confront the administration on its policy towards El Salvador. The continued killing, the absence of meaningful reform—and the Reagan administration's refusal to acknowledge this—are reasons enough. But more importantly, the significance of El Salvador far exceeds its size. We must challenge the wisdom of further aid to El Salvador because what is happening there is a metaphor for First and Third World relations. It is primarily a North-South, not an East-West struggle, one that is defined more by economics and hunger than by geopolitics.

When I left El Salvador in 1983, there were 10,000 civilians living on the slopes of the Guazapa volcano. Last spring, Salvadorean army commanders boasted that the area had finally been pacified. The only peace it knew was the peace of the dead, the "disappeared," or those that had finally fled. The government considered the peasants there subversives, terrorists, or communists. Most of them, however, would not know Marx, whether Groucho or Karl. Their struggle is not about ideology, so much as it is about a suitable standard of living and human dignity. Their existence has reached the point where their deaths had as little meaning as their lives.

When I worked in El Salvador, one *campesino*, puzzled by my commitment to nonviolence, told me:

You gringos are always worried about violence done by machine guns or machetes. I used to work on the finca over there and my job was to care for the dogs. I would put a bowl of meat or milk before them as I went to the fields, unable to feed my own children. I would take them to the veterinarian, while my own child died for lack of medical attention with a nod of sympathy from the landlord. If you do not come to understand the violence of the spirit that comes from helplessly watching your children starve to death, you will never understand nonviolence or violence.

By this time tomorrow, 40,000 more children will have died of malnutrition-related causes in the Third World. In places like South Africa, the Philippines, and El Salvador their parents will pick up rifles and fire them at multimillion dollar jets. If we continue to watch them and wonder where they get their rifles, instead of understanding the desperation that would lead them to such an act, then we will remain the "911" (the police telephone number for emergencies) for repressive regimes that cry "Communism!" when their privilege or status is threatened. We must understand that there is nothing inherently attractive about communism except that it offers hope to those who are desperate.

President Ronald Reagan has said that if it were not for the Soviets, there would not be any hot spots in the Third World. Consequently, the Reagan doctrine sees places like El Salvador as an arena for East-West confrontation; the aspirations of its people have no context. The United States will not allow a negotiated settlement in El Salvador for fear that it might signal that we lack resolve. The Salvadorean people sent a stronger message to the contrary when they responded to President Duarte's campaign pledge of a dialogue that could lead to peace by giving the Christian Democratic Party an absolute majority in the National Assembly.

There was a similar protracted and polarized violent civil war in Rhodesia in the late 1970s. There too, elections were held and democracy proclaimed, but the insurgents refused to put down their arms because meaningful political participation was impossible. The fifteen-year bloody conflict of Marxists versus capitalists and black versus white eventually came to an end through dialogue. Rhodesia became Zimbabwe with ballots rather than bullets. This did not occur until Great Britain, the dominant regional power, brokered a negotiated settlement that ensured the safety of all participants in the political process.

What prevents a similar solution in El Salvador is the lack of will on the part of the dominant regional power—the United States. El Salvador is desperate for our help. We must honestly ask the question: Is the United States using all the leverage that $2.5 billion in aid buys to end this conflict?

NOTE

1. This analysis, including data and quotations, is based on Charles Clements' testimony on April 21, 1987, to the Subcommittee on Foreign Operations of the Committee on Appropriations, U.S. House of Representatives.

PART III
CHANGE

11

New Social Movements in Central America: Perspectives on Democratic Social Transformations

James Petras

The most significant and least understood political development in Latin America over the past decade and a half has been the growth of a wide range of autonomous social movements. These movements represent a distinct departure from previous political patterns in the region in several crucial aspects.

1. The new social movements exist outside of the control of the party-parliamentary-electoral-state framework which has previously dominated popular mobilizations. They embody the democratic practice around which the future society they envision will be organized. The movements are a means and an end. In contrast, party-electoral mobilizations or movements have been subordinated (or became means) to securing political office for upwardly mobile professionals, to strengthening the bargaining position of party professionals, to gaining access to state patronage for would-be and existing entrepreneurs, etc. Traditionally such political movements were levers for alien ends.

2. The new social movements are led by rank and file leaders who are tied to the day-to-day struggle of the organization, who are directly controlled by popular assemblies or other forms of direct controls. While they may or may not have charisma, their leadership depends on their qualities to organize and articulate their deep-felt interests—not to mystify their followers through brilliant rhetorical but vacuous flourishes. These leaders are not middle-class lawyers, building a base for future careers in Parliament, using their legal skills and work among the "downtrodden" as a trampoline for an illustrious ministerial position. The leaders of the new social movements follow a different career path: they share the life-style and standard of living of their members—are

often jailed, beaten, and not infrequently, the most obvious target of death squads. Unlike the career-building professionals, international campaigns are seldom organized when leaders of these new social movements are arrested, kidnapped or disappear. These grass-roots leaders are best known by their constituents; they usually do not get invited to deliver papers at international conferences.

3. The movements embrace a vast constituency, they proliferate throughout the country, and they politicize and activate their membership on a continuous basis on the issues of most concern to their members: their educational programs pivot around a discussion of the relationship between everyday squalor, state violence, and the class character of the state. The new social movements collectively have become the "street parliaments" of all those groups outside of official politics. They meet in houses, neighborhoods, street corners, run-down theatres, soccer fields, parks, squatter land sites, construction building lots, in and around popular markets. They place a premium on providing an open arena for exchanging views without the mediation of party, state, university, professional or religious hierarchs.

4. The structure and organization of the new social movements are profoundly democratic, an *ongoing* democracy that continuously raises new, or revises old, issues. They respond to state and elite violence— assaults and assassinations—with renewed mobilizations. Solidarity neutralizes state intimidation. The organizational tasks are performed, duplicated, or triplicated by a multiplicity of self-mobilized militants as jailings, killings, flight, clandestinity, and decisions to opt for other forms of struggle (guerrilla or electoral) lead to constant turnover. The great majority of the rank and file continue the struggle. The process of direct participation, of ongoing discussion, and lateral alliances with other movements that share common conditions and pursue similar goals converge to deepen the level of politicization and commitment to unprecedented levels.

5. These new movements have spread from one sector of the economy to another, from productive activity to distributive, from economic to social life, from older neighborhoods to improvised housing sites, from factories to sidewalks. As the message of the movement spreads, it envelops layers of society never before organized by the traditional left parties—the bootblacks, the laundresses, the lottery sellers join in mass demonstrations that fill the largest plazas of the capital to overflowing— plazas that often become the sites of midday massacres: emptied by machine guns and left with bloody cobblestones and abandoned shoes.

6. The proliferation of the movements and their capacity to extend and link the most oppressed and occupationally diverse population is based on the existence of a vast army of informal "opinion leaders": self-educated, articulate, and outspoken working people. The washerwoman

at the stream who exposes the exorbitant prices that belie the demagoguery of United States-educated civilian presidents—the same presidents that deny the complicity of the military with the death squads; the squatter settler who organizes the homeless to occupy speculator-owned terrain; the unemployed teenagers protecting their neighborhoods from state violence, seizing the tear gas canisters and hurling them back at the police; the mother who leads other mothers to break the state curfews to obtain bread for crying children—baring her breast, defiantly challenging peasant soldiers to shoot or ignore the curfew. These are the daily "discourses" of the movement people engaged in class struggle on the ground. They give concrete expression to the idea that each member is an organizer, the secret of the success of the new social movements. Self-mobilization is what nourishes their capacity to sustain struggle against the death squads and disappearances, their capacity to regroup after bloody massacres and to take the streets once more. During the past decade and a half we have witnessed the great crimes of our time—the orgy of state violence that has been unleashed against these same social movements. Mass terror has become the norm of state behavior from Chile to Guatemala. Washington and its clients are engaged in a war to exterminate these newest and most profound challenges to their domination. Against the comprehensive participatory movements they use the unrestrained violence of total warfare. The very scope and depth of the social movements are the measure of state violence. Directed against the populist chieftains of the past, the dead numbered in scores, the jailed and exiled in the hundreds. The rest, the populist clientele, were told to "return to their shacks, the carnival was over." With the new social movements the "chieftains" number in the tens of thousands, the program of struggle is in the minds of millions, the families, neighborhoods, churches, villages. As a consequence whole villages are burned, families assassinated, by the besieged state—security doctrine dictates that they are all subversives.

SOCIAL MOVEMENTS: FROM THE 1970S TO THE PRESENT

The 1970s was the decade of the new social movements. Though inordinate attention was paid to the regimes which presided during the growth of the movements, it was the movements themselves which represented the real break with the self-perpetuating cycle of alternating elite power—reformist, reactionary, or even radical. It was the movements that carried the left parties to power. In Chile, under Allende it was the social movements that broke new ground, opening up alternatives to private/public ownership with new forms of self-management of industry. The movements challenged the resistance of the speculators

and wholesalers by organizing new distribution networks. Industrial belts
(not the parties, ministers or trade union executives) broke the employers'
boycott by taking over thousands of plants. New social movements created parallel structures of authority in the municipalities, while the traditional parties were negotiating cabinet positions with their future grave-
diggers in the military.

In Guatemala, El Salvador and Nicaragua, the seventies witnessed the
unprecedented growth of autonomous social movements on a massive
scale. In the highland Indian communities of Guatemala, tens of thousands of women and men formed unions and cooperatives, organized
marches, politicized households, villages, regions—and converged on
the capital city. They joined artisans, slum dwellers, Christian base communities. In 1978, Guatemala City witnessed the biggest demonstration
in its history: over a quarter of a million people demanded democracy,
land reform and national sovereignty. All the parties, trade unions, per-
sonalities, vanguard and rear-guard leaderships were dwarfed. The people marched and spoke for themselves. For that crime, over 50,000 were
murdered in the next eight years, and the elections have not stopped
the state killing machine. Nor can the people forget. Unable to speak
with their own voice, they voted for the Christian Democratic politician
Cerezo—a 70 percent landslide against the terror. They are awaiting an
opening for the social movements to rise again massively. That is a cer-
tainty.

In El Salvador, over 250,000 people demonstrated in 1980—the coming
together of scores of movements from all over the country, Christian
peasant communities, trade unions, school teachers. This was the culmination of a decade of grass roots organizing that dominated Salvadorean political life in a way that the Christian Democrat, Social Democratic and Communist parties never had and never would. From the
mountain villages to the back alleys of overcrowded slums and markets
the movements formed, dominated the streets, and threatened to take
the palaces of injustice and the ministers of violence. Sixty thousand
were killed over the next five years to empty the streets of the social
movements. Close to a million were driven into refugee camps, exiled,
or crowded into city slums. Fifteen thousand joined the guerrillas. Neither napalm bombings nor death squads nor U.S. helicopter gunships
nor Duarte's demagogy has succeeded: in 1986, fifty thousand persons
marched in San Salvador, attacking the state, its war and its economic
policies. In 1986, trade union unification brought together 500,000 working people. The movements began to fill the streets again.

Nicaragua is the country par excellence of the social movements: one
of them, the Sandinistas, took state power. The trade union leaderships
were negotiating collective bargaining agreements with Somoza's partners. The Christian Democrats were following the protest led by the

bourgeoisie, petitioning Somoza to resign. The Communist Party was denouncing Somoza and attacking the Sandinistas as adventurers . . . and plying their "democratic slogans" in alliance with the Christian Democrats and the employers. The driving force of the Nicaraguan Revolution was the social movements in the towns, cities and villages, and among the aggressive street fighters who never found a job, the teenagers, the self-employed artisans in Monimbó, Estelí, León. The movements set the terms for the shopkeepers, workers, and business people to join the struggle.

THEORETICAL REFLECTIONS ON THE ASCENDANCY OF SOCIAL MOVEMENTS

What accounts for the growing importance of the social movements in shaping Latin American political life? The most obvious answer is the inadequacy of existing political organizations. Neither so-called "corporatist" structures, nor political parties, nor "interest groups" or trade unions have been capable of responding to increasing participation and involvement of broad sectors of the population. Related to this growing mass involvement was the rapid and comprehensive structural, demographic and economic changes that were taking place in Latin America. The structural changes and ensuing new attitudes did not "fit" with the preexisting style of politics. The programs of the existing parties, their structures and mode of action did not attract and engage the emerging new social forces. The third factor influencing the growth of the social movements was the political changes within these new social constituencies—their experiences, political education, and ties to new political actors and approaches—which propelled them toward new forms of "movement politics" and away from traditional party, electoral, and state-client politics. The interaction of rapid structural and demographic changes, unresponsive political organizations and new forms of political education and practice converged to engender the "movement phenomena." If we were to sort out the political and social experiences of Latin America, with specific reference to Central America, over the past two decades, the most striking feature is the degree to which social changes and institutional innovations which further the interests of the populace have been a product of the activities of the social movements.

On the other hand, the great bulk of those policies and institutions that have adversely affected the populace have been the result of military tyrants, foreign and domestic bankers, *caudillos*, presidents, technocrats and political ideologies of the market place. Through prisons or death squads, through executive orders and legislative measures, they have commanded reductions in the standard of living. Liberals and conservatives, reformers and democrats, dictators and populists have allowed the invisible hand to gracefully fatten the investors' bank accounts. The ideologies vary—from liberal to social democracy, authoritarianism to capitalism—but the results are consistent. Against these institutional forces, the social movements emerged as the only force capable of creating new forms of popular participation against the cycles of disintegrating populism and elite dominance. The social movements, charged by the energies of their newly aroused constituencies, refused to be harnessed to the existing populist electoral machines, to be educated by the orthodox left on the virtues of a prolonged apprenticeship under the direction of the progressive democratic bourgeoisie. Nor did the social movements heed the advice of the ex-leftists of the sixties who, having thrown in their lot with the postmilitary civilian regimes, counselled austerity and realism and who condemned any popular movement or protest from below as a provocation and threat to . . . democracy. These intellectuals in retreat celebrated their newly attained individual freedoms by absolving the democratic regimes for all their savage attacks on living standards, their outrageous transfer of income from the poor to the foreign debt holders, their de facto grants of immunity for the torturers and generals in the name of realism and normality. These regime provocations to the conscience of the people isolated the intellectual apologists of the compromised democracy from the burgeoning social movements. The elections have not ended the social movements, they reemerged as it became clear that the civilian regimes were continuing the same basic socioeconomic policies as the dictatorship—relying on the same torturers and kidnappers to enforce the new democratic and sovereign subordination to the banks.

The continued bankruptcy of institutionalized politics, its incapacity to provide the channels to activate the populace, to engage them in a struggle to rupture relations with their repressive state and exploitative bankers, has created enormous political space on the left—which is being filled by the social movements.

The movements are not tied to a static concept of democracy based on alliances between professional politicians and the military, backed by the State Department, alliances that empty the state coffers to fill the overseas bank accounts of fleeing investors.

The abandonment of the political space of active popular mobilization is also clearly visible among the parties and trade unions of the left and populist groups. For them the populace is a source of recruitment for votes and electoral campaigns—to fill plazas, to listen to speeches, to act according to the discipline and logic which fit the current dialogues and alliances with the titular democratic regimes (who in turn consult with the military and the International Monetary Fund before deciding any consequential issue).

Even some of the guerrilla groups cannibalize the movements, recruiting militants and waiting for the struggle to move to a "higher stage"—toward an elite, centralized, military formation. This is a step backward from the autonomous democratic mass movements with their open assemblies. The military struggle is an extension of this collective action, not its replacement by an elite military vanguard. In Nicaragua, the proliferation of insurrections in the cities and towns grew out of the mass movements and represented a continuation of its democratic politics through military means.

The immobilism of the traditional party-state form of political activity came into conflict with the existence of new forms of political education: the idea of popular empowerment based on the dialectics of Christian and secular base community organizing and everyday experience. The political generation of the 1970s—those between the ages of fifteen and twenty-five—were sandwiched between political structures that offered mostly rhetoric, elections, and defeats before the military onslaught and catastrophic deterioration of economic conditions. They had no escape in the foreseeable future. The movements were able to attract all those forces—in most cases the overwhelming majorities of the urban and rural poor—by engaging them in daily struggles, open discussions, assemblies, and in the street movements. The flexible format and political openness of the movements best suited the concrete struggles and advanced consciousness of the urban poor. The intensity and drive of the movements reflected the direct style of participation and the close identity between the social class of the member, the leadership and the rest of the activists: solidarity is born of common conditions, shared experiences and self-mobilizing struggles. It is this combination which has sparked the rebirth of open and democratic currents within the masses of Central America, and which will continue to play a major role in the reshaping of that troubled region. Their organizational level is excellent (for every leader killed there appear several more), and their commitment is unquestionable. They represent an increasingly important political factor in the development of Central America.

12
Liberation Theology as a Force for Change

Blase Bonpane

These observations are based on many years of experience as a Maryknoll priest in Guatemala, from where I was expelled when I began to denounce the horrific realities of life and death there. In Guatemala when the poor attempt to organize, they are called communists. Many people whom I served as a priest in Guatemala died because they were called communists. I once asked a death squad leader why one of our most promising students had been selected for torture and death. "Because he is a communist," was the reply. When asked how that was determined, I received a second answer: "We heard him say he would give his life for the poor." According to these standards, Jesus is a communist in Guatemala. We cannot say the Lord's Prayer and fail to do the will of God on earth. In Guatemala today, a new person is being formed. This new, revolutionary person insists that human values be applied to government. This leads to a ruthless reaction from government. Important freedoms are lost, and undesirable "freedoms" are acquired. Children should not be free to die of malnutrition. No one should be free to die of polio or malaria. Women should not be free to be prostitutes. No one should be free to be illiterate. The loss of these "freedoms" is essential for a people to make their own history. An important tool in bringing these changes about is the theology of liberation—the kind of theology that made the early Church an immediate threat to the Roman Empire.

That form of theology, by its very essence, is confrontational—if it is to be true to its calling of liberation. Take, for instance, the issue of violence in Central America. Do we create violence by virtue of a parlor game in which we say: "those in favor of violence sit on this side and those opposed to it on that side, and we will now discuss whether we want violence or not?" We could do the same thing with disease, and say all those in favor of disease on the planet stay here; those opposed to disease go there. In doing so, however, we don't discuss whether there *is* disease, because clearly it exists. What we discuss is how to deal with it, and some of the logic we get—especially from church sources— often evades the central issue, asking us not to talk about violence, because violence is evil. One could pursue this line of reasoning, asking people not to become doctors, because disease is evil.

We acknowledge that there is disease and violence on the planet, and we ask: what are we going to do about it? Forty thousand people died today of violence, principally by starvation. We should note that they died in places that have freedom of the press. Ironically, many of them couldn't read. Most of them would have enjoyed the freedom of the press—if they had owned the printing press. In light of these facts, we can appreciate the great many myths about what democracy is, or isn't. Democracy enshrines the right to be free of the violence of starvation, and that right is an important one. Liberation theology in Central America needs to state this clearly and unequivocally—despite the confrontation (and church censure from certain quarters) that will result. To avoid one's responsibility in so stating is to be a poor Christian.

"Sharing" is a central theme of liberation theology. The very term "liberation theology" is really only what most of us learn to appreciate by living with the poor. We attempt to explain our understanding through orthodox theology; it's an attempt at honest theology. I learned it by experience, by being called into the Cardinal's office in Guatemala City where Cardinal Casariego told me to stop my students from getting involved in politics. I delivered that message to the students at the University of San Carlos. After some discussion, the consensus of the students was to request that I, in turn, advise the Archbishop that he was abusing his position in the hierarchy, and should himself stay out of politics. It is extremely important to see this, because liberation opens the dialogue. No more monologue from any entity. No monologue from the hierarchy. No monologue from political figures. No monologue from authority figures, but rather a dialogic future—communication.

Democracy springs, then, from this cultural context of liberation theology: we're thinking of Jesus saying, "where two or three are gathered in my name, I will be there, in the midst of them, and bless them." And people have been gathering that way in Latin America now for some time, forming their small communities to reflect together, to make decisions together, to pledge their lives together, to come to some clear theological conclusions together, and to integrate their spiritual and political lives. In Chaletenango, in El Salvador, the political unit of governments is actually the base community. As the FMLN began to gain ground, they didn't want to structure a whole new political entity in that area, so they asked the *campesinos* through their base communities to keep law and order.

Liberation theology is also nonsectarian, embracing people of all faiths, and encouraging them to work together for the well-being of all. It doesn't necessarily respect titles, somewhat like the theology of Michelangelo who painted the Sistine Chapel. He painted and painted—and when the scaffolding was removed, to the surprise of many, it revealed popes in hell, bishops in hell! It was very strong theology, very clear theology, telling powerful people that their titles were meaningless, that their hierarchy would not save them. What mattered was their conduct—not their rank.

A personal experience taught me the value of this blend of democracy and dialogue. It was in Quiché and the students were assigning various priests and sisters to different parts of that Indian area. I was supposed to be in charge there, and in my hierarchical way resented their arranging everything. However, the students knew the area. I had no confidence about what was what in Quiché, and if I had assigned tasks in a hierarchical fashion I would have made assignments and I could have killed somebody because I didn't know the Indian areas as well as the students did. Liberation theology demands, then, dialogue and cooperation.

Liberation theology is also extremely transcendental in the sense of saying: "Yes, we are theists—we want to relate in some way to God, we are believers." It is conservative theology. It is not a European type of theology which attempts to theologize about God by dealing with the Creed, by spending twenty years discussing the virginity or nonvirginity of Mary. The focus is not on trying to dissect the Holy Trinity, but rather on the conduct demanded of us at this time, with the imperatives that are all around us. Theology is not private enterprise. It is not God and myself. It is a collective enterprise. It is a matter of identifying with one another as members of the same family, and of identifying the common good.

Unlike its orthodox equivalent, liberation theology is quite prepared to make value judgments. We don't want to be humanoids any longer, we want to be human beings. We will continue making decisions, and we will make mistakes, but we will make value judgments about everything—about the tax system, about the refugee system, about the military, about everything we do every day. Why? Because that's a mark of an educated human being, to be able to say what one likes and what one doesn't like. It is also a form of theology which encourages people to form an opinion: we have to have an opinion. What do you think about the rape of Central America? If you don't have an opinion, you need to get an opinion, and make value judgments. That's part of this theology.

The theology of liberation contrasts with what can be called the "theology of empire." What does empire want of people? It wants first and foremost, nonaction. It wants people to do nothing. It wants conformity. It wants people to let some authority figure make decisions. It wants to pacify everybody. Much of theology has been oriented toward pacification. First and foremost, the wholesaling of guilt ("You are very evil"), to be compensated for gradually by the retailing of forgiveness, very slowly. This accompanies the skillfully crafted sermons heard in most of our churches: first of all perfect yourselves, then someday you'll be able to change someone else. So, we don't do anything today because we're not perfect yet, and the same is true for tomorrow, and so on. By waiting until we are perfect before doing anything, inaction goes on forever.

Liberation theology, on the other hand, maintains that people are on this earth to make history. They are not here as spectators at a football game; they are here to participate in the football game. The future created will depend on each of us. We are co-creators with the Almighty. The creative force of God is with us.

When we go out to evangelize, we bring good news to the poor. The good news includes democracy, a democracy that, first and foremost, means the right to eat. That right is beautifully crafted into the new Nicaraguan Constitution, together with the right to a job, a decent house, free medical care, and free education. It's incredible what poor countries can do. Why can't the United States do the same?

Liberation theology knows that God is on the side of justice and when injustice is done, that is un-Godly. We know that God is on the side of peace. We know what side God is on and we can make the necessary judgments. Don't fall into the liberal trap, saying both sides are the same. No, they are not the same. I have been observing the Central American revolution in one form or another for some twenty-five years. The two sides have nothing in common. They are not the same at all. One side works for the children of Central America. The other side practices rape and torture and summary execution. Look at them, and learn to discern.

Liberation theology is diametrically opposed to the trend known as "fundamentalism," because fundamentalism believes that humanism has nothing to do with Christianity. Liberation theology enters into the hopes, desires and anxieties of a people, wherever that may lead. This requires being incarnational, it requires a juncture. Liberation theology encourages the cooperation of atheist and theist alike, coming together with common goals and common objectives. On the other hand, a religion that tries to condemn what it thinks is secular humanism in books winds up being both anti-intellectual and fundamentalist. It is often headed by very dangerous people who are filled with hatred because they claim to have *the* truth ("We know the truth and any outside of us are the unsaved; what we have to do ultimately is to kill them. We must kill them. We really have to kill the Nicaraguans because they don't have freedom of the press, so we must kill them. We have to kill people, because they are communist people and they are witches and we must kill. . . .") This is the game of tag and kill—a game played throughout history.

The Golden Rule stipulates that we treat others the way we want to be treated. The Golden Rule also applies between countries. Do I want to be interfered with? If I think that Canada should not be interfered with, then I think that Canada should not interfere with someone else. And that applies to empires as well. There's a growth in spiritual life that goes even further than this relationship because of its involvement in faith and in scriptural reading; and that is, not only do we treat others the way we want to be treated, but we believe in a very mysterious way, that our only relationship to God is through our brothers and sisters. *That* is our only relationship. There is no other gauge. There is no other measure. We can go to a much higher level, which is sometimes called "the illuminative way," which means that God begins to enlighten the soul when we accept the fact that our relationship to other people, individually and collectively, is precisely and distinctly our relationship to God. That's a very high level to reach. It does not accept anyone who demonizes the communists. You either relate to others as you relate to God, or you don't, but you have to choose.

The illuminative way is possible; and that illumination can be brought into our theology; it can be brought into our political perspective, which never includes fostering or making an institutional church rich. Institutional churches do not need to be rich; they don't need buildings. Jesus was never seen promoting the building of churches, nor did He travel around promoting church attendance terribly much. We should therefore ask ourselves: should we build the church as we know it as an institution, or should we build the kingdom? The answer, of course, should be to build the kingdom. Let's build clear signs of peace. In the United States, where has the kingdom been? It's been in the streets, in the civil rights movement, in the peace movement: these are movements whose people have been crucified. Look at the example embodied in the assassination/crucifixion of Martin Luther King. He opposed the Indo-China war, twenty years ago, and he said that our country was on the wrong side of these revolutions. We should be with these revolutions around the world, he claimed—and he was right.

For liberation theologians, the New Testament is much more meaningful in our times. We should not allow any institutions—including the churches—to oppress or to enslave. We should not allow them to instruct us about what to do with our conscience. The individual has to make those decisions. To do that, we must free ourselves from the stifling bureaucratic side of organized religion; we can then become free persons and participate in some of the rites that we loved, and appreciate them more than ever. In Guatemala I decided one day, after baptizing a few scraggly-looking babies, near Chichicastenango, not to baptize any more hungry babies. Before anything else, these children needed vaccinations. After that they needed to be assured of food, and after they looked healthy, and were healthy, then we could talk about baptism. Until then it would simply be an empty exercise.

Liberation theology is divisive, pitting friends and relatives against each other. Far from being unhealthy, though, these divisions are absolutely essential: they were essential for Martin Luther; they are essential now. You have to decide who represents the truth—someone who speaks in the name of power from the episcopacy or a few peasants who gathered together to read the Gospel. Was the former Archbishop of Managua who defended the Somozas because "all authority comes from God" to be believed, or the *muchachos* who fought against *somocismo*? Revolution really begins the moment people read and discuss the Gospel and come to decisions on what they are going to do about their lives.

In the case of Central America, liberation theology, the struggle for peace and social justice—what many understand as the revolution—exists to help bring about the Kingdom of God. We can achieve this goal. It's not simply a matter of the glorification of a specific political struggle, but rather of saying that people have the *right* to that specific political struggle, and of our seeking to understand—selflessly and objectively— their goals. As Christians, though, we need to stop simply thinking of our personal sins, of being shocked by four-letter words and not nuclear missiles. We have to define what sin is, and we have to identify the real sins. A real sin is the fact that 40,000 children died today who did not have to die—that's a sin. The real sin is that there are diseases that are tolerated in El Salvador, while hundreds of millions of dollars are spent in military aid. That is a crime. As we begin to attack the visible real devils of the world we live in (and not the false ones our governments, the media, and the churches present before us), we'll discontinue the practice of reciting silly little personal peccadillos to the clergy—and become more holy in the process.

13

The Sanctuary Movement
in the United States

Mary Ann Lundy

The Sanctuary movement in the United States began in 1982 as a service to the refugees, a movement to help people who were coming into this country in great numbers, particularly in the southwest. Its goal was to respond to the mass deportation of refugees after they had been put into detention centers. At that time, most refugees were Salvadoreans, who were placed in detention centres largely without legal counsel and were then sent back to El Salvador. The first members of the movement to oppose this policy happened to be from religious groups—Presbyterians, Methodists, United Church of Christ, a Jewish congregation, and Quakers. They began to understand that the whole border in the southwest was a series of detention centers, and that most Americans didn't realize it. They began to try, particularly in Tucson—a city close to the Mexican border—to prepare bonds for refugees and to bail them out.

The U.S. government has asked why the Sanctuary movement didn't *start* by pursuing legal avenues. The answer is that Sanctuary did precisely that. Sanctuary members said, "Let's get these people bonded out, and get them to apply for asylum." Community groups raised about $850,000 the first year and a half, bonded out refugees, and then tried to get them into the process of applying for asylum. When they went to the immigration offices, however, they discovered that these were never open the same hours, never open five days a week, let alone on the weekend. Sometimes the offices would open for only two hours a day, maybe from 2:00 to 5:00 on one afternoon, and from 9:00 to 10:00 on the next day. Sanctuary members began to realize that not only was there substance to the charge that refugees who applied didn't get asylum, but also that U.S. immigration officials simply didn't want them to apply for asylum.

The religious communities began to ask questions, build coalitions, and raise concern about basic issues. What happens, for example, when refugees are sent back? What else can we do? We seem to be trying to stop the flow of blood, but we don't seem to be asking about the root cause of the exiles' presence in North America. The Sanctuary movement sprang from coalitions of religious people deciding that they couldn't simply keep trying to deal with the end results. We had to ask: "what is happening that is making this influx of refugees grow greater and greater in our area?"

Our members came to realize that the ancient religious right of sanctuary was one of the answers to the plight of the refugees. The idea was that refugees could come into religious communities for protection, into a community of support. The community would agree to house them and they, in turn, would agree to be open in speaking about their lives. Telling your story, the story of your life, thus became the theme of the Sanctuary movement. The refugees would agree to be visible—a very, very high risk for them. Hundreds of thousands of refugees, of course, are in North America and have become absorbed into our communities. One of the things that we didn't realize was that indeed the world would hear and the Sanctuary movement would grow.

My own involvement in Minneapolis began when my husband's church was considering becoming a Sanctuary church. John Fythe, one of the ministers in the southwest, came to us and spoke about the movement. At that point, there were six Sanctuary groups, and John asked us if we would consider taking in a refugee. We debated the issue, and decided to help. All of a sudden we got a phone call and were told that we had a refugee; he had to leave the southwest, and Minneapolis seemed a good place because nobody would look for Central Americans there. What has happened since is a marvelous story of one congregation of 400 people being very involved in saving the lives of Central American refugees. Put quite simply, a coalition was born in Minneapolis and it's been duplicated in cities all over the United States.

New communities—or new reformations in communities, if you will—have emerged. What happened to us through giving this service, to use the religious term, is that we were saved—and that's been true all over the United States. The church is alive and very, very well in these communities, because we learned what it means to be a community. We learned what it means to be a community in the midst of persecution and death, and we learned what it is to be faithful at a time when faith is in short supply. And the marvelous part of the Sanctuary movement is that it's a phenomenon of middle America, the middle-aged, middle-spread mainstream of society—people like me who have been very much involved in learning about the situation.

My own "case history" illustrates clearly this learning process. For my actions I received five subpoenas to force me to testify in Arizona against church coworkers who had helped refugees. At the pretrial hearings, and when the trial opened, the U.S. government tried to paint a picture of the Sanctuary movement as left wing, "leftover people" who really were on the fringe of America. That picture quickly fell flat on its face. They also tried to portray Sanctuary as a three-tier movement with generals at the top, colonels in the next rank (those happened to be mostly nuns), and sergeants at the base. We came from small towns in Iowa and Missouri—hardly the hotbeds of revolution. That has been one of the amazing and marvelous things of the Sanctuary movement, for people respond when they are told about the reality of Central America. When the issue becomes a person and when you understand that it means life and death, the debate ends.

The Sanctuary movement in the United States has grown until it now includes about 380 churches, true communities of faith. One must also remember that when a congregation declares sanctuary in any of these communities, then at least sixty other groups endorse the action by voting to support that congregation, increasing by at least sixty the number of communities. What results are new coalitions of justice and religious groups that take a prophetic stand in the face of an unjust law. We started somewhat late—using techniques employed by the "underground railroad" of the U.S. Civil War—but thank God we are spreading like wildfire, and will continue to spread.

14
Four Themes and
an Irony

Walter LaFeber

A number of general themes, somewhat resembling a streak of red sur-
gical thread running through torn flesh, tie together the 150-year relations
between Central America and the United States. One of these themes
is a *dependency* relationship between Central Americans and North
Americans, a dependency that appeared so emphatically that El Salvador
seriously considered applying to Washington for statehood in the mid-
nineteenth century. Some 130 years later, El Salvador is so dependent
on U.S. economic aid that if this "fix" were removed, the once proud
and internally controlled Salvadorean economy would collapse overnight.

A second theme can be termed *neodependency*, that is, the historic ea-
gerness of U.S. officials to use military force directly on a Central American nation whenever it tries to break the dependency relationship or in
other ways move out of Washington's orbit. Such military intervention
began in the nineteenth century, accelerated during Theodore Roosevelt's
and Woodrow Wilson's presidential terms, and reached an historic peak
under Ronald Reagan. More than any of his thirty-nine predecessors in
the Executive Mansion, Reagan has been willing to use military power
to maintain what remains of the United States domination of the Central
American region. Neodependency has meant substituting direct force
to continue that domination after the usual dependency controls of cultural, political, and, especially, economic levers have lost their prowess.
The sources of U.S. neodependency policy are varied, but most instruc-
tive. They include the historic preference of North Americans for using
force instead of having to become involved in political compromises,
and also a preference for unilateral, military action instead of multilateral,
regional negotiations—particularly in a region Washington officials have

long considered their "backyard." North Americans are never more isolationist than when they go abroad alone to kill other peoples.

A third general theme has been Washington's stern opposition to revolution. This theme appeared relatively late. The Monroe Doctrine of 1823, contrary to what the Reagan administration has asserted, welcomed Latin American revolutions and pledged that the United States would not become involved in them. These were questions for Latin Americans, not North Americans, to decide, according to Monroe and his highly realistic Secretary of State, John Quincy Adams. By the 1890s, however, the Monroe-Adams approach had given way to a new policy that assumed Latin American revolutions ran counter to United States interests. This change is one of the (perhaps *the*) most important turns in the nation's diplomatic history. It long predated the appearance of communism in Russia, and it focused on the Caribbean-Central American region. The new antirevolutionary policy became apparent when the United States entered Cuba in 1898 not only to evict the rapidly crumbling Spanish empire, but also to stop an indigenous Cuban revolutionary movement. In Central America, the new policy most notably emerged in 1909–12 when President William Howard Taft dispatched troops to control change within Nicaragua. Taft's decision led to a twenty-year U.S. occupation of Nicaragua, and helped set a precedent for the interventions of Wilson, Coolidge, and Reagan.

Wilson added a vital dimension to the new policy by arguing that its ultimate objective was to teach Latin Americans how to become democrats. The result of the policy turn for Central Americans so far has been, with few exceptions, death and dictatorships, but democracy remains a talisman brandished by U.S. presidents whenever they employ military force. None of the nations of Central America—with the possible exception of Costa Rica—has been democratic (when measured by the standard criteria in a political science textbook). Nevertheless Washington has used "democracy" (on its own terms) as a true talisman—a device of irrational occult power warding off criticism of the militarily-enforced antirevolutionary policy.

A fourth theme might also be suggested, especially as the bicentennial of the United States Constitution is celebrated: that during the past century, U.S. intervention in Central America has increasingly been open to charges of unconstitutionality. Without exception, the questionable actions have been taken by the Executive branch of government. The sad but dangerous facts about the Reagan administration's actions uncovered in 1987 by the Tower Commission Report, the special House-Senate hearings on the Iran-Contra scandal, and the Special Counsel's findings of that scandal have deep roots in United States diplomacy.

The framers of the Constitution carefully gave Congress the most vital foreign policy powers: the powers to declare war, to tax, and to pass money bills to pay for those wars and other foreign involvements, and to regulate commerce. The institution of the presidency appeared late in the founders' deliberations—not quite as an afterthought, but certainly as an institution whose key foreign policy powers were to be made available only by Congress. The president's authority as commander-in-chief of the nation's military forces, an authority Mr. Reagan has employed to dispatch U.S. troops throughout the Central American region, was a power the framers believed would be used only after Congress declared war or the United States was directly attacked.

That power dramatically changed, however, between 1890 and 1920, and the arena for change was the Caribbean-Central American region. Theodore Roosevelt instructed U.S. military forces to halt a possible revolution in Santo Domingo in 1904–05 and then to seize the customs houses on which the country's government depended for revenue. When Congress refused to approve Roosevelt's actions, he went ahead anyway. His acts not only helped transform the Monroe Doctrine from a prorevolutionary to antirevolutionary tradition, but did so through the exaltation of presidential—and the evasion of Congress's—powers. Taft, Wilson, and Coolidge used Roosevelt's precedent to justify repeated military action in Central America. Congress did not oppose such intervention by passing legislation; there was no early version of the Boland Amendment that in the 1980s prohibited or restricted the use of military threats against sovereign, recognized governments. By the mid-twentieth century, the president's authority to deploy force whenever and wherever he wanted went unchallenged.

Then a new power appeared. The secret use of covert military operations by Executive-controlled agents was not new in 1954, but the Central Intelligence Agency's overthrow of an elected Guatemalan government that year proved to be a watershed in U.S.-Latin American relations. That success led directly to the Bay of Pigs operation of 1961, the "perfect failure," as it has been rightly termed. The Guatemalan intervention is also the backdrop for understanding the intensified covert activity more recently in Costa Rica, Honduras, El Salvador, Guatemala, and, especially, Nicaragua. These activities, which have produced fatalities and the attempted overthrow of sovereign governments, appear to many as acts of war which should require formal declaration by Congress. Certainly a strong argument can be made that the framers of 1787 viewed such acts that way.

Central America has thus been a laboratory in which presidents have experimented to see how far they can go in removing constitutional restraints on their power. To change the metaphor slightly, the region has historically been both a training ground for U.S. military intervention and a guinea pig for presidents to discover the tolerance of the public for their attempts to accrue power. Obviously these actions have been taken with less concern for Central Americans than for increasing executive power and establishing U.S. "credibility" in the eyes of more powerful allies and adversaries. When viewed from this perspective, Washington's policies have been destructive for Central America because, among other reasons, they were not primarily concerned about that area. The officials viewed Central America as a mere means. Or as Secretary of State Alexander Haig argued in 1981, Central America could be the place where President Reagan won an easy victory militarily and thus demonstrated new North American will to the more important observers such as the Soviet Union.

Given these beliefs—that the president has long acted as if he has extensive constitutional powers that allow him to proceed without Congressional authority, and that these powers can be easily exercised in Central America as warning signs to more distant adversaries—the revelations of the Iran-Contra investigations have a long historic preface. When the Reagan administration wished to circumvent Congress's powers, it moved policy out of the State Department, whose officials can regularly be held accountable before the legislature, and into the National Security Council (NSC) which is accountable only to the president. So, for the same reason, was the actual direction of covert operations against the Nicaraguan government moved from the Central Intelligence Agency bureaus to the offices of Lt. Col. Oliver North of the NSC. And when Congress finally challenged the Executive's activities, the president's office declared that the legislature's laws did not apply to the president. Senator Orrin G. Hatch (Rep.-Utah) even declared that the president is "the sole person to whom our Constitution gives the responsibility for conducting foreign relations."

Given the record of the 1787 Convention, Senator Hatch's position is indefensible. But given the record of post-1890 U.S. foreign policy in Central America, a record redolent not only of Executive acquisitiveness in seeking war powers, but Congress's supineness in surrendering those powers, evidence can be found for the Hatch thesis. Thus an interesting irony: while North Americans viewed Central America as a mere backyard that was a dependency, Central American affairs were subverting rights and constitutional restraints that North Americans have historically considered most important for their own personal freedoms: the right for themselves or their elected representatives to decide when and where they are to fight and die, and for which causes their money is to be taxed and spent.

15

The Reagan Administration and Its Attempts to Thwart Change

Wayne S. Smith

Behind the turmoil and bloodshed which have so afflicted Central America over the past decade lies that region's desperate need to cast off the old order, characterized by economic underdevelopment, social injustice and repressive governments, and to replace it with something more attuned to the modern world. While Mexico and most of the major South American countries have emerged as modern nation states, as of 1979, much of Central America remained in a quasi-feudal condition, as backward as ever. Only Costa Rica boasted a flourishing democracy and a socioeconomic system which provided a decent life for the majority of its people.

Clearly, it was in the interest of the United States to encourage and facilitate the transition of the Central American states to modernity. What the United States wanted (or should have wanted) in Central America was a group of nations that was economically healthy, politically stable, and moving forward confidently to a brighter future with a more equitable distribution of goods, justice for all, and popular participation in government.

The United States got a late start in trying to bring all this about—if, indeed, it ever really did get started. For fifty years, the United States cared not a fig about democracy in Nicaragua; rather, it enthusiastically supported the dictatorship of the Somozas. In Guatemala, it overthrew the progressive government of Jacobo Arbenz in 1954 and afterwards happily cooperated with one military dictatorship after another. El Salvador had one of the most unjust societies in the world. A few wealthy families occupied most of the land and, with the help of the military, bloodily suppressed any among the peasant masses who might dare protest or dream of change. The United States accepted that unjust society with complete equanimity. Honduras received virtually no attention. It would remain poverty-stricken forever for all the United States seemed to care.

While it was true that the transition to modernity was in the interest of the United States (whether or not the United States recognized it), it was also clear that the old order was not likely to give way without a struggle; the bloodier and more protracted the struggle, the more polarized the societies would be and the less likely that moderate, middle-of-the-road governments would fill the vacuums left by the collapse of the old order. Nicaragua was a case in point. There, as Somoza fled the country in 1979 following a full-scale civil war, no one doubted who would dominate the political landscape in the postrevolutionary period: the Sandinistas, a revolutionary group farther to the left than Washington would have preferred, but for whose arrival to power Washington bore its full share of responsibility.

The Carter administration made some effort to move away from past policies of support for right-wing governments and indifference to poverty and social injustice. It announced a new American interest in human rights and an aversion to dictatorships. Policy actions, as opposed to rhetoric, in fact changed little, but at the very least, in 1979 when the Sandinista government came to power in Nicaragua, the Carter administration was sufficiently pragmatic to be willing to work with it, rather than try to overthrow it, as past administrations probably would have done (and as the Reagan administration, in fact, has tried to do).

As the Reagan administration entered office in January of 1981, it faced a difficult task in Central America, but one which was entirely manageable. The region was in turmoil, yes, but, from Washington's perspective, headed in the right direction. In El Salvador, a supposedly all-out guerrilla offensive had just been defeated with the guerrillas already beginning to indicate a willingness to negotiate with the government. A skillful use of the leverage provided by U.S. economic and military assistance to the Salvadorean government ought to have enabled the new administration to encourage sweeping reforms and, eventually, a negotiated solution to the war. This, however, would have implied a direct challenge to the deeply-entrenched power of the oligarchy and their right-wing military allies.

In Nicaragua, the Sandinistas had acceded to the Carter administration's demands that they halt assistance to the Salvadorean guerrillas. In doing so, they stressed the value they placed on their relations with the United States and their willingness to negotiate the various areas of disagreement between the two countries. The way was open to constructive diplomacy.

Endemic guerrilla warfare continued in Guatemala, fed, more than restricted, by the Guatemalan Army's indiscriminate slaughter of tens of thousands of peasants. The military had, nonetheless, indicated its intention to hold elections and return power—albeit a circumscribed power—to a constitutional government. The United States ought to have sought, through careful diplomacy, to indicate its support for democratic forces and to expand the parameters within which an elected government would operate. Certainly it ought to have condemned in the strongest terms the slaughter of innocents.

In Honduras, the military was already moving to hold elections and return power to a civilian government. Honduras, moreover, had managed to hold itself aloof from the turmoil around it. To abandon that policy seemed as clearly counterproductive to Honduras' interests as Cambodia's forced involvement in the Vietnamese conflict had been to its development. Nor was it necessary to abandon it. The new Nicaraguan government had indicated its desire to reduce tensions along the border and suggested a series of talks to work out ways of doing so. The Sandinistas made it clear that they wanted no trouble with Honduras.

Unfortunately, rather than taking advantage of the opportunities thus available to it in the region, the Reagan administration completely misread the situation, squandered the opportunities available to it and went off on a tangent which worsened Central America's problems and further complicated the U.S. position there.

The crisis in Central America was essentially regional in nature and sprang from the internal ills discussed above. There *was* an East-West component to the problem—seen principally in the special relationship between the Sandinistas and the Cubans. This component, however, was of secondary—perhaps even tertiary—importance and could have been dealt with easily through diplomatic means. But the Reagan administration had an ideological agenda of its own. It thus described the situation in Central America in starkly East-West terms. What we faced, its spokesmen insisted, was nothing less than Soviet aggression and expansionism articulated through Moscow's Caribbean surrogate, Cuba. Unless we reacted vigorously, the administration warned, the whole area might be swept into Moscow's sphere of influence. This was absolute rubbish. The Soviet Union had shown little interest in the area. It had given few, if any, arms to the Salvadorean guerrillas. It refused to provide hard-currency support to the Sandinistas and eventually even cut back on its petroleum shipments to Nicaragua. It was, of course, willing to provide limited amounts of military equipment, of which it had a surfeit. Cuba sent military advisers as well as doctors and teachers. Both Havana and Moscow emphasized, however, that they were willing to reduce their presence and severely limit military ties as part of a negotiated settlement. Moreover, Nicaragua said it was ready to sign an agreement with the United States prohibiting the operation of any Soviet weapons systems from Nicaraguan soil and in other ways addressing U.S. security concerns.

Unfortunately, the Reagan administration had not the slightest interest in a negotiated solution. Rather, its objective, as signalled by the Republican platform in 1980, was to get rid of the Sandinista government altogether, not to deal with it and thereby restrain it. Thus, only a few weeks after entering office, President Reagan authorized the CIA to begin operations against the Nicaraguan government, and by the summer of 1981, the Agency was beginning to organize the Contras around a nucleus of former officers from Somoza's National Guard. From that point forward, the administration's central thrust was to use the Contras to oust the Sandinistas, or to cause such havoc inside Nicaragua that the whole governmental system would begin to disintegrate. Since the Contadora process (begun in 1983) aimed at a regional settlement satisfactory to all sides and thus would have left the Sandinistas in power, its objectives and those of the administration were mutually exclusive. The administration could not just refuse to cooperate with the Contadora process; at all costs it had to prevent its successful conclusion. This it managed to do simply by keeping the Contra war going. As long as the United States refused to shut down its aid to the Contras as part of a negotiating process, the Sandinistas could not sign a regional accord which would tie their own hands militarily.

The central fallacy in such a policy was that it simply left us in a box. As suggested above, the administration could not achieve legitimate U.S. security objectives through negotiations because it refused to negotiate. But neither could it achieve them through its chosen instrument—the Contras—because the latter did not have and were never likely to have the military capability to do more than harass the Sandinistas. The administration was thus left with no workable options at all.

Further, it was a deceitful policy from the beginning—one which required that the administration say one thing but do another: to say, for example, that it was simply trying to pressure the Sandinistas to negotiate, when all along it was aiming to overthrow them; to say that it supported the Contadora process, when all along it was working to undermine it. Since deceit so often leads to more deceit, the revelations of Irangate should have come as no surprise. As the administration had been perfectly willing to lie about the nature of its policy, so did it not hesitate to circumvent the Congress and violate the law of the land in pursuit of that policy.

Deceit is not without its costs. The Reagan administration's Nicaragua policy not only resulted in Irangate—the administration's most damaging domestic crisis—but also brought down on the United States the humiliation of being condemned for the first time in its history by the World Court. All for nothing, since the policy that led to such a pass was totally ineffective and advanced no discernible U.S. objective. It did, however, lead to widespread suffering in Nicaragua and to the death of tens of thousands of Nicaraguans, thus raising the old maxim of international politics, that to spill blood needlessly and to no end is the highest form of immorality.

In pressing its contra war against Nicaragua, moreover, the administration succeeded in dragging Honduras into the conflict, as the Nixon administration had dragged Cambodia into the Vietnamese war. The Contra army was organized and trained on Honduran territory and launched its raids into Nicaragua from base camps inside Honduras. This sharply raised border tensions between the two countries. The United States also began to base thousands of its troops in Honduras (under the guise of conducting maneuvers), and built airstrips and other forward-basing facilities to be used against Nicaragua. This emphasis on military activity strengthened the hand of the Honduran officers against the civilian government and thus impeded, rather than facilitated, Honduras' transition to full democracy.

In Guatemala, rather than condemn the military government's atrocities, the Reagan administration seemed to condone them—President Reagan at one point even saying that Rios Montt, the dictator of the moment, was a fine fellow who had "been given a bum rap by the U.S. media." This, at a time when the dictator's troops were massacring Indians in the highlands. And after the election of a civilian, Vinicio Cerezo, to the presidency in 1984, the administration's surrogate war against Nicaragua and its resulting regional tensions made it more, rather than less, difficult for Cerezo to broaden the parameters of what was tolerated by his own military establishment. Again, as in Honduras, the administration's policy impeded, rather than encouraged, the transition to democracy.

And finally, in El Salvador, despite some initial successes, the administration's approach left it right where it had started. Military assistance to the Salvadorean army did enable the latter to fight the guerrillas to a stalemate—rather than losing the war, as in 1983 the army seemed about to do. And the holding of democratic elections, which brought a popular face—José Napoleón Duarte—to the presidency, improved the image of the government. In order to consolidate these gains, however, it was necessary to press ahead with sweeping economic and social reforms, and to begin talks with the guerrillas in hopes of bringing about an end to the fighting. This would have meant a confrontation with the military and the oligarchy, however, and this the Reagan administration wanted no part of. It failed, therefore, to use military and economic assistance to El Salvador as leverage in favor of reforms and negotiations. Indeed, it seemed little interested in a negotiated settlement to the civil war. Reforms stagnated, and with them, the image of Duarte. By late 1987,

Duarte's political capital was spent, his popularity in tatters. El Salvador's economy was in desperate straits and the guerrillas were again on the rise. With Duarte's term in the presidency almost up and his personal health poor, El Salvador's future was ominously uncertain—perhaps even more uncertain than when the Reagan administration had first laid hands on El Salvador, for peace seemed now more distant than ever.

Any overall evaluation of the Reagan administration's Central America policy, then, would have to give it the lowest of marks. It was—and is—a policy which was not only immoral, illegal, and unsupported by our friends and allies, but also ineffective; indeed, even damaging to United States interests. Worst of all, perhaps, it pits the United States unnaturally against the momentum of history. Central America is going through the turmoil and agonies of change. It must do so. Rather than trying to facilitate what is in any event an inexorable process, the Reagan administration is attempting to stand in its way. That effort can only fail.

16
The U.S. War in
Central America

Ed Asner

I'm an average citizen watching what my government is doing with my tax money in Central America, and with America's reputation and honor. I am, however, privy to many sources: academic reports, analyses, members of Congress, and so forth. I'm fed what the average citizen is fed from Washington and the media but I also have a chance to peek at the truth, to get some inside information. Because of the ongoing "Gippergate" revelations, the general public, and the world, is starting to find out the truth. Until now it's been like looking at an intricate tapestry from the back side, at the loose threads and indistinguishable patterns. Now we've walked around to the front and can see the horrendous picture that Ronald Reagan and this government have woven—the lies, the misused money and power. The common thread all through the tapestry is the administration's motto: it's easier to get forgiveness than permission. But it's time we stopped forgiving; it's time we stopped giving permission. The public has become much more aware of the modus operandi of this administration, of the overall image Reagan has tried to put forth. We must continue to demand radical, fundamental changes in what passes for a Central American policy.

The Reagan administration knows full well the impact of entertainment and the media. Ronald Reagan has been our most skillful president in using the media to his own ends. He is, as Robin Williams likes to say, "Disney's last wish," a product of the media. But while his showbiz persona has made him into one of the most popular presidents, it's also turned out to be one of our biggest problems. Others have been writing his scripts for him. He merely hits his mark and says the line.

I know I'm caught in 'contra'diction, if you'll pardon the pun, when

I point a finger at Reagan for the mess in Central America, and then pull back and seem to indict his naivete. I think the truth lies somewhere in the middle. On one level, Reagan knows the sure outcome of backing a government like Duarte's in El Salvador, knows about the human rights violations and inequity suffered by the people there. He must know that cutting back on educational funding in favor of the U.S. military build-up will leave the next generation of Americans even further behind the rest of the world. His priority, and I believe that Reagan is fully sincere in this, is stopping "the dreaded spread of communism." Toward that end he can think of *nothing* that is more important, including the state of the nation.

On a more covert level, the mess we're in in Central America has more to do with power and money. The tapestry of this administration is a picture of a huge family tree, an incestuous bunch of mercenaries prof-iteering together long before Reagan and the presidency came along. But make no mistake, the administration has given the nod to this group, all in the name of stamping out communism. All or most of the names are familiar by now: North, Secord, Shapley, Singlaub, Hakim, Niece. Their business is assassination, drug running, manipulation, and money.

What makes it worse is the attitude of many of our members of Congress. Unfortunately, Congress does not represent the 65 percent of the American people who don't wish the engagement in Nicaragua to continue. We have a weird fluke in our country: ever since the State Department was pilloried and persecuted during the McCarthy era for "letting China go communist"—as if they could have done anything to stop it—any other nation that hovers at the edge, and does go socialist or communist, causes tremendous problems for the progressives of our world. Anyone vulnerable to indictment for "losing" a country must run for their very life. Our Congress is so paralyzed by the fear that someone will accuse them of participating in the takeover of a country by communism, that they will do everything in the world, including voting for Contra aid, to escape that label. A couple of years ago, it became unbelievably ludicrous and humorous to watch anti-Contra members of Congress always preface their speeches with "I loathe the Sandinistas"; "I hate communism but. . . ."

Here's a movie plot for you. The camera pans a countryside. Music swells—Latin music. We're in a poor Central American country. Camera cuts to a man, frightened, wary, entering a smoky barroom. He cautiously approaches a stranger at the bar. He asks for help in escaping. The man explains he was part of a guerrilla group trying to overthrow the government, was then drafted into a smaller special unit, sort of an international brigade based on the coast at a sprawling ranch of a rich American. We hear a voiceover of the man's explanation as we see a montage of the ranch—crates of guns and ammunition being loaded, unloaded, and stored—explosives. Several limousines without license plates hover nearby, but the voiceover continues—he never meant to become involved in drug running. We see huge amounts of cocaine being loaded into planes destined for Miami, Memphis, New Orleans. The profits, he explains, come back to finance more of the covert war, not only in Latin America, but in other places around the world. The men in the bar are spotted, captured and taken to the ranch where they are questioned for hours. At darkness, they escape amidst a hail of bullets. Through the help of friends, the second man from the bar flees the country with his family. The special units man goes into hiding. The stranger later learns the man was recaptured, brought back to the ranch to be beaten, tortured to death and buried. This is just one true incident from Daniel Sheehan's report—his affidavit. He is the chief attorney of the Christic Institute (an interfaith center for law and public policy in Washington, D.C.) investigating the real-life sordid saga. The rich American's name is John Hull and his ranch, the gun running, assassination plots and drug running are all real—all set up through the secret team of North, Secord and friends.

In reading the affidavit for the first time a couple of weeks ago, it struck me how much it sounded like a Chuck Norris movie. And this is the stuff of which movies are made; it's juicy; it's intriguing. The problem lies with the syndrome that *New York Times* columnist William Safire calls "the MEGO theory"—My Eyes Glaze Over. It's one thing to watch this kind of action in the movies; it's another when it's true, because the thought that our government sanctions and abets such actions, including the murder of thousands of people, the double-dealing with terrorists, the duplicity—it does make our eyes glaze over. It's overwhelming. Dan Sheehan calls it "infotainment"—information much like the Watergate days that is released bit by bit to give people information, but giving it to them in parcels that they can digest and accept. You can't risk disrupting what Sheehan calls "the people's world-view"—their entire dependence on, and confidence in, our system.

And if there's one thing we need now it's confidence in our system of government—that is, the original system, the first system, the way it was intended. This administration has trouble remembering those good intentions. In true Reagan fashion, those good intentions were misquoted radically in a press conference Reagan gave not long ago, trying to justify our support of the Contras. Reagan quoted John Quincy Adams as saying, "Wherever the standard of freedom and independence has been or shall be unfurled, there will be America's heart, her benedictions." However, Adams added a big "but" immediately following which Reagan didn't:

But she goes not abroad in search of monsters to destroy. She is the champion and vindicator only of her own; she will recommend the general cause by the countenance of her voice and by the benignant sympathy of her example. She well knows that by once enlisting under other banners than her own, were they even banners of foreign independence, she would involve herself beyond the power of extrication in all wars of interest and intrigue, of individual avarice, envy and ambition which assume the colors and usurp the standards of freedom. The fundamental maxims of her policy would insensibly change from liberty to force. She might become the dictatress of the world. She would no longer be the ruler of her own spirit.

Writer Charles Russell echoed John Quincy Adams' words when he wrote, "Guard and protect your land, for there is no afterlife for a place that started out as heaven."

I'm glad to see Americans take up that challenge, insisting that we intend to take back the rule of our own spirit, take our tax dollars and our permission away from those who hold avarice, envy, and ambition above the Constitution. We must protect the freedoms we have, and guarantee that people in other countries have the same right of self determination. We must not continue, as Uruguayan writer Eduardo Galleano wrote, "to sentence people because they committed the crime of not being us." If there is to be any change in Central America, our collective cooperation in realizing it both there and in North America is essential. We have much to do.

17
Obstacles to the Peace Process in Central America

Sandor Halebsky and Susanne Jonas

The road to a negotiated settlement of the conflict in Central America has been a long and tortuous one. Such efforts began as early as the summer of 1981 in Managua, but have foundered on the opposition of the United States to anything short of the destruction of the Sandinista government.

The search for peace during the last six and a half years has made clear the differences in the meaning and importance of negotiations to Nicaragua and the United States. For Nicaragua, successful negotiations are a means of putting an end to death and destruction. They offer the opportunity to move ahead with development efforts and the creation of a better life for the Nicaraguan people. For the United States, negotiations are a problem in public relations.[1] They reflect the need to appear to be a nation open to reason, one seeking peace while continuing to wage war. Negotiations also serve to placate Congress and manipulate public opinion. It is in response to the intransigence of the United States that the Latin American, and ultimately, even the Central American nations, had to take a number of unprecedented initiatives toward a settlement of the conflict.

The search for peace has been pursued through a number of channels. It has included the unsuccessful efforts of Nicaragua to negotiate directly with the United States, the elaborate Contadora process, and most recently the August 1987 Esquipulas Accords of the Central American presidents. The following discussion describes each of these approaches.

The present account necessarily focuses on the peace process in Central America. To understand fully the obstructive role played by the United States in that process, however, one must see the Reagan administration's obsession with Nicaragua and their opposition to a negotiated settlement in terms of the broader global strategy represented by the so-called "Reagan doctrine." The current administration developed this strategy in response to the weakening of U.S. hegemony following its defeat in Vietnam and the heightened domestic opposition to involving U.S. troops in foreign adventures. The doctrine seeks to reverse revolutionary or communist "advances" almost anywhere in the world where American power can be more or less safely projected by aiding counter-revolutionary forces, as in Angola; or by the direct application of U.S. troops where their role and number can be controlled, as in Grenada. As former Under Secretary of Defense, Fred Iklé, has pointedly remarked, "containment has been outflanked . . . it doesn't work in the Third World." He denounced any effort to "contain communism within Nicaragua" as a "terrible idea." What is sought is not the containment of change but its reversal. The choices, in his apocalyptic world view, were between "appeasement" and "freedom."[2] Similar sentiments have been echoed in the rhetoric of the president. Nicaragua thus finds itself as the prime test case for the Reagan doctrine of aggressively seeking the rollback of any national change identified as communist or even suspect in its loyalty to the United States.

REJECTING SERIOUS NEGOTIATIONS WITH NICARAGUA

From August 1981 to the end of 1984 Nicaragua attempted to resolve its differences with the United States and to end the fighting. These efforts failed because the Americans were not interested in negotiations, despite Nicaragua's acceptance of U.S. security concerns in the region.

Characteristic features of United States behavior in regard to negotiations emerged as early as the summer of 1981.[3] Talks with Assistant Secretary of State for Inter-American Affairs, Thomas Enders, began in Managua in August 1981, and finally broke off in October, presaging later experiences. Hard-line, aggressive American attitudes and behavior characterized the discussions, including demands which "flabbergasted" even Arturo Cruz, (an outspoken critic of the Sandinistas); the subsequent withdrawal of positions offered; the absence of written or official statements of positions establishing preconditions for negotiations; and division within American officialdom over whether to negotiate at all. The United States showed no great alacrity in renewing talks. Seven months elapsed between the departure of Ambassador Lawrence Pezzullo from Managua in the fall of 1981 and the arrival of the new ambassador, Anthony Quainton, on March 15, 1982. Meanwhile, during the course of 1981 the United States initiated covert efforts to develop and support an armed counter-revolutionary force.

American unwillingness to negotiate became increasingly clear from 1982 on as U.S. representatives essentially rebuffed initiatives by Nicaragua and other Latin American countries. By the spring of 1982, the administration policy had clearly hardened. In February, the efforts of Mexican President José López Portillo to outline peace terms were perceived as an annoyance by the Reagan administration. In response to the Mexican initiative, however, it felt compelled to offer an 8-point proposal in early April. When Nicaragua responded on April 14 with a 13-point proposal for discussion, it evoked little interest or action by the United States. The Nicaraguan proposal sought to meet U.S. concerns over security and arms shipments and offered to negotiate all disagreements without preconditions.[4] They also requested the participation of Mexico in the discussion as a "moderator" or "witness." The United States stalled and avoided actual negotiations. A September effort by Mexico and Venezuela to initiate talks was greeted with "great interest" but in effect was turned aside by the Reagan administration.

In 1983, Nicaragua continued its efforts to engage the United States in negotiations. Its proposals attempted to meet U.S. concerns in the region. In April, however, the United States turned down the Nicaraguan request for talks with the United States and Honduras, with United Nations Secretary General Pérez de Cuéllar, serving as mediator.[5] Then, on July 19, 1983, the fourth anniversary of the overthrow of Somoza, Nicaraguan President Daniel Ortega, reversing earlier Nicaraguan reluctance and responding to American demands, announced Nicaragua's willingness to participate in multilateral talks and to accept verification by the United Nations of any accords reached. He outlined a wide-ranging 6-point peace plan to end hostilities, arms shipments, and military assistance in the region.[6] Foreign bases were to be prohibited, and on October 20 Nicaraguan Foreign Minister Miguel d'Escoto delivered to Washington four draft treaties reflecting and extending the earlier July announcement. They addressed all U.S. security-related concerns and fell within the framework for peace developed by Contadora, including a provision for the Contadora nations to monitor compliance.[7] (See below for a discussion of the Contadora peace process initiated by Mexico, Panama, Venezuela, and Colombia in January 1983.)

On December 1, 1983 Nicaragua also provided the Contadora mediators with a draft proposal dealing with a freeze on arms, the size of armies, and the development of democracy and representative political institutions in Nicaragua and Central America. This followed an announcement two days earlier by Interior Minister Tomás Borge, who stated Nicaraguan agreement to the withdrawal of all Cuban military advisers if a regional agreement were reached. During the last two months of 1983, the Nicaraguan government also initiated liberalization measures within the country—among them amnesty, the announcement of forthcoming elections, and easing of press censorship.[8] In effect, the Nicaraguans indicated a willingness to meet United States strategic, military, and security concerns, as well as some of its demands regarding internal political forms.

How did the Americans respond to these concrete proposals? A special negotiator, Richard Stone, flew to Panama to meet with Contra leaders and "to help forge a unified Contra position on negotiations with the Sandinistas."[9] In a January 19, 1984 speech, Ambassador Langhorne Motley contemptuously dismissed the Nicaraguan overtures. In June 1984, eight months after it was offered, special envoy Harry Shlaudeman officially rejected the October treaty proposal.

The United States assumed an equally negative stance in bilateral negotiations with Nicaragua in Manzanillo, Mexico from June to November, 1984. These were held at the urging of the Contadora nations. As one astute student observed, however, "the American negotiating positions were so extreme that again the U.S. participation appears to have been simply a charade to placate the Mexicans."[10] Finally, on January 17, 1985 the United States walked out of the Manzanillo talks. In July, the United States rejected the request of the Contadora Foreign Ministers for resumption of negotiations with Nicaragua. Secretary of State George Shultz later had the audacity to state, at the Organization of American States meeting on December 2, 1985, that Nicaragua sought to use the bilateral talks to "undermine" the Contadora peace process "so we don't intend to go back to that."[11] In fact, Nicaragua had made the Contadora proposals the basis of its negotiating position.[12] In August, the intransigent Assistant Secretary of State for Inter-American Affairs, Elliott Abrams, arrogantly stated that, "it is preposterous to think we could sign a deal with the Sandinistas to meet our foreign policy concerns and expect it to be kept."[13]

BEATING BACK CONTADORA INITIATIVES

The United States also responded negatively to the Contadora initiative. Mexico, Panama, Venezuela, and Colombia, nations more or less bordering on Central America, initiated this effort on January 8, 1983. It reflected their concern with achieving stability, security, and peace in the region, and their determination to buttress the principles of self-determination and nonintervention by foreign powers. The destabilizing effects of the Reagan doctrine and continuing warfare in Central America—and potentially within their own states—heightened these concerns.

In September 1983, the Contadora nations secured the agreement of Costa Rica, El Salvador, Guatemala, Honduras, and Nicaragua, to a 21-point "Document of Objectives" in the areas of security, economic cooperation, and politics. In January 1984, working groups began drafting a formal accord, and on September 7, 1984 finally presented a draft treaty. It prohibited arms smuggling and support for guerrilla movements, the presence of military advisers and foreign military bases, the importation of arms, and the holding of military exercises. It provided for a verification commission to go anywhere in Nicaragua, and required the holding of free elections.[14] In effect, it met many of Washington's concerns.

At first, the United States appeared to respond positively. It began to raise objections, however, when Nicaragua unexpectedly signed the agreement on September 21; and then launched a successful effort to torpedo the draft treaty—a proposal which capped nearly two years of work by the Contadora countries. In October, the administration could congratulate itself on having once again subverted an effort at a negotiated settlement of differences, even while proclaiming its support for negotiations and the Contadora efforts. Thus, in a secret October National Security Council document, revealed by the *Washington Post* on November 6, the NSC proudly proclaimed that "we have effectively blocked Contadora group efforts to impose the second draft to the Revised Contadora Act. . . . We have trumped the latest Nicaraguan-Mexican effort to push signature of an unsatisfactory Contadora agreement."[15] The United States thus rejected a treaty that would have ended hostilities with Nicaragua while meeting its own stated concerns. The treaty failed to win American acceptance because it did not satisfy the real American objective—the destruction of the government of Nicaragua.

Given the preceding events, it is not surprising that in spite of considerable efforts by Contadora after 1984 the United States continued to block a negotiated settlement of their differences with Nicaragua. The opposition persisted even when the "Support Group" of Argentina, Brazil, Peru, and Uruguay added their support to the Contadora initiative, thus bringing nations with 90 percent of the Latin American population behind these efforts. The Contadora effort had become a Latin American-wide initiative. It signaled an even more fundamental Latin American initiative (evidenced in the 1986 and 1987 meetings and pronouncements of the eight nations' heads of state in Rio de Janeiro and Acapulco) to establish an organizational presence and policies independent of the United States.

The Contadora process weakened in 1985 because of U.S. pressures, but peace efforts revived early in 1986 at Caraballeda, Venezuela. Foreign Ministers of the Contadora and Support Group nations met on January 12 and reiterated a number of previous proposals that addressed the Nicaraguan need for peace and security. The Caraballeda declaration also included a plea for "national reconciliation" in Nicaragua, which could be interpreted as talks between Nicaragua and the Contras. On February 10, in an attempt to secure the American return to negotiations, the eight Foreign Ministers of the Caraballeda Group travelled to Washington and presented these proposals to Secretary Shultz. They were rejected.[16]

During this period, Washington pressed the Latin American nations to resist the Contadora proposals. In April 1986, the respected *Latin American Weekly Report* stated that "some governments were offered the carrot of substantial United States aid; some were delivered cryptic warnings about difficulties which could arise in their countries if their attitudes did not change."[17] In early June, *The New York Times* reported on the continuing pressure by "American diplomats" on the Central American nations, "telling them to maintain a firm position against Nicaragua. . . ."[18]

The Contadora peace process temporarily gained new life in late 1986 and early 1987 when the Secretaries General of the United Nations and the Organization of the American States, Javier Pérez de Cuéllar and João Clement Baena Soares, offered the services of their organizations to the peace effort. These included, among other activities, monitoring the border, supervising military withdrawal, investigating arms trafficking, and seeing to the fulfillment of any agreement reached. Together with the foreign ministers of the eight Contadora and Support Group nations, Pérez de Cuéllar and Baena Soares visited the five Central American nations to urge, unsuccessfully, their return to the bargaining table.[19]

By midyear, however, Central American governments began to change their attitudes toward peace. The shift reflected the weakening of the Reagan administration by the Iran/Contragate scandal, the awareness that the Democratic-controlled Congress might reduce—or refuse—additional support to the Contras, and the internal political and economic exigencies of the Central American nations themselves.

CHANGING TRENDS AND THE PEACE PROCESS[20]

Early in 1987, attention focused on a new proposal, from Costa Rican President Oscar Arias Sánchez. Initially, the Arias Plan was seen as an alternative to Contadora, one that would be acceptable to (and controlled by) the United States. The Arias Plan, however, has developed a dynamic of its own, particularly since August 1987 when the Central American presidents signed Peace Accords based largely on the plan. What began as an alternative to Contadora has become, in some respects, its continuation.

The four pro-American presidents braved open and intense U.S. opposition to sign the Peace Accords with Nicaraguan President Daniel Ortega in Guatemala City on August 7. Unlike the Contadora proposal, the Accords provide for domestic changes within the Central American countries (ceasefires where there are armed insurgencies, internal dialogue with unarmed opposition groups, amnesty, national reconciliation commissions, democratization measures, guarantees to returning refugees—as well as a cut-off of foreign assistance to the Nicaraguan Contras and other insurgent movements, and an agreement by each country not to serve as a base for attacking neighboring countries.

The Accords initiated a fluctuating and contradictory peace process but they reflect profound changes now taking place in Central America—including a redefinition of relations with the United States. The fresh peace efforts also reveal the bankruptcy of the Reagan administration's Central American policy. These emerging trends are becoming clear to actors and observers throughout Central America and internationally.

First, the United States, not Nicaragua, is isolating itself in Central America. It retains significant power to block peace and to pressure individual governments. Nevertheless, to one degree or another, each of the Central American governments is questioning whether its interests are best served by deeper hostilities with Nicaragua, or by support for the Reagan administration's attempts to destabilize and overthrow the Nicaraguan government. Indeed, they have found these policies, and, above all, the threat of war in the region, to be destabilizing to themselves—a message which the Contadora governments have tried to convey to Washington for several years.

On the contrary, accommodation with Nicaragua would serve the interests of the other Central American governments despite their very conservative domestic policies and anticommunist global orientation. For their own reasons, they have come to accept the existence of a revolutionary government in Nicaragua, and seek peaceful coexistence among varied political systems in the region. In principle, peaceful coexistence with Nicaragua should increase the possibility for ceasefires in El Salvador and Guatemala, where revolutionary/popular insurgencies have pressured the governments for years. In practice, the extent to which either of these governments desires such an outcome remains to be seen.

Economic considerations are no less important. Regional peace implies the revival of economic integration and increased trade among all five countries, and offers concrete benefits to governments plagued by years of economic crises. It is increasingly difficult for these governments to achieve their major domestic objectives—which are conservative—without regional stability, and hence a redefinition of their stance toward current U.S. policy.

The extent to which Washington is out of step with even its closest allies in Central America was revealed in the massive tactical blunder in August 1987 of unloading the Reagan/Wright Plan on the eve of the Presidents' meeting. The maneuver not only failed to change the agenda, but also created a situation in which any Central American president who blocked a regional accord would be seen as an open puppet of the United States.

Since the signing of the Peace Accords, the Reagan administration has further isolated itself in the international arena (where the Accords have been greeted with near-unanimous enthusiasm) through statements that the agreements are "fatally flawed" and actions ranging from "boycott" to outright subversion and vengeance. Reagan administration obstructionism provoked Guido Fernandez, the Costa Rican Ambassador to Washington, to say of Elliott Abrams: "either he underestimates the capacity of the five Central American presidents to write an agreement or he doesn't understand the text." The administration retaliated against Costa Rica for its role in the peace process by suspending in 1987 all economic assistance (up to $140 million in a tiny and battered, debt-ridden economy) and exerting pressure to block international bank credits and trade relations.

During the implementation of the Peace Accords, there have been increased U.S. maneuvers, pressures, and retaliations. These can retard, but they cannot permanently reverse, the growing tendency of each Central American government to act in its own interests, whether or not those coincide with the interests of the United States. These are signposts of what many regard as a long-range structural shift in Central American (and Latin American) relations with the United States—a redefinition of the terms of U.S. hegemony and an assertion of "relative autonomy."

Second, the agreements make official what was already an explicit and pervasive view in Central America (and, for that matter, virtually everywhere in the world outside the United States): the Contras are both discredited and nonviable; and as long as U.S. funding keeps them alive, the chances for peace in the region are greatly reduced. Furthermore, Costa Rican President Oscar Arias clearly disagrees with the Reagan policymakers—the Contras are the problem, not the solution in Nicaragua. It is the Contra war that has increased tensions between Nicaragua and its neighbors and made democracy more difficult to achieve in Nicaragua.

These are the reasons why the Accords call for an end to Contra funding. Costa Rica and even Honduras have reconsidered the wisdom of allowing their territory to be used as bases for U.S.-directed Contra activity—especially now, in the wake of the political/military debacle of the Contra operation and the political weakening of the Reagan administration.

In Honduras, conservative forces—coffee growers in the southern part of the country near the border with Nicaragua, and even spokesmen for the government party—have taken the lead in denouncing the Contra presence and activities. The Contras have displaced 12,000 Honduran peasants, caused serious economic losses, and threatened the safety of their families. The Honduran government has particular cause for concern about the Contras, as their future prospects and viability as a fighting force inside Nicaragua are virtually nil.

Third, the Nicaraguan government has made clear its political will and commitment to implement the Accords, and, no matter how controversial it may sound in the United States, this has been widely recognized in Central America since August 1987. (In fact, all who attended the presidents' meeting recognized that Nicaraguan President Ortega had come prepared to take major steps toward a peace process.) The weekend after the signing, Nicaragua withdrew its claim against Costa Rica in the World Court and moved immediately to establish the Reconciliation Commission with representatives of the opposition political parties and the church.

By early October, the Sandinistas had taken concrete measures to re-open *La Prensa* and Radio Católica, and to declare a ceasefire. Further concessions, including direct negotiations with Contra leaders (something the Sandinistas had vigorously and repeatedly rejected) and a broader amnesty law, were also offered in January 1988 as evidence of their commitment to the peace process by the Nicaraguan government. These actions bear out their repeated promises to implement the provisions of the Accords ahead of schedule, as a sign of good faith. They have also begun a campaign of public education based on the theme that the implementation of the Accords is the program and the priority of the FSLN for the coming period of time. Debates have been held in the National Assembly and there is widespread discussion in the base-level mass organizations.

None of this surprises Central Americans as much as it does North Americans. Certainly there is a spectrum of views about Nicaragua, ranging from great skepticism, to pragmatism, to firm trust that Nicaragua will implement the Accords. What is strikingly absent from most discussions in Central America is the extreme ideological demonization of the Sandinistas or "Sandinista-bashing" that characterizes the discourse even of many Contra opponents in the United States.

Does the above mean that the peace process will succeed? Not necessarily—and certainly not unless the terms of the Accords are applied by the other Central American governments—and respected by the United States. In many significant respects, these governments are much farther than Nicaragua from meeting the standards set by the Accords for both peace and democratization. To mention only a few examples:

—Honduras has a major problem in complying with the stipulation of not aiding insurgent movements in neighboring countries. In fact, dismantling the Contra bases in Honduras presents the most difficult practical problem for such implementation, since it ultimately requires some willingness on the part of the United States to end its war against Nicaragua.

—Full-blown political democracy of the kind being demanded of Nicaragua can hardly be said to exist in the other countries—for example, in Guatemala, where even moderate and legalized opposition forces never know whether they will suffer reprisals by security forces for voicing protest, or where refugees have no assurances for a safe return. And El Slavador has a vastly more powerful insurgency on its hands than Nicaragua. In both El Salvador and Guatemala, the war has intensified since the signing of the Peace Accords.

—Salvadorean President Duarte has attempted to use the Accords to argue that there is a "symmetry"—i.e., that the situations in El Salvador and Nicaragua mirror each other. By this reasoning, if the Salvadorean government meets face-to-face with the FMLN, Nicaragua must do likewise with the Contras. In January 1988, the Nicaraguans offered to negotiate with the Contras even though this flies in the face of some basic realities in the region. The Contras owe their existence and continued operation to an outside power (the United States), while the FMLN and the FDR in El Salvador are indigenous forces. "Power-sharing" makes sense as a demand in El Salvador, since the FMLN and FDR are a major internal political force with a large social base; the situation of the Contras in Nicaragua is simply not comparable.

These points are important for several reasons. First, it is clear that each country will have to implement the Peace Accords in relation to the particularities of its social and political reality, not in relation to an artificial "symmetry" which is not part of the written Accords. Second, the argument for "symmetry" has itself become a means by which other governments, within the framework of the Accords, pressure Nicaragua.

The latter highlights an instability in the peace process which stems from the fact that it makes peace contingent upon democratization measures in Nicaragua as defined by other governments—some of which, until now, have been extremely susceptible to U.S. pressures. Although the United States cannot achieve its active goal (overthrow of the Sandinistas), it does retain considerable power to torpedo the Peace Accords—by continuing to fund the Contras, by preventing Honduran compliance, by constantly upping the demands on Nicaragua, or by attempting to reconstitute the "Tegucigalpa Group" (the other Central American governments minus Nicaragua). It is for this reason that the battle must still be won *in the United States,* as a precondition for a lasting peace in Central America.

By late 1987, the initial thrust for peace in Central America had been weakened by the unrelenting U.S. assault on the peace process (directly and indirectly). Internal conflict within the Central American countries also remained unresolved. Amidst gloomy predictions, the Central American presidents met in January 1988 and, with major concessions from Nicaragua, kept the peace process alive. As the process follows its tortuous and uncertain route, it reflects both fundamental change in Central and all Latin American relations with the United States, and an overwhelming desire for a negotiated settlement to a debilitating war in Central America.

NOTES

1. See Dennis Gilbert, "Nicaragua," in *Confronting Revolution: Security Through Diplomacy in Central America*, eds. Morris Blachman, William LeoGrande, and Kenneth Sharpe (New York: Pantheon, 1986), 88–124

2. Iklé quotes are from Sidney Blumenthal, "The Reagan Doctrine's Strong History," *Washington Post*, 29 June 1986, C2.

3. See Roy Gutman, "America's Diplomatic Charade," *Foreign Policy* (Fall 1984): 3–23; and Dennis Gilbert, "Nicaragua," in *Confronting Revolution*; and Thomas W. Walker, "The Nicaraguan-United States Friction: The First Four Years," in *The Central American Crisis: Sources of Conflict and the Failure of United States Policy*, eds. Kenneth Coleman and George C. Herring (Wilmington, Del.: Scholarly Resources, Inc., 1985), 157–89.

4. *New York Times*, 15 April 1982, A1; *Washington Post*, 9 May 1982.

5. *New York Times*, 6 April 1983, A8; ibid., 12 April 1983, A11.

6. *New York Times*, 20 July 1983, A1.

7. *New York Times*, 21 October 1983, A10; *Washington Post*, 12 October 1983, A1.

8. *New York Times*, 21 November 1983, A8; ibid., 27 November 1983, A15; ibid., 28 November 1983, A17; ibid., 1 December 1983, A13; ibid., 5 December 1983, A8

9. "United States Nicaragua Talks: Going Through the Motions," *International Policy Report* (Washington, D.C.: Center for International Policy, December 1983), 8.

10. Wayne S. Smith, "Lies About Nicaragua," *Foreign Policy*, no. 67 (Summer 1987): 87–103.

11. *New York Times*, 3 December 1985, A3, also source of Shultz quote.

12. Ibid., 99, and William Goodfellow, "The Diplomatic Front," in *Reagan Versus the Sandinistas*, ed. Thomas W. Walker (Boulder, Colo.: Westview Press, 1987): 143–156.

13. *New York Times*, 3 December 1985, A3.

14. "Contadora: The Treaty on Balance," *International Policy Report* (Washington, D.C.: Center for International Policy, June, 1985).

15. *Washington Post*, 6 November 1984.

16. *New York Times*, 11 February 1986, A3.

17. *Latin American Weekly Report*, (April 25, 1986), 1.

18. *New York Times*, 8 June 1986, A8. Also see the *Washington Report on the Hemisphere*, 25 June 1986.

19. *New York Times*, 22 December 1986, A9.

20. This part of the article is based on direct observation of the peace process highlighted by the Central American Presidents' meeting in Guatemala in August 1987. It was written in the fall of 1987 and updated in January 1988.

Appendix

CENTRAL AMERICA: SOCIO-ECONOMIC STATISTICS

	Costa Rica	El Salvador	Guatemala	Honduras	Nicaragua	Panama	United States
Population (millions) 1985	2.6	4.8	8.0	4.4	3.0	2.2	239
Rural Popul. (% of total pop.)	55	57	59	61	45	44	23
Average Household Size (# persons)	5.0	5.0	4.7	5.4	6.9	4.0	2.8
Labour Force (1000s)	715	1785	2465	850	940	1160	110,000
Un/Under-employment (% of L.F.)	25	40+	65+	75+	25	45	8-10
GNP per capita (1985) (Million $US)	1300	820	720	680	770	2100	16,690
GDP per capita (1984) (Million $US)	1570	710	1190	750	870	2020	14,690
Foreign Debt (1985) (Million $US)	4191	1736	2595	2713	5615	3550	—
Energy Consumption (kg/per capita)	580	210	220	240	280	730	11,630
Infant mortality (deaths per 1000 live births)	19	53	70	87	43	22	12
Life expectancy (1985)	74	64	60	62	59	72	76
Terms of trade (1985) (1980 = 100)	97	98	91	95	89	94	114
Daily calorie supply per capita	2803	2148	2294	2211	2425	2419	3663

Sources: Statistical Yearbook for Latin America, ECLA/UN 1983; World Development Report, IBRD, 1987; Statistical Abstract of Latin America, vol. 23, 1984; Economic and Social Progress in Latin America, IDB 1985.

Selected Bibliography

The following is a list of sixty volumes of English-language printed material that, in our opinion, will provide any concerned reader with solid and wide-ranging background information for understanding the ongoing crisis in Central America and the transformative potential of the region. Like this volume itself, the "top 60" represents a broad variety of positive approaches to the issues of democracy, development and change; in sometimes differing ways, all selections are from perspectives that favor change in Central America toward popularly controlled human development.

Each entry is very briefly commented upon. All are currently available in paperback; all have been published within the last six years.

Acker, Alison
1986   *Children of the Volcano* (Toronto: Between the Lines Press). Moving accounts of children's lives in Guatemala, El Salvador, Honduras, and Nicaragua.
Amanecida Collective
1987   *Revolutionary Forgiveness: Feminist Reflections on Nicaragua* (Maryknoll, New York: Orbis Books). A feminist, personal, and religious encounter with the Nicaraguan revolution.
Argueta, Manlio
1983   *One Day of Life* (New York: Aventura). A fine novel centered upon a Salvadorean grandmother.
Bagley, Bruce M.
1987   *Contadora and the Diplomacy of Peace in Central America* (Boulder: Westview). A good introduction to Contadora and all its difficulties.
Barry, Tom
1986   *Low Intensity Conflict: The New Battlefield in Central America* (Albuquerque, NM: Inter-Hemispheric Education Resource Center). United States' new strategic war strategy as applied to Central America.

Barry, Tom and Deb Preusch
  1986   *The Central America Fact Book* (New York: Grove Press). Relatively com-
          prehensive especially with respect to ownership issues.
Bermann, Karl
  1986   *Under the Big Stick: Nicaragua and the United States Since 1848* (Boston:
          South End Press). Thorough review of seven generations of U.S. coer-
          cion in Nicaragua.
Berryman, Philip
  1985   *Inside Central America: The Essential Facts, Past and Present, on El Salvador,
          Nicaragua, Honduras, Guatemala, and Costa Rica* (New York: Pantheon).
          The best primer.
  1984   *The Religious Roots of Rebellion: Christians in Central American Revolutions*
          (Maryknoll, N.Y.: Orbis Books). The best overview of the revolutionary
          Christian stance.
Blachman, M. J., William M. LeoGrande, and K. Sharpe (eds.)
  1986   *Confronting Revolution: Security through Diplomacy in Central America* (New
          York: Pantheon Books). A number of leading U.S. scholars argue that
          it is in the U.S.'s best interests to negotiate rather than coerce.
Black, George
  1984   *Garrison Guatemala* (New York: Monthly Review Press). An analysis of
          the militarization/fascization of Guatemala.
  1981   *Triumph of the People: The Sandinista Revolution in Nicaragua* (London: Zed).
          Incisive study of the struggle to overthrow Somoza.
Bonner, Raymond
  1984   *Weakness and Deceit: U.S. Policy and El Salvador* (New York: Times Books).
          Revealing and authoritative account of the United States policy and role
          in El Salvador.
Bonpane, Blase
  1985   *Guerrillas of Peace: Liberation Theology and the Central America Revolution*
          (Boston: South End Press). A central statement, in autobiographical
          form, of the revolutionary Christian response to Central American con-
          ditions.
Brody, Reed
  1985   *Contra Terror in Nicaragua* (Boston: South End Press). A lawyer presents
          the evidence.
Brown, Cynthia (ed.)
  1985   *With Friends Like These: The Americas Watch Report on Human Rights and
          U.S. Policy in Latin America* (New York: Pantheon). Documents and cri-
          tiques state terror from a human rights stance.
Burbach, R., and P. Flynn (eds.)
  1984   *The Politics of Intervention: The United States in Central America* (New York:
          Monthly Review Press). Situates Central America within the history of
          U.S. control over the Caribbean Basin.
Burns, E. Bradford
  1987   *At War in Nicaragua: The Reagan Doctrine and the Politics of Nostalgia* (New
          York: Harper & Row). An analysis of the United States war in Nicaragua
          placed in a broader world perspective.

Cabezas, Omar
  1985   *Fire from the Mountain: The Making of a Sandinista* (New York: Crown
         Publishers). A sometimes humorous autobiographical account.
Camarda, Renato
  1985   *Forced to Move: Salvadorean Refugees in Honduras* (San Francisco: Solidarity
         Publications). Accounts of terror and solidarity.
Chomsky, Noam
  1986   *Turning the Tide: The U.S. and Latin America* (Montreal: Black Rose Books).
         Focuses on thoroughly critiquing the U.S.'s self-proclaimed "fifth free-
         dom" to determine other people's lives in the interests of the U.S. im-
         perial state.
Collins, Joseph
  1986   *What Difference Could a Revolution Make? Food and Farming in the New
         Nicaragua,* 3rd edition (San Francisco: Institute for Food and Develop-
         ment Policy). An exemplar of serious, committed analysis.
Dixon, Marlene (ed.)
  1985   *On Trial: Reagan's War Against Nicaragua* (San Francisco: Synthesis Pub-
         lications). Testimony from the Permanent People's Tribunal, an inves-
         tigative body comprised of some of the world's most respected people.
Dixon, M. and S. Jonas (eds.)
  1983   *Revolution and Intervention in Central America,* revised edition (San Fran-
         cisco: Synthesis Publications). A strongly argued overview that includes
         important documents.
Dunkerley, James
  1982   *The Long War: Dictatorship and Revolution in El Salvador* (London: Verso).
         An analysis of the economic roots of the war in El Salvador, the role
         of the United States, and the wider ramifications of the war.
Frank, L. and P. Wheaton
  1984   *Indian Guatemala: Path to Liberation* (Washington, DC: EPICA). Discusses
         the role of Christians in the indigenous revolutionary process.
Fried, J. L., M. E. Gettleman, D. T. Levenson, & N. Penchenham (eds.)
  1983   *Guatemala in Rebellion: Unfinished History* (New York: Grove Press). A
         representative collection of historical and contemporary materials.
Guadalupe Carney, Padre J.
  1985   *To Be a Revolutionary* (San Francisco: Harper & Row). An autobiography
         of a revolutionary priest and former U.S. citizen in Honduras who is
         now presumed murdered.
Handy, Jim
  1984   *Gift of the Devil: A History of Guatemala* (Toronto: Between the Lines). A
         fine history that is well written.
Jonas, S., E. McCaughan and E. S. Martínez (eds.)
  1984   *Guatemala: Tyranny on Trial* (San Francisco: Synthesis Publications). Tes-
         timony from the Permanent People's Tribunal condemning the actions
         of that horrifying "killing machine," the Guatemalan army.
Kornbluh, Peter
  1987   *The Price of Intervention: Reagan's War Against the Sandinistas* (Washington,
         DC: Institute for Policy Studies). Details the wide-ranging United States
         effort to overthrow the Sandinista government.

Lapper, R. and J. Painter
   1985 *Honduras: State for Sale* (London: Latin America Bureau). A critical overview of the "Pentagon Republic."
LAWG
   1985 *An Anti-Intervention Handbook: Canadians and the Crisis in Central America* (Toronto: Latin American Working Group). The best intro for Canadians; should be produced annually.
   1983 *Central American Women Speak for Themselves* (Toronto: Latin American Working Group). The struggles and gains, similarities and differences within Central America of women's liberation and development; in need of updating but very inexpensive.
LeFeber, Walter
   1984 *Inevitable Revolutions: The United States in Central America* (New York: Norton). Perhaps the most incisive analysis of the crisis of U.S. intervention.
Leiken, R. S. and B. Rubin (eds.)
   1987 *The Central American Crisis Reader* (New York: Simon & Shuster). More background.
Levie, Alvin
   1985 *Nicaragua: The People Speak* (South Hadley, MA: Bergin & Garvey). Many viewpoints from a broad cross-section of people.
McClintok, Michael
   1985 *The American Connection, Volume 1: State Terror and Popular Resistance in El Salvador* (London: Zed Press). Strong material, strong argument.
   1985 *The American Connection, Volume 2: State Terror and Popular Resistance in Guatemala* (London: Zed Press). Strong material, strong argument.
Menchú, Rigoberta
   1984 *I . . . Rigoberta Menchú: An Indian Woman in Guatemala* (London: Verso) An autobiography of this important revolutionary.
Montgomery, Tommie Sue
   1986 *Revolution in El Salvador: Origins and Evolutions* (Boulder: Westview). Analysis of the origins and unfolding of the struggle in El Salvador.
Morris, James A.
   1984 *Honduras: Caudillo Politics and Military Rulers* (Boulder: Westview). An overview of the last thirty years in Honduras.
North, Liisa
   1985 *Bitter Grounds: Roots of Revolt in El Salvador* (Toronto: Between the Lines). A fine historical overview.
Pearce, Jenny
   1986 *Promised Land: Peasant Rebellion in Chalatenango. El Salvador* (London: Latin American Bureau). A carefully detailed account.
Randall, Margaret
   1984 *Risking a Somersault in the Air: Conversations with Nicaraguan Writers* (San Francisco: Solidarity Publications). Moving accounts of cultural work.

Robinson, William I. and Kent Norsworthy
  1987   *David and Goliath: the U.S. War Against Nicaragua* (New York: Monthly Review Press). Details of the U.S. war against Nicaragua and the defense mounted by that nation.

Romero, Archbishop Oscar
  1985   *Voice of the Voiceless; The Four Pastoral Letters and Other Statements* (Maryknoll, NY: Orbis Books). Thoughts of an assassinated Christian.

Rosset, P. and J. Vandermeer (eds.)
  1986   *Nicaragua: Unfinished Revolution—The New Nicaragua Reader* (New York: Grove Press). Wide-ranging material and perspectives in this excellent collection.

Russell, Philip L.
  1984   *El Salvador in Crisis* (Austin, TX: Colorado River Press). History and current reality.

Schlesinger, S. and S. Kinzer
  1983   *Bitter Fruit: The Untold Story of the American Coup in Guatemala* (Garden City, NY: Anchor Books). Documents the 1954 overthrow of yet another democratically elected government by the United States.

Spaulding, Rose J. (ed.)
  1987   *The Political Economy of Nicaragua* (Boston: Allen & Unwin). Wide-ranging examination of the dynamics of revolutionary economic transformation.

Studemeister, Margarita (ed.)
  1986   *The New El Salvador: Interviews from the Zones of Popular Control* (San Francisco: Solidarity Publications). A short introduction to life in the areas liberated by the FMLN.

Thomson, Marilyn
  1986   *Women of El Salvador: The Price of Freedom* (London: Zed Press). Written in coordination with the Human Rights Commission of El Salvador; sometimes horrifying, sometimes hopeful.

Vilas, Carlos M.
  1986   *The Sandinista Revolution: National Liberation and Social Transformation in Central America* (New York: Monthly Review Press). Well-argued, if somewhat controversial, account of what the revolution is and is not.

Walker, Thomas W. (ed.)
  1987   *Reagan Versus the Sandinistas: The Undeclared War on Nicaragua* (Boulder: Westview). More materials on U.S. intervention and its impact.
  1985   *Nicaragua: The First Five Years* (New York: Praeger). A comprehensive university text book with a wide variety of stances.

Woodward, Ralph L.
  1985   *Central America: A Nation Divided*, 2nd edition (Oxford: Oxford University Press). A standard text that argues for Central American unification.

Yanes, G., M. Sorto, H. Castellanos Moya and I. Sorto
  1985   *Mirrors of War: Literature and Revolution in El Salvador* (Toronto: Between the Lines). Prose and poetry springing from the revolution.

Zwerling, P. and C. Martin
  1985   *Nicaragua: A New Kind of Revolution* (Westport, CT: Lawrence Hill & Company). Forty-five interviews with "key spokespeople."

SELECTED LISTS OF OTHER RESOURCES

Bibliographic and Research Guides

Grieb, Kenneth, *Research Guide to Central America and the Caribbean* (Madison: University of Wisconsin, 1985).

Human Rights in Latin America (Washington, DC: Library of Congress, 1984). A bibliography of "literature of protest and opposition."

Handbook of Latin American Studies, Hispanic Division of the Library of Congress (Austin: University of Texas Press, annual). The most comprehensive bibliography in the field.

Hispanic American Periodicals Index: Articles in English, Vol. 1: 1976–80 & Vol. 2: 1981–82. (Westwood, MA: Faxon Press). A regularly published bibliography surveying approximately 50 English language periodicals. Drawn from the HAPI that includes about 200 additional periodicals in Spanish.

Inter-American Review of Bibliography (Washington, DC: Organization of American States). Quarterly review containing articles, book reviews, and bibliography organized by topics.

Latin America in Books (New Orleans: University of New Orleans, Dept. of Anthropology & Geography). A semiannual review offering feature articles and annotations for books about Latin America.

Latin American Politics (Santa Barbara, CA: ABC-Clio). Contains more than 3,000 abstracts of journal literature for 1973–82.

Resource Directories and Handbooks

Directory of Central American Organizations (Austin, Texas: Central American Resource Center, 1985). Provides information on more than 800 groups in the United States active around Central America and/or United States policy toward the region.

Latin America and Caribbean: A Directory of Resources, eds. T. P. Fenton and M. J. Heffron (London: Zed Books, 1986). An essential source for organizations, books, periodicals and audiovisual materials.

Third World Resources: A Quarterly Review of Resources from and about the Third World (Oakland, CA: Third World Resources). Updates the type of resources provided in Latin America and Caribbean while offering coverage for all regions of the world.

Weekly and Annual Summaries and Reviews

Inter-American Development Bank, *Economic and Social Progress in Latin America* (Washington, DC: Inter-American Development Bank, 1961–). Annual report on regional economic and social developments, including updated statistics and country by country summaries.

Latin America. Facts on File, 1972–. Annual summaries of events in Latin America and the Caribbean.

Latin America and the Caribbean Contemporary Record (New York: Holmes & Meier,

1981–). Comprehensive annual reviews by the leading scholars on Latin America offering thematic essays on current issues, country by country profiles, and a reprinting of important documents and updated economic and social statistics.

Latin America Newletters (London, 1979–). Useful, authoritative summaries of political and economic issues and events published in a number of series. Two of special interest are the weekly *Latin American Weekly Report* and the monthly *Latin American Regional Report: Mexico and Central America.*

Statistical Abstract of Latin America (Los Angeles, CA: CLS Latin American Center Publications, 1961–). A comprehensive annual statistical review, plus several special topic essays in each number.

Journals and Newsletters

Central American Bulletin (Berkeley, CA: Central American Research Institute). A monthly review of news plus feature articles.

Central American Update (Toronto, Ontario: Latin American Working Group and Jesuit Center for Social Faith and Justice). Excellent bimonthly offering regular update of information on Central America.

Envío (Washington, DC: Central American Historical Institute, Georgetown University, Intercultural Center). Excellent monthly produced in Nicaragua providing detailed accounts of developments in that nation.

ICCHRLA Newsletter (Toronto, Ontario: Inter-Church Committee on Human Rights in Latin America). Five-times-a-year survey of human rights conditions in Latin America and the Caribbean; also includes Canada's external relations in that region.

Latin American Perspectives (Beverly Hills, CA: Sage Publications). A quarterly offering progressive and readable scholarly analyses of Latin American developments and social and political structures.

NACLA Report on the Americas (New York: North American Congress on Latin America). Bimonthly critical analyses of contemporary Latin America with each number including one issue treated in detail.

Washington Report on the Hemisphere (Washington, DC: Council on Hemisphere Affairs). A biweekly newsletter on Washington's Latin American politics as well as regional news.

News and Journal Reprint Publications

CAPA Clipping Service (Toronto, Ontario: Canada-Caribbean-Central America Policy Alternatives). Monthly package of selected clippings principally from English-language Canadian newspapers, plus additional articles and documents.

ISLA: Information Services on Latin America (Oakland, CA: Data Center). Provides 450–500 articles a month from nine of the world's major newspapers, principally from the United States.

Central America Monitor (Oakland, CA: Data Center). Biweekly packets of articles selected from some 100 journals and magazines.

Audio-Visual Sources

Film Distributors

Cinema Guild of New York
1697 Broadway
New York, NY 10019

DEC Films
427 Bloor St. West
Toronto, ON
M5S 1X7

ICARUS Films
200 Park Avenue South, Suite 1319
New York, NY 10019

IDERA Films
2524 Cypress Street
Vancouver, BC
V6J 3N2

Audio Tapes

David Barsamian
1415 Delwood
Boulder, CO 80302
Extensive catalogue of Central American and other Third World-related audio
tapes.

The Other Americas Radio
P.O. Box 85
Santa Barbara, CA 93102
Excellent one-half to two-hour audio tapes from Santa Barbara, CA radio
station devoted to coverage of Latin America.

Index

About the Contributors

ED ASNER, distinguished stage, screen, and television actor, is a former president of the Screen Actors Guild and recipient of five Golden Globe Awards and seven Emmy Awards for his work on the "Mary Tyler Moore" series, the mini-series "Roots," "Rich Man, Poor Man," and "Lou Grant." He serves on the Board of Directors of the Office of the Americas and has contributed greatly to efforts to educate North Americans about the realities of Central America.

BLASE BONPANE is a former Maryknoll priest who was assigned to and later expelled from Central America. He is Director of the Office of the Americas, an educational foundation striving to achieve peace in the Americas. A professor at the University of California, Los Angeles, Professor Bonpane is the author of *Guerrillas of Peace: Liberation Theology and the Central American Revolution* (Boston: South End Press, 1985).

CHARLES CLEMENTS is the Director of Human Rights Education for the Unitarian Universalist Service Committee in Boston, Massachusetts. He is an Air Force Academy graduate, a Vietnam veteran, and a physician. In 1982–83 he worked as a physician in a rural area of El Salvador largely controlled by guerrilla forces. He is the author of *Witness to War: An American Doctor in El Salvador* (New York: Bantam Books, 1984).

SANDOR HALEBSKY is a professor of sociology at Saint Mary's University, Halifax, Nova Scotia. He received a Ph.D. in sociology from Cornell University. Dr. Halebsky is the coeditor of *Cuba: Twenty-Five Years of Revolution, 1959–1984* (New York: Praeger, 1985); the author of *Mass*

Society and Political Conflict: Towards a Reconstruction of Theory (Cambridge, England: Cambridge University Press, 1976); and editor of *The Sociology of the City* (New York: Charles Scribner's Sons, 1973).

JIM HANDY is an assistant professor of history at the University of Saskatchewan. He obtained his Ph.D. from the University of Toronto. Dr. Handy is the author of *Gift of the Devil: A History of Guatemala* (Toronto: Between the Lines, 1984). He has also served as Central American Coordinator for Amnesty International Canada.

SUSANNE JONAS, who teaches in the Latin American studies program at the University of California, Santa Cruz, received her Ph.D. in political science from the University of California, Berkeley. An editor of *Contemporary Marxism*, Dr. Jonas has published widely on Central America, including "Guatemala" in Ronald H. Chilcote and Joel C. Edelstein, ed., *Latin America: The Struggle with Dependency and Beyond* (Cambridge, MA: Schenkman Publishing Co., 1974); *Guatemala: Tyranny on Trial* (San Francisco: Synthesis Publications, 1984), coeditor; and *Guatemala* (Boulder, CO: Westview Press, forthcoming).

JOHN M. KIRK is associate professor at Dalhousie University, Halifax, Nova Scotia. He holds a B.A. in Hispanic studies from the University of Sheffield, an M.A. in Latin America literature from Queen's University, Ontario, and a Ph.D. in Latin American studies from the University of British Columbia. He is the author of *Between God and the Party: Religion and Politics in Revolutionary Cuba* (Gainesville, FL: University Presses of Florida, 1988); coeditor of *Cuba: Twenty-Five Years of Revolution, 1959–1984* (New York: Praeger, 1985); author of *Jose Marti, Mentor of the Cuban Nation* (Gainesville, FL: University Presses of Florida, 1983); and the coeditor of *A Fist and the Letter: Revolutionary Poetry from Latin America* (Vancouver, BC: Pulp Press, 1977).

H. E. SERGIO LACAYO, a lawyer, is Nicaraguan Ambassador to Canada.

WALTER LAFEBER is Marie Underhill Noll Professor of American History at Cornell University. A distinguished historian of American foreign policy, his publications include *The American Century: A History of the United States Since the 1890's* (New York: Alfred Knopf, 1986), coauthor; *Inevitable Revolutions: The United States in Central America* (New York: W. W. Norton & Co., 1983); *The New Empire: An Interpretation of American Expansion, 1860–1898* (Ithaca, NY: Cornell University Press, 1967); and *The Panama Canal: the Crisis in Historical Perspective* (New York: Oxford University Press, 1978). Dr. LaFeber received his Ph.D in history from the University of Wisconsin.

MARY ANN LUNDY currently serves as the Director, Women's Unit, Presbyterian Church of the United States. She has been the Coordinator of the National Student Movement of the YWCA, an organizer for Amnesty International, a staff person in the Church and Society Division of the National Council of Churches (1979–82) and a member of the American Indian Concerns Task Force (1986). From 1982–87 she participated actively in the Sanctuary Movement.

W. GEORGE LOVELL is associate professor of geography at Queen's University in Kingston, Ontario. He received his Ph.D in geography from the University of Alberta. A leading scholar on the colonial experience of the indigenous people of Guatemala, Dr. Lovell's publications include *Conquest and Survival in Colonial Guatemala: A Historical Geography of the Cuchumatan Highlands, 1500–1821* (Montreal: McGill-Queen's University Press, 1985) as well as articles in the *Latin American Research Review, Canadian Geographer, Transactions of the Institute of British Geography,* and *Journal of Historical Geography,* among other journals.

MORRIS H. MORLEY is a lecturer in political science at Macquarrie University in Sydney, Australia, and a senior research fellow at the Council on Hemispheric Affairs in Washington, D.C. He is the author of *Imperial State and Revolution: The United States and Cuba, 1952–1986* (Cambridge: Cambridge University Press, 1987) and *Crisis and Confrontation on a World Scale: Ronald Reagan's Foreign Policy* (Totowa, N.J.: Rowman and Littlefield, forthcoming). He is the coauthor (with James Petras) of *The United States and Chile* (New York: Monthly Review Press, 1975) and *The Nationalization of Venezuelan Oil* (New York: Praeger, 1977).

LIISA L. NORTH is an associate professor of political science at York University in Toronto and a Fellow at its Centre for Research on Latin America and the Caribbean. Dr. North received her Ph.D. in political science from the University of California, Berkeley. A former president of the Canadian Association of Latin American and Caribbean Studies, her publications include *Bitter Grounds: Roots of Revolt in El Salvador* (Toronto: Between the Lines, 1981); *Negotiations for Peace in Central America: A Conference Report* (Ottawa: Canadian Institute for International Peace and Security, 1985); and *Civil-Military Relations in Argentina, Chile, and Peru* (Berkeley, CA: University of California International Studies, 1966).

JAMES PETRAS is professor of sociology at the State University of New York, Binghamton. He obtained his Ph.D. in political science at the University of California, Berkeley and has traveled extensively throughout Latin America. Dr. Petras has published scores of articles and books, including *Class, State and Power in the Third World* (Montclair, NJ: Allonhead Osmun & Publishers, 1981), coauthor; *Latin America: Bankers, Generals and the Struggle for Social Justice* (Totowa, NJ: Rowman and Littlefield, 1986), coauthor; *Cultivating Revolution: The United States and Agrarian Reform in Latin America* (New York: Random House, 1971), coeditor; *Critical Perspectives on Imperialism and Social Class in the Third World* (New York: Monthly Review Press, 1978), coauthor; *Political and Social Forces in Chilean Development* (Berkeley, CA: University of California Press, 1969); and *Politics and Social Structure in Latin America* (New York: Monthly Review Press, 1970).

GEORGE W. SCHUYLER is director of the International Education Centre, Saint Mary's University, Halifax, Nova Scotia. He holds a B.A. in history from Yale University, an M.A. in international relations from Johns Hopkins University, and a Ph.D. in history from Stanford University. He served as a Ford Foundation official in Colombia and Venezuela and as Director of the Ibero-American Studies Program, State University of New York, Stony Brook. He is the author of *Hunger in a Land of Plenty* (Cambridge, MA: Schenkman Books, 1980); coeditor of *Rethinking Caribbean Development* (Halifax: International Education Centre, 1988); and author of two popular histories of Saint John, New Brunswick as well as several articles and reviews.

WAYNE S. SMITH is a professor at Johns Hopkins University's School of Advanced International Studies in Washington, D.C. A career diplomat for 25 years, Dr. Smith was the U.S. State Department's top expert on Cuba when he left the diplomatic service in 1982. He was chief of the U.S. Interests Section in Cuba from 1979 until 1982. Dr. Smith holds a Ph.D. from George Washington University. He has written extensively on recent U.S. policy in regard to Central America and Cuba. His major study is *Closest of Enemies* (New York: W. W. Norton & Co., 1987).

GUILLERMO MANUEL UNGO is head of the Democratic Revolutionary Front, the civilian arm of the struggle to liberate El Salvador. Dr. Ungo is a lawyer, former university professor, and leader of the social democratic National Revolutionary Movement in El Salvador. He was a member of the first governing junta following the coup of October 1979. Dr. Ungo lived in exile during the early 1980s, but returned to El Salvador to continue his political work early in 1988.

JUDITH A. WEISS is an associate professor of Spanish at Mount Allison University, Sackville, New Brunswick, Canada. She obtained her Ph.D. at Yale University. A long-time student of Cuban popular culture, her publications include *Casa de las Americas: An Intellectual Review in the Cuban Revolution* (Chapel Hill, NC: Estudios de Hispanofila, 1977).

W. GORDON WEST is an associate professor of sociology in education at the Ontario Institute for Studies in Education, University of Toronto. He received his Ph.D. in sociology from Northwestern University. An area of major interest has been that of education and social justice in Nicaragua. Dr. West has published in the *Canadian Journal of Education*, *The British Journal of the Sociology of Education*, *Interchange*, and in a number of Spanish language journals.

ANTHONY WINSON is assistant professor of sociology at Guelph University. He has published on rural development, politics, and the state. Dr. Winson is the author of *Coffee and Democracy in Modern Costa Rica* (London: Macmillan, forthcoming) and has published articles in *The Canadian Journal of Sociology*, *Comparative Studies in Society and History*, *Economy and Society*, *Latin American Perspectives*, and *Studies in Political Economy*. He received his Ph.D. in sociology from the University of Toronto.